PREPARE
TO BE A MILLIONAIRE

$1,000,000 dire

PREPARE
TO BE A MILLIONAIRE

Tom Spinks, Kimberly Spinks Burleson, and Lindsay Spinks Shepherd

Health Communications, Inc.
Deerfield Beach, Florida

www.hcibooks.com

Library of Congress Cataloging-in-Publication Data

Spinks, Tom.
    Prepare to be a millionaire / Tom Spinks, Kimberly Spinks Burleson, and
Lindsay Spinks Shepherd.
        p. cm.
    Consists of stories adapted from *Millionaire Blueprints* magazine.
    ISBN-13: 978-0-7573-0714-0 (hardcover)
    ISBN-10: 0-7573-0714-0 (hardcover)
    1. Success in business—United States. 2. Entrepreneurship—United States.
3. Millionaires—United States. 4. Success in business—United States—Biography.
5. Entrepreneurship—United States—Biography. 6. Millionaires—United States—
Biography. I. Spinks Burleson, Kimberly. II. Spinks Shepherd, Lindsay.
III. Millionaire blueprints. IV. Title.
HF5386.S7526 2008
332.024'01—dc22

                                                                2007041645

Publisher: Health Communications, Inc.
            3201 S.W. 15th Street
            Deerfield Beach, FL 33442-8190

Book cover design by Sherry Leigh
Inside book design by Sherry Leigh
Inside book formatting by Dawn Von Strolley Grove

This book is dedicated to Mom,
Barbara Lindsay Spinks,
the cheerleader, the rock, and the believer
in all dreams that any of us have ever had.

———

We are grateful to the many people
who have a role in making the
Millionaire Blueprints *vision a reality.*
Together, we are "dream makers."

CONTENTS

ACKNOWLEDGMENTS

We would like to personally thank Imal Wagner, who was instrumental in making this book a reality. She has been wonderful to work with. Thank you to Peter Vegso and the staff at HCI for their professionalism and kindness. Thank you for believing in *Prepare to Be a Millionaire* and its potential to help millions of readers achieve success in business and in life.

Thank you to the millionaires who so graciously gave their time, advice, and information to help empower new entrepreneurs with detailed steps and great motivation. Thank you to our team—the researchers, the interviewers, the transcribers, the writers, the editors, the copyeditors, and the designers—in making each story a usable blueprint.

A special thank you to our senior editor, Kipp Murray—you are great at what you do and have worked so hard on this project! You give all of us peace of mind about what goes out there to the world. Thank you to Greg Summers—you bend over backward to help us with our mission to help people achieve tremendous success. Your passion is infectious and your friendship a gift. Brittany Gaydos and Bonnie Daman, thank you for doing so much legwork for this book and for doing it all with a smile!

Lastly, thank you to Sherry Leigh—you are a gift from God. You are one of the most gifted artists and one of the smartest business women we have ever known. Our father, Tom, loved you like a daughter and was so proud of you. We couldn't have done this without you.

INTRODUCTION

I am writing down the words that come from my father's lips as he lies in a bed battling cancer. I sit here with my body bent forward, notes in hand, as I listen silently to his words, not wanting to miss anything he says. The one person he continues to speak of is someone he has chosen to honor in the foreword of this, our first book. In my father's words, this man is a dream maker. But I will wait to share his identity with you.

I take my father back to his early memories of days spent playing football with his best friend, Terry Bradshaw. I ask him if this was his first dream—to play in the NFL. To my surprise, he says, "No. That was Terry's dream." My father had always dreamed of playing professional baseball. He had great potential to achieve this dream. He was an all-star pitcher and won every award that could be bestowed upon a young baseball player.

My father then quietly says to me, "I caught Terry's dream. Most of us don't realize the dream that lies within us until a fateful friendship or connection happens with another person. Then you somehow catch that person's dream, because dreams are contagious."

My father tells me that one dream is not enough for a person—that we must see many dreams unfold. I ask if he had ever dreamed of being a business giant. He softly replies, "No. The circumstances of my life forced me to find new dreams that involved business."

What many of you did not know is that my father was Terry Bradshaw's receiver and his best friend since eighth grade. Through junior high, high school, and college, they were a phenomenal duo. They went on to play together for the Pittsburgh Steelers. Art Rooney, Sr., then owner of the Steelers, told my father that he had the best receiving hands he had ever seen in his years of owning an NFL team. While playing with the Steelers, my father ran a route during a practice that ended his dream. He blew out his knee. While trying to make a comeback, he carefully hid his pain so his coaches wouldn't send him home. He would wrap the injured knee so tightly that it would cause him to lose all feeling in his leg right down to his toes. After a second blowout with the same knee, he realized it was time to go home and search for new dreams.

So my father began to walk down the pathway of life that most people can identify with. In the midst of great successes, while founding and developing three NFL weekly newspapers and three college football newspapers, a multi-level marketing company that had tens of thousands of distributors, an educational film company, and an accounting lead generating company, my father lived through many ups and downs in the business world. At times, he experienced the stress of not being able to pay the bills, of waking up in the middle of the night knowing that the electricity would be turned off the following afternoon if he didn't find the money to pay the bill. He experienced the feeling of what it was like to be taken advantage of, as well as the anger and pain that came along with it, after an employee embezzled funds from one of his companies. But he says that his most painful memory was telling his young children that one particular Christmas was going to be "slim."

I actually remember this "slim" Christmas conversation. Christmas has always been my father's favorite time of the year. He loves having many presents under the tree, and has always asked my mom to wrap everything separately. The pants to every new outfit would go in one box, and the tops would go in another—just so the tree would be overflowing with gifts. You can only imagine how difficult it was for him to talk to us. He sat us down and became choked up as he explained and apologized. It didn't matter to us, however, because we knew Santa would come through! Ha! I'll tell you the kind of family we are blessed to have. When all of our aunts, uncles, cousins, and grandparents arrived to celebrate Christmas with us the next day, they brought in bags full of wrapped presents. I remember seeing my dad's eyes fill with tears as our tree became surrounded with gifts.

Each of these experiences—the good, the bad, the exceptional, and the painful—was necessary. It was necessary to go through these times in order to see a real need. The need was for real information. As an entrepreneur over the course of almost forty years, my father had read every book and magazine ever published on business and marketing tools. What he found was more frustration. He realized that the key could not be found by reading articles about the seven secrets to success, or about the ten reasons why someone isn't successful. The key was in giving real information to people who wanted to succeed.

Words we have heard my father say on a regular basis around our office are: "No fluff; we will not give the readers fluff content. We will only give the readers information they need." My father saw many business magazines on the rack with blurbs that read something like: *"John Doe started his company working out of the basement of his home with $200. Today, he is worth over $200 million."* He would flip to each article as quickly as possible. And each time, he would be sorely disappointed by the lack of detail he found there. He would say that the right questions were not being asked!

Through this frustration, *Millionaire Blueprints* became a new dream for my father. It is a dream that my sister, Lindsay, and I "caught," and we work daily to make this family vision come to life. It is a dream that emerged from a real need. My father has always believed that the true nature of all human beings is to help one another. So he decided to ask self-made millionaires to teach him exactly how they built their businesses and how they became successful. He created *Millionaire Blueprints* in hopes that it would become the vehicle through which the world could learn those teachings. He was so right. This simple act of relaying the right information to readers has changed thousands of lives. It has not only changed the lives of the "givers," the self-made millionaires we feature in each issue of our magazine, but also the lives of the readers we are able to arm with the real information they need to succeed in business. It has changed our lives as well. You see, we are able to meet other dream makers through *Millionaire Blueprints* magazine.

The person my father wants to honor in this book is Peter Vegso, the biggest dream maker ever to come into our lives. He is this book's publisher and the founder of HCI Publishing. He is the driving force behind famous book titles and the faces of their authors whom we see at book signings or on television. When people hear of publishing greats like Peter, they envision big money, private jets, horses, and luxurious homes. What you may not know is that Peter started out like most of us—with a dream and nothing else. He started his company as a kid operating out of a small car with his friend and the co-owner of his publishing company, Gary Seidler. Peter has also seen the ups and downs of his company and experienced the fear of not knowing what lies ahead. He follows his gut instinct and takes risks on individuals he believes in. He is the person who has helped us make this dream of *Prepare to Be a Millionaire* come true. We will be forever grateful to Peter for his belief in our vision.

As I begin to speak of Peter, my dad raises his head, opens his eyes and says, "Peter and I have created a new dream. This book and the books that will follow have the ability to impact so many lives by creating footsteps that each reader can follow."

As my father looks upward toward the sky, he whispers, "Do you realize that the people who will read these books and follow the blueprints of these millionaires will be the very people we will feature in future books? Doesn't that blow you away?" I press my cheek to my father's hand and say, "Yes, Dad, that blows me away."

Our dream is for this book, *Prepare to Be a Millionaire,* to do just as the title reads. We hope it provides you with the information you need to propel yourself toward becoming the millionaire you see yourself being—and the millionaire we see you becoming.

It became very difficult for my father to speak the day after
he and I had this beautiful conversation that I have shared with you.
Five days later, he lost his battle with cancer.
I will continue on with his vision and dream for *Millionaire Blueprints.*
I have been blessed to be his business partner and
his "right arm," as he called me.
I have been most blessed to be his first child.
I will love him forever.
This book is a tribute to the life of my father,
Thomas Allen Spinks, October 29, 1948–August 26, 2007.
Kimberly Spinks Burleson

1

True Stories of
INTERNET MARKETING
Millionaires

Diane
BINGHAM

Savvy eBay pioneer Diane Bingham rises to success.

BUSINESS NAME:
FromGlobalToYou.com

TYPE OF BUSINESS:
E-Commerce and Antiques

LOCATION:
Provo, UT

ADAPTED FROM:
Millionaire Blueprints magazine article,
"Turn $20 Into $1 Million: Savvy eBay Pioneer
Diane Bingham's Rise to Success,"
May/June 2006

2

W*hen destiny met Diane Bingham, she was just a girl in the coal mining town of Price, Utah. Bingham's stepfather, Charles Ferrero, owned an antique store. "He taught me all about business," she recalls. "He would say, 'You buy something for twenty dollars; you sell it for forty-five dollars. If you can get sixty dollars, go ahead. Always ask for more; settle for a bit less. You can go down, but you can't go up.'"*

Bingham learned valuable tips about bartering and successful business practices from her stepfather and his friends. She had no idea these tips would transform her life years later. In 1998, Bingham and her husband, Michael, were struggling to support their family of five children on one income.

"Michael would hand me just ten dollars a day or twenty dollars a day to buy dinner," Bingham says. "One day, he handed me an extra twenty dollars and said, 'Why don't you see what you can do with this?'" Bingham took the opportunity. She visited a local thrift store, Deseret Industries in Price, Utah, and used the twenty dollars to buy antiques. She then went to a local antique store and sold the items for a profit. "I probably made a couple hundred dollars out of that twenty," Bingham says. "I bought fifty dollars worth of groceries and took the rest and put it back into the company."

In just a day, Bingham had started a business. The skills her stepfather taught her as a young girl quickly came into play. Within a few years, she would transform this new antique business into a million-dollar success. Her story and her business know-how will help anyone seeking to start or improve a business on eBay.

THE MERCHANDISE

How did you pick items to resell the first day you visited the thrift store?

I knew a little bit because my stepfather owned an antique store. I found glassware, porcelain, and books. In the antique world, they call them "smalls." I went to a local antique store, sold them, and turned a profit.

How did you know what to purchase?

I'd watch HGTV and look at the trends. I learned a lot just watching what people were paying the big bucks for. I looked for things that were beautiful—things that didn't have chips or cracks. After a while, I took some of my money and bought books to learn about antiques. I learned what was valuable, how to age it, date it, and that kind of thing.

How did you sell the items you had bought?

For the first four months, I drove my little truck everywhere to sell all my goods. I'd go everywhere from 100 to 200 miles away with my boxes. I'd unpack my boxes, show the antique stores my goods, and then drive home.

When did you get a computer?

In 1998, I asked my stepfather for a loan so I could buy a computer. I needed $3,000, and that was a lot of money. He cosigned the loan. I knew the Internet was the future, and I was a pioneer on eBay. They didn't even have a million items on yet when I joined. For the first six months, I did nothing but buy off eBay. And all I was buying were antiques—just the small things that I could ship real easily.

THE GOODS

Were you still finding items to sell on eBay at thrift stores?

Thrift stores, yard sales, and garage sales—I was buying everything I saw. I was at the yard sale before the yard sale opened. My strategy was to get there first.

What type of items did you find at garage sales?

Most people don't know what they have. I was buying gorgeous brooches for twenty-five cents with Schiaparelli on the back. We're talking a thousand bucks for a Schiaparelli brooch. I'd look these people square in the eye and say, "Are you sure you want to sell this for twenty-five cents? This is valuable." And they'd say, "Oh yeah, I don't need it."

THE E-COMMERCE

How do you run so many auctions on eBay at once?

I hire people to run my auctions. I give them pictures and a template, and they set it up and send it in. We upload it from the office.

Who do you employ to run your eBay auctions?

I employ as many single mothers as I can. I train single moms to set up my auctions and do research. They sign a noncompete, nondisclosure for two years. (See resource page.) I also hire addicts and alcoholics who are in recovery. Your state can give you an employee who's been out of recovery for six months, and the state will pay half their wages if you train them.

THE OVERSEAS BUSINESS

Is it important to have personal contacts if you want to buy from people overseas?

If you think you're just going to find someone in Europe with a webpage and they want money up-front, you're going to get duped. Don't do it.

When you found an antique seller in Europe, what was your next step?

I said, "Hey, listen, you're in the antique business now. This is what you're going to do. You're going to go to these markets and fairs, you're going to buy everything you can, and I'm going to send you money."

THE MARKETING

Did you keep everything in your home or somewhere else?

We rented a warehouse for $600 a month. We filled the warehouse and built two stages—one black and one white—so we could have a contrast with our pictures.

Are pictures important on eBay?

Oh, huge. If your pictures aren't good, you've got a problem. You won't sell anything without good pictures.

The business lessons Bingham learned as a girl in her stepfather's antique store paved the way for her success. Today, she strives to give back what she's been given. The first item she sold on eBay was given to her by a woman who appreciated her determination to set her life right after alcoholism. In the years since this act of kindness, Bingham has reached out to others in a similar way. She has hired people in need and helped them get back on their feet.

"You just keep helping people, keep doing right by people, and everything falls into place," she says. "There are little miracles around you all day, every day, and you can see them if you just open your eyes."

THE ADVICE

How do you determine what your antique dealer will buy for you?

With as many people as there are in this world, it doesn't matter what I buy. It will sell, ninety-eight cents, no reserve. You can't make a mistake. It is foolproof.

Are you telling me that no matter what you sell, you put it at ninety-eight cents, no reserve?

I can't believe I am telling you this, but that is what I do for everything. I normally get bids that exceed the price I want.

What one piece of business advice do you believe is most important?
Never accept the word, "No." If somebody says, "No, it can't be done," just turn "No" into "On," and go forward.

THE PLAN TO FOLLOW

STEP 1

Seek out items in all possible outlets, including thrift stores and garage sales. Make a high offer, and then compromise down.

NOTE: Bingham strives to be the first person to arrive at a garage sale. She plans and maps out garage sale days in advance.

STEP 2

Turning a profit on eBay takes tenacity and lots of research. Compare bidding trends, patterns, and bidders to learn new tactics.

NOTE: Bingham advises that you not put a reserve on an item for sale on eBay.

STEP 3

Learn strategy from other eBay sellers. Research current market values, and progressively narrow your search when you find a new item.

NOTE: Bingham advises that you refer to completed auctions for comparison.

STEP 4

Take good quality pictures of your items for sale on eBay.

NOTE: Bingham warns that without good pictures, nothing will sell. Once you can afford it, hire a photographer.

STEP 5

When importing furniture from Europe, try to use your network for referrals. You have to learn how to get a broker, deal with customs, and get shipping containers.

Here's how it usually works: First, the overseas shipping line takes the container to the person selling you the goods. You pay for the warehouse. Then it's loaded into the container, and you've got to pay the trucker to take the container to the steam line so it can be shipped overseas. Then it goes to Union Pacific and is put on the train from a regional port. Then you've got to pay another trucker to take it from there to wherever you live. You're looking at $5,000 to ship a $10,000 container to your door. And then you have to find a customs broker.

NOTE: Bingham points out that you have to trust people sooner than later, but do not ever send money up-front to the person scouting your goods overseas. To find an antique dealer, you may need to go overseas yourself to meet people at a furniture trade show. There are trade shows in China, Egypt, and Europe, as well as in High Point, North Carolina, and Las Vegas. Just do an Internet search on "furniture trade shows." (See resource page for more details.) Bingham points out that antique dealers frequent trade shows and will import from just about any country.

STEP 6

You can find a customs broker by going to Google, searching for "customs broker," and putting your state in the search. (See resource page for more details.)

NOTE: For an overseas shipping line, Bingham uses Maersk (**www.maersk sealand.com**) or APL (**www.apl.com**). Bingham also says that if you need an interpreter for your overseas trip, consider contacting the Mormon Church in Utah (**www.lds.org**) and telling them you want to hire a returning missionary who is looking for a job. A returning missionary will speak the language fluently and will usually know the area.

THE HIGHLIGHTS

- Price an item to sell by always asking for more than you paid and by compromising the price down.
- After turning a profit, always put a percentage back into your business.
- Buy anything—valuables are to be found at the most common garage sale and thrift store.
- Do your research, and learn from other sellers on eBay. Review completed auctions for market values and bidding trends.
- Be forward and decisive in your actions when bidding and importing.

THE RESOURCES

MORE INFORMATION ABOUT DIANE BINGHAM

From Global to You
www.fromglobaltoyou.com
Diane Bingham's website.

eBAY BUYING AND SELLING TIPS

eBay Learning Center
http://pages.ebay.com/education/index.html
The eBay Learning Center is for people who are new to eBay. Courses provide a quick overview of how to buy and sell with confidence.

eBay University
http://pages.ebay.com/university/index.html
eBay University offers classes across the country or in the comfort of your own home.

eBay Merchant Solutions
http://pages.ebay.com merchantsolutions
This eCommerce Merchant Solutions Center provides a fast, easy, and cost-effective way to increase sales and reach more customers.

eBay Selling Tips
http://pages.ebay.com/education/sellingtips
An easy, four-step process for the beginning seller.

THRIFT STORES AND GARAGE SALES

To find thrift stores in your area, simply run a search on **www.yahoo.com** for "thrift stores." A Yahoo! shortcut will appear at the top of the page for "thrift stores near you." Or run a search with the following terms: "thrift stores," your city, and your state.

The Salvation Army
www.satruck.com/findstore.asp
Enter your zip code to find The Salvation Army location nearest you.

Goodwill Industries International
www.goodwill.org
Enter your zip code to find a Goodwill nearest you.

To find garage sales and yard sales, simply check your local newspaper's classified section on Thursdays for listings of weekend garage and yard sales.

Garage Sale Planet
www.garagesaleplanet.com
Find garage sale listings anywhere across the country.

Garage Sale Hunter
www.garagesalehunter.com
Find a garage sale, or join an e-mail list to receive a daily e-mail of local garage sales.

Yard Sale Search
www.yardsalesearch.com
National listing of thrift stores and yard sales with live chat, maps, and a bargain forum.

TIPS ON FINDING ITEMS AT YARD SALES, GARAGE SALES, AND THRIFT STORES

HGTV Yard Sale Tips
www.hgtv.com/hgtv/pac_ctnt_lnb_gutter/text/ 0,1783,HGTV_3938_12265,FF.html
Contains articles on bargain hunting, books, and a message board.

LOANS

Most people will not need loans to start an eBay business. However, the following resources are helpful if needed.

America's Business Funding Directory
www.businessfinance.com
Search for business and capital sources.

U.S. Small Business Administration
www.sba.gov
Tips on starting, expanding, and financing your small business.

TAX TIPS FOR EBAY SELLERS

eTaxes
www.etaxes.com/ebay.htm
An article and Q&A section on this site answers questions regarding eBay taxes. You will need to pay taxes on items you sell through eBay.

MARKETING AND SALES TRENDS

MarketResearch.com
www.marketresearch.com
800-298-5699
A comprehensive collection of published market research. This site lets you browse categories to learn about a variety of trends.

KnowThis.com
www.knowthis.com
This marketing resource has business information and tips in more than 130 categories.

eBay Marketplace Research
http://pages.ebay.com/marketplace_research/ index.html
Marketplace Research enables buyers and sellers to gather intelligence on buying and selling trends on eBay for a low subscription fee.

PHOTOGRAPHY

eBay Photography Discussion Board
http://forums.ebay.com/db1/forum.jspa?forum ID=98
Discuss photography with other eBay members.

SHIPPING (DOMESTIC AND INTERNATIONAL)

United States Postal Service (USPS)
www.usps.com
Features shipping and mailing tools, online tracking, and more.

United Parcel Service of America, Inc. (UPS)
www.ups.com
UPS is another great option for shipping items.

Maersk
www.maersksealand.com
One of the largest overseas shipping companies with ports all over the world.

APL Limited
www.apl.com
One of the top leaders in global ocean transportation services.

CUSTOMS BROKERS

FedEx
www.fedex.com/us/services/ftn/brokerage.html
Use a customs broker through FedEx.

U.S. Customs and Border Protection Broker List
http://apps.cbp.gov/brokers/index.asp?port Code=2834
An extensive list of customs brokers across the country.

Cleared and Delivered
www.clearedanddelivered.com
A licensed online customs brokerage and clearance specialist.

INTERPRETERS

The Church of Jesus Christ of Latter-Day Saints
www.lds.org
Reference Desk: 801-240-2584
Ask for references for returning missionaries who may need employment and who are fluent in foreign languages.

FURNITURE TRADE SHOWS

Events Eye
www.eventseye.com/fairs/event_t_361.html
Search for furniture trade shows across the world by location or date. (These searchable categories are in the right column.)

FINDING AND HIRING EMPLOYEES

Workforce Services
To find workforce services in your state, run an Internet search on "workforce services" and enter your state.

America in Recovery
www.americainrecovery.org
Matches applicants' résumés with small business owners looking to hire those who are ex offenders or who are in substance abuse recovery.

Noncompete and Nondisclosure Forms Online
www.lawdepot.com
Create a noncompete, nondisclosure form online.

Millionaire Blueprints neither endorses nor recommends any of the companies listed in the resource section. Resources are intended as a starting point for your research.

Titus
BLAIR

Titus Blair started a lucrative online business with as little as $100.

BUSINESS NAME:
Swords Online

TYPE OF BUSINESS:
Sword Sales Online

LOCATION:
Bakersfield, CA

ADAPTED FROM:
Millionaire Blueprints magazine article,
"Swashbuckling Success,"
May/June 2006

12

"*I'll always stand behind the idea that free is the best way to sell something,*" *Titus Blair says. That marketing strategy turned a random gift into a million-dollar business. Blair had no previous interest in swords, but began to think about them after his father, an inventor who often attended trade shows, picked some up for him as a gift. Fresh from closing out a partnership, and looking for a new idea, he decided to give it a try. "When he gave me those swords, the wheels just started turning," Blair says.*

Blair began learning computer skills from his father when he was sixteen years old. By the time he was eighteen, he was teaching 3D animation and computer programming at a local community college. That led to his first business venture, ipitimi Animation, where, with a partner, he created a computer-coloring book for kids that sold on QVC. Then it was on to swords. After starting with $100 and considerable computer skills, Blair grew one step at a time to reach revenues of $3.25 million in 2004.

THE BEGINNING

What year did you start thinking about creating Swords Online?

Around 1997. It was after *Braveheart* came out, but before *The Lord of the Rings*. I think lots of people liked swords, but you couldn't really find them. Now they've gained popularity. There's a new "sword" movie every year. One of the things I worked on previously was website design, so I knew how to put a site together. I started thinking about selling swords. I realized that they're easy to ship and that not many stores carry them. So I decided to put a few on the Internet as kind of a test market.

THE WEBSITE

What were your initial steps?

First, I bought the domain name. My first choice was taken, so I bought **www.swordsonline.com** instead. Then I began looking on the Internet for companies that manufactured swords. I found some factories in Pakistan and China. I contacted them, but we were too small to order directly so they referred us to their U.S. distributors. I called the distributors and said, "I'm interested in creating a wholesale account to buy swords."

THE BUSINESS

Did you have to do anything special to buy swords wholesale?

I had to sign up as "doing business as" (DBA) in the county where I lived. I started out as a sole proprietor under the name Blair Enterprises. I didn't incorporate until later. Once you get a DBA, you can open a business bank account and get a seller's permit, which allows you to sell a product. The seller's permit number is what you give the distributors to be able to buy wholesale and not pay sales tax. That's the same for any business. I didn't have to do anything special in the beginning to sell swords.

THE PRODUCT

How did you handle shipping to your customers?

When I started out, I was sharing a room in a house, and I did everything from there. I wasn't holding on to much inventory, so I did a lot of "just-in-time" shipping. This means that when I received an order from a customer, I'd place that same order with the distributor and then ship it to the customer as soon as it arrived. Most days, I spent the morning doing customer service and placing orders. Then I'd go surfing for three or four hours, come home, and ship product in the afternoon. I wasn't making a lot of money, but it was enough to pay my bills.

How did you find manufacturers?

We create designs that are manufactured exclusively for us. There are manufacturers around the world. We found our manufacturers online. Once you're in business, you naturally find more and they start to find you.

THE MONEY

What did you spend the $100 on to get started?

That covered everything, from buying my first product to getting the DBA, to opening the bank account. The minimum order was $50, so that's what I ordered. I had a catalog, and the swords looked good, so I ordered a couple to check shipping and product quality. I took pictures of them to use on my site. The cool part about the Internet is that I just scanned in several other photos from the catalog, and I put them on the site too. I only had a small amount of inventory, but I had a large selection on the web.

THE MARKETING

How did you get customers when you started?

I used search engine optimization strategies to become number one in Yahoo!.

You also started giving away swords?

Yes, I believe that if I can give you one sword, you'll probably buy two more—one for yourself, and one for a friend. Word of mouth spreads for only two reasons: awesome prices or fervor. We created the fervor by giving away free items. The winners were asking their friends, "Hey, do you like swords? You should go check out this site." We give away one sword a month to the people who sign up to win, which is relatively cheap no matter what the cost of the sword. We pick a random person, and then we pick a random item from their wish list.

What advice do you have for people about creating contests?

It's rare to find someone who likes something and who doesn't have friends or family with the same interests. Dedicate your marketing to finding the people who love what you sell, and then give it away. That's what we did. We gave away as much as we could. One word of caution is that you have to make people feel passionate about the item and about your company at the same time. If you make them feel passionate only about the item, they can usually go somewhere else to buy it. If you make them feel passionate about you, then you've got a dynamite combination.

What do you do with all the names you collect in your contest database?

We send out monthly e-mails. To enter the contest, you have to agree to receive e-mails; if you don't want them, you're not in the contest. People always read them to see if they won. Of course, we use the e-mails to promote our products, and we highlight whichever "weapon of the week" is currently featured online with a little write-up about it. We also have flash sales, which are low prices on items. We try to keep the volume of e-mails low. The more e-mail, the lower the impact will be.

What other ways do you advertise?

We use keyword advertising like AdWords (**www.adwords.google.com**) and Overture (**www.searchmarketing.yahoo.com**). We also market to customer groups like Renaissance communities. Look up websites for people who are interested in what you do, but who don't sell it. For example, look up a website aimed at sword aficionados that doesn't sell swords. We run some magazine ads, and we've had booths at conventions such as Renaissance and sci-fi shows. We constantly run contests giving away swords through magazines, radio shows, and our website. Thousands of people sign up to win. We also get a lot of public relations because of what we sell. To me, free PR is the best. Spend some of your time, your sweat, and your labor to get it for free.

THE GROWTH

So how did you grow once you got rolling?

As sales increased, I needed help. Instead of hiring an employee, I hired a company to handle drop shipping for me. The volume eventually got too big for them, and then the company was sold. So I had to do the order fulfillment myself once again. I hired a couple of friends and some students to help me. Then I decided I wanted to open a retail store.

How did the retail store do?

It was breaking even. My four employees and I worked out of the basement, and the store was on the level above. We stayed there for a year and kept growing. Then we moved to a bigger facility. We got serious about the store at the next location where we had a bigger warehouse.

How much warehouse space did you have at that point?

We had 2,000 square feet, plus 600 square feet for the store. Our most popular thing is a table of "scratch-and-dent items," like swords that were dented during shipping or that have a loose handle. People eat that stuff up because we sell an item for twenty dollars that's normally fifty dollars. We still make a small profit because the items are well priced, but mostly it allows us to clear out damaged items.

How did you advertise the store?

Once I opened the new store, I started doing local television ads. They're great for promoting any local business. What's great about that is you can pick where your ads are shown. We wanted our ads to play during sword movies like *Highlander,* so they always reached the right market. There's a dramatic change when the ad runs. We see a quadrupling of traffic.

THE PLAN TO FOLLOW

STEP 1

Register your domain name. Obtain a DBA, seller's permit, and business bank account.

NOTE: Blair suggests that you make a list of backup domain names in case your name is taken.

STEP 2

Find a supplier for your product.

NOTE: Blair suggests that you search the Internet to find a manufacturer. If your company is not large enough to purchase straight from the manufacturer, ask for a list of distributors.

STEP 3

Develop an e-commerce website that can accept payments online.

STEP 4

Market your site through pay-per-click Internet advertising. Also, hold contests on your site to encourage word-of-mouth advertising and to build an e-mail contact list. Send e-mails to your contact list on a regular basis with announcements and offers.

NOTE: Blair says it's rare to find someone who likes something and who doesn't have friends or family with the same interests. Dedicate your marketing to finding the people who love what you sell, and then give it away to encourage word-of-mouth advertising.

THE HIGHLIGHTS

- You need very little startup capital to launch an online business.
- Encourage word-of-mouth marketing, and create fervor by giving away free items.
- Build your e-mail contact list through online contests and strategic marketing.
- Keep e-mail volume low for higher impact on potential sales.
- Market to people and groups that you know will be interested in your product.

THE RESOURCES

MORE INFORMATION ABOUT TITUS BLAIR

Swords Online
www.swordsonline.com
Blair's website tells you where to purchase cool swords.

HOW TO FIND PRODUCTS MADE OVERSEAS/ONLINE INNOVATIONS

TPage
www.tpage.com
The single most comprehensive source to post and to search for data regarding trades and market research.

BuyKorea
www.buykorea.org
Korean products and import/export trade leads.

Importers.com
www.importers.com
Maintains a directory of international importers and exporters called "TradePages."

North American Wholesale Co-Op Association
www.nawca.org
Members have access to live supplier and drop ship directories, a web-wide product search, and a surplus and liquidation finder.

HOW TO IMPORT PRODUCTS

Worldwide Legal Directories
www.hg.org

Going Beyond Borders (webcast)
www.globalspeak.com/html/video.htm

IMPORTING HONG KONG (CHINA) PRODUCTS TO THE UNITED STATES

U.S. Commercial Service
www.customs.gov

U.S. Department of Commerce
www.buyusa.gov/hongkong/en/faqs.html
Lists FAQs regarding Hong Kong business protocols. (Link may also be found via the U.S. Commercial Service website listed above.)

CMS Corporate Management Services
www.cmshk.com/hkcompany.shtml
Full-service company providing detailed information for international business ventures, including Hong Kong taxes.

HOW TO DESIGN A DO-IT-YOURSELF (DIY) WEBSITE WITH A SHOPPING CART

Web Design Software
www.diywebkit.com
DIY web-kit is a complete solution that enables you to design a webpage in minutes. Its web design software contains everything needed to create a website.

Register.com, Inc.
www.register.com
A DIY website-building tool to grow your business online.

Creative Cart Internet Shopping Cart Service
www.creativecart.com
Split hosting, secure order processing, cut-and-paste interface, and very low cost is offered here.

Charge.com
www.charge.com
Your application is quickly completed online. This company offers many free services.

HOW TO ADVERTISE YOUR WEBSITE RANKINGS/SEARCH ENGINE

Paramount Webmasters
www.paramountWebmasters.com/ search_engine_optimization.php
Analyzes webpages and gives advice on how to improve them for search optimization.

Google AdWords
www.adwords.google.com
This site provides a wealth of information concerning AdWords' advantages, success stories, cost, news, and demos.

Overture
www.searchmarketing.yahoo.com
Marketing research tools.

Carmen Maranon (the "Marketing Chick")
www.marketingchick.com
Produce better results from your marketing efforts. A good source of website tools and aids.

Intelligent Web Marketing, Inc.
www.i-web-marketing.com
Information on increasing traffic to your website.

Pay-Per-Click Advertising (PPC)
www.goclick.com
Click on the beginner's guide link for complete detailed instruction on PPC advertising.

AddMe! Free Search Engine Submission
www.addme.com/submission.htm
This site allows you one website submission to the top fourteen search engines and directory free of charge.

Web Decal
www.webdecal.com
Car decals, static cling decals, and bumper stickers to enhance your website promotion efforts by advertising on your car.

Millionaire Blueprints *neither endorses nor recommends any of the companies listed in the resource section. Resources are intended as a starting point for your research.*

Ryan
LEE

His knack for marketing and for pursuing big ideas propelled him to the top of his industry. Now he's planning to change the way we approach–and gain access to–personal training.

BUSINESS NAME:
Personal Trainer University

TYPE OF BUSINESS:
Fitness Information Products Online

LOCATION:
New Canaan, CT

ADAPTED FROM:
Millionaire Blueprints magazine article,
"The Future of Fitness,"
January/February 2007

When Ryan Lee created a website for his personal training services back in 1998, he never dreamed where it would lead. He was one of the first in his field to have his own site, which he created to promote what he thought would always be a side business. Little did he know that the income from his side business would grow to dwarf his regular salary, and that he would be able to do what he loved full time and never look back.

Lee started working out with his dad in their basement when he was twelve years old, and he's been hooked on fitness ever since. While most of his early jobs related to fitness in one way or another, it was working for himself as a personal trainer that led him to the success he enjoys today. In an industry where many personal trainers have no idea how to market themselves, Lee seems to have an innate ability for it. Lee's Rolodex now contains the names of all of the top people in the health and fitness industry, including those who train actors and professional athletes. Lee tells us about how he made it to the top and what he plans to do next.

THE BEGINNING

How did you get involved with the Internet?

I started a website to promote the personal training company I was running on the side. I asked some friends I had in the industry to contribute articles to my site, and I started studying a lot about Internet marketing.

How did you get people to come to your site?

I don't really know how they found me in the beginning. That first site had maybe thirty or forty articles, so I guess people were finding me through the search engines. I started getting e-mails from people all over the world, and that's when I really started to get into it and work on the marketing. I did some targeted pay-per-click ads on GoTo, which became Overture, and now it's Yahoo! Search Marketing. Back then, you could get ads all over the Internet for a penny a click.

Ads for a penny a click?

Yeah, I got a thousand people for ten dollars. It was great. And then I started doing some e-books. The way I first started making money online was through a relationship with an equipment company. They sold workout equipment, and I started selling their products through my site. As my site grew, I got more confident. I wanted to do something big, so I asked the equipment company to put me in their catalog and promote me. I was declined, so I had to come up with something else.

What was your sales pitch?

I went to the biggest company in the world for training products, called Perform Better (**www.performbetter.com**). I called them and told them what I was doing. I landed a meeting with the guy, and we ended up striking a deal.

I said, "I reach a lot of trainers and coaches right now, and you do, too, but I can help you reach even more. I will sell your products and promote you all over my site and in my newsletter. And in return, I ask two things. The first is that you give my members a 10-percent discount. The second is that at your live seminars, I can have a booth with my laptop where I can tell people about my site."

That's a pretty aggressive marketing idea. How did it work out?

I figured I had nothing to lose, and it's been a great relationship. I have a half-page in their catalog where they promote my products, and I speak at most of their events.

Then your company was bought in 2000?

Yes. It was bought by an Internet company called Eteamz (**www. eteamz.com**). They had seen my website and were really interested in what I was doing. I was making maybe $30,000 at my hospital job, and the salary they offered was more than double that, plus lots of stock options. The cash up front was nothing, maybe $1,000, but the incentives were good. I did it to be a part of something big and because it was a new challenge. I was there for about two months, and then the Internet bubble burst.

THE WEBSITE

Were you running your website again on the side?

Yes. Luckily, the company that had bought it gave it back to me after the bubble burst. Then around that time, I saw a site called Global Health & Fitness (**www.globalfitness.com**). It was a membership site where people paid to access their content on health and fitness. I had already reserved the domain name SportSpecific.com, and I wondered if I could create a membership site about strength and conditioning for athletes.

What did you have to do to make it a paid site?

Basically, I had to make it secure. So I used a password protection script. It's basically just something that protects your pages, so that people need a password to enter it. You can find them online by typing "password protection script" in any search engine. And then I needed a way to process credit cards. I used ClickBank. So people would go to ClickBank and pay forty-seven dollars for a one-year membership, and it would take them right to this password script where they got a username and password. I also had people who had signed up for my newsletter and who were reading the content for free. Having a list and developing a good relationship with them is vitally important. And the best way to keep people on an e-mail list is to have good content.

THE MARKETING

How were you marketing, besides to your e-mail list?

ClickBank has a built-in affiliate program, so I looked for sports-related sites online that seemed like a good fit with what I was doing. Then I contacted them and said, "Hey, we have this affiliate program. We're paying 50 percent. Would you like to do a promotion? You could use some articles for free."

THE AFFILIATE PROGRAM

What is an affiliate program?

It's basically like having thousands of salespeople who are purely commission-based. They have the referral link. If they sell it, they get ten dollars and you get ten dollars. If they don't sell it, you might still get a lead anyway.

THE IDEA

When did you start doing this full time?

In June 2002, after I'd worked at the school for a year and a half. I wanted to wait until I had at least six months of consistent revenue from the Internet that was double my pay at the school. I wasn't sure if I should leave the job or not, because at that time it was paying around $50,000. I thought if I did both, I could really make a lot of money. But then I thought, if I can make this much part time on the Internet, imagine if I did it full time.

How are you putting all of this together?

Since I've been in this industry and online for so long, I have a huge network of fitness professionals, and I'm contacting them saying, "Create the workouts. We'll pay you." I have a couple of staff members who are organizing everything, and I'm outsourcing all the web design. We're going to do some really interesting things where high-level trainers will have their own membership sites. For example, if you want to go in and see Alwyn Cosgrove, the guy who writes for *Men's Health*, you could see his workouts at this site.

THE INFORMATION

How do you create all of these websites?

For the membership sites, I use software called MemberGate. It's a program for creating membership sites. It handles secure servers and content management, and they design the sites for you.

Why are membership sites so profitable?

They're great because you get recurring income. I think it's the perfect business because you can help thousands of people at one time, and you can work from anywhere, as long as you have Internet access.

Once someone has a passion and a niche, what's next?

You're an expert in your field, so start writing and publishing articles. Educate the consumer. You also want to put it in article directories like *EzineArticles*. Article directories publish articles for every market imaginable. If you search Google for "article directories," hundreds will come up, and you just submit them. And, of course, this whole time you should have your website set up. Even if you don't have any products yet, you can at least send out some sort of weekly or biweekly e-mail.

THE ADVICE

What advice can you give us about starting a membership site?

Rule number one is get involved with something you're passionate about. I truly believe that, because you're going to have to live and breathe this. Rule number two is to be as specific in that niche as possible.

THE PLAN TO FOLLOW

STEP 1

Find your niche. Be very specific about who your target market will be.

STEP 2

Set up a basic website. You can add extra features at a later date once you have formed a product.

NOTE: Even if you don't have any products yet, send out a weekly or biweekly e-mail.

STEP 3

Begin writing and publishing articles that will educate the consumer.

NOTE: Start with the top ten things you need to know about your area of expertise.

STEP 4

Contact sites that might be interested in posting your articles.

NOTE: You also want to submit your articles into directories. Lee uses *EzineArticles*.

STEP 5

Start your affiliate programs.

NOTE: You need to develop something you can sell. Lee suggests an e-book.

THE HIGHLIGHTS

- You can work from anywhere, as long as you have Internet access.
- Find your specific niche, and start writing your articles.
- Keep your website and articles up to date.
- You can have other people promote your site through affiliate programs.
- With a membership site, you will bring in reccurring income.

THE RESOURCES

MORE INFORMATON ABOUT RYAN LEE

Ryan Lee
www.ryanlee.com
This is a portal with links to all of Lee's sites.

Workout Pass
www.workoutpass.com
This site offers you access to tens of thousands of workouts created by Lee and his team of fitness experts.

Membership Site Boot Camp
www.membershipsitebootcamp.com
Lee's two-day program teaches you exactly how to start up your own profitable, paid membership site.

Nutrition Generator
www.nutritiongenerator.com
This is where you can discover how to follow a simple balanced nutritional program using your favorite foods.

Personal Trainer U
www.personaltraineru.com
This membership site is for fitness professionals looking for the latest profit-building strategies.

MARKETING

Yahoo! Search Marketing
http://searchmarketing.yahoo.com

PASSWORD-PROTECTION SCRIPTS

A password-protection script keeps people from accessing the content on your website without your permission. Once they've signed up, they are assigned a username and password to log in to the portions of your site that you want to restrict access to. Listed below are just a few of the sites that offer these scripts, which we found when we did a quick Internet search.

The JavaScript Source
http://javascript.internet.com/passwords/

JavaScript Kit
www.javascriptkit.com

Simply the Best
www.simplythebest.net/scripts/

DEVELOPING MEMBERSHIP SITES

Membership sites can provide steady monthly income, but there's more to it than meets the eye. Check out the companies listed below, and do your own online search for software, articles, tips, and tricks to develop a membership site that will provide paying clients indefinitely.

MemberGate
www.membergate.com

Interlogy Internet Technologies
www.interlogy.com

Membership Site Advisor
www.membershipsiteadvisor.com

AFFILIATE PROGRAMS

Affiliate programs allow other people to help you sell your products and services for a cut of the profits. There are thousands of them online. Do some research to find the one that matches your needs.

ClickBank
www.clickbank.com

Affiliate Guide
www.affiliateguide.com

Affiliate Programs
www.affiliateprograms.com

Affiliate Scout
www.affiliatescout.com

ARTICLE DIRECTORIES

One great way to start getting your name out there is to submit articles for free online. We did a quick search and have listed just a few of the article directories and helpful sites that came up.

Article Writing Tips
www.articlewritingtips.com

EzineArticles
www.ezinearticles.com

Article Dashboard
www.articledashboard.com

Go Articles
www.goarticles.com

Millionaire Blueprints *neither endorses nor recommends any of the companies listed in the resource section. Resources are intended as a starting point for your research.*

Jennifer
NICHOLS

While planning her wedding, Jennifer Nichols uncovers a million-dollar business.

BUSINESS NAMES:
My Wedding Favors and Kate Aspen

TYPE OF BUSINESS:
E-Commerce for the Wedding Industry

LOCATION:
Birmingham, AL, and Atlanta, GA

ADAPTED FROM:
Millionaire Blueprints magazine article,
"A Fortune in Favors: While Planning Her Wedding,
Jennifer Nichols Uncovers a
Million-Dollar Business,"
March/April 2006

29

For some people, planning a wedding can feel like a full-time job. For Jennifer Nichols, it became exactly that. When she found the perfect venue for her upcoming wedding, she approached the owner about creating a website that would market the venue in exchange for a deal on the booking. He accepted and unwittingly launched her lucrative entrepreneurial career. At the time, Nichols was working in corporate sales. Her fiancé, Brad Fallon, was working as a successful search engine consultant. That marriage of skills later proved itself a match made in heaven.

In her search for wedding favors, Nichols encountered another opportunity disguised as a challenge. Looking for creative mementos to give her guests, she found that the supply simply did not meet the demand. Retail stores rarely stocked 100 to 250 of any one item, and most online retailers seemed compromised by poor quality and dull, uninspired packaging. Inspired and undeterred, Nichols then started My Wedding Favors.

Just one month later, they received $10,000 in orders. Now, with both Brad and Jennifer working full time on the business, the website averages monthly sales of $350,000. In January 2005, they followed their first success with its wholesale counterpart, Kate Aspen.

Starting with a great idea that was sparked by her approaching nuptials, Nichols tapped into numerous resources to take a random observation, apply combined talents, and create fortune.

THE BEGINNING

When did you open for business?

We started My Wedding Favors in December 2002. That January, we did $10,000 in sales. Then, in February, we did $30,000 in sales. The wedding cake candle was one of our first bestsellers. I couldn't keep them in stock.

THE E-COMMERCE

How did you pursue the idea of an online wedding favors business?

I found out that you could go to Overture (**www.overture.com**) to see what people were searching for online, and to see how many were searching for it. I looked up wedding favors, and I saw that tons of people were also searching for them. I was learning about search engine optimization (SEO) from my husband. This means structuring the content on your website so that search engines list it at, or near, the top in the results of a search. Then I researched competitors and their products—and read a great e-book via Yahoo! Store Profits (**www.yahoo-store-builder.com**). I took everything I learned and used Yahoo! Merchant Solutions to create my website. Then I rented a reception hall to take pictures of the items.

Where did you get products to sell?

I actually thought I could buy products "off the shelf" and sell them for a profit online, but I soon realized that wasn't going to work. That's when I decided to go to The Mart (**www.americasmart.com**). AmericasMart in Atlanta is one of the largest wholesale marketplaces in the world.

Can anyone go to The Mart?

You have to be a reseller. I got a license and a reseller's tax ID. (See resource page.)

THE SUPPLY CHAIN MANAGEMENT

What exactly does "drop ship" mean?

When a customer places an order on our website, we forward the order to the wholesaler. The wholesaler then ships the package directly to the customer with our name on it. We don't touch the package. It all happens seamlessly. Some retailers require a minimum order of maybe $150 to drop ship, otherwise they might charge a drop-ship fee of $10. But some drop ship for free with no minimums. There aren't many people in the drop shipping business, so they are hard to find. You usually don't find them on the Internet. One thing you can do is order a product from another site. When you get it, you can figure out where it came from by the labels.

What challenges did importing present?

Ordering is always a gamble because you don't always know what will be hot. We usually order 10,000 pieces to start a new item. But if everyone wants them, you just can't get 50,000 pieces from China next week. It takes time. We had problems at first with tariffs. Some were up to 30 percent. (See resource page.)

How many suppliers do you have in China?

We have manufacturers for candles, soap, silver-metal items, and a few others. We have backups for all of them. The first manufacturer may not be available when we need to reorder a hot item right away, so we go to our second choice. It generally takes about thirty days to produce an order of 10,000 pieces, and then another thirty days to ship it by ocean freight.

How do you buy things there? Is it like going shopping?

In China there are two ways to buy products: off the shelf or customer-designed. Many of our wholesale competitors buy everything off the shelf, but we like to design pieces ourselves. The production costs are the same whether you design it yourself or not, but you might have to pay for a sample and create a mold for production. Molds for candles and poly resin items are only $40 to $100, but a mold for a metal item can cost a couple thousand dollars.

What is the process for designing an item?

Basically, you just create a design, send it over, and they'll manufacture it for you. Most of the suppliers will do it from a picture, if that's all you have. My advice is to send as much information as possible such as photos, dimensions, and colors. Be very specific. If you can create a mold, that's ideal.

THE WHOLESALE

How did you get into wholesaling?

When I couldn't get the wedding cake candle, I said, "Let's create a better one, and see if we can buy it overseas."

How did that change things?

We started ordering direct from China for My Wedding Favors. Originally, we imported items for the retail site, but we saw the potential for a wholesale business right away. We had a hard time finding suppliers in the United States, and knew that most of the companies were run by men who didn't seem to pay as much attention to the aesthetics of attractive packaging and printing. We figured if we were having that problem, other wedding favors sites must be having the same problem. We made up the name Kate Aspen. We thought it sounded like a designer's name. Then we set it up as a separate company.

How do you get your name out there as a wholesaler?

We call everyone that is on the first, second, and third page of a Google search for wedding favors. We can tell from that search who is doing the most business, so we call them. You'd think more drop shippers would do that. We send e-mails, and we try to market so that they can find us. Plus, we sell to our own retail site. My Wedding Favors buys about 50 percent of its products from Kate Aspen. Some of our wholesale customers were concerned since we own both companies, but it hasn't been a conflict.

THE MARKETING

How did you bring customers to your website?

Through Internet advertising. We began using pay-per-click (PPC) advertising right away, which is bidding for your little ad to come up next to search results on places like Google and Yahoo!.

How do you get customers now?

Most of our sales come from Internet advertising, but we also advertise the retail site in bridal magazines. It's good for branding.

What have you done to increase profits?

One great thing we did was find out what our conversion rate was, which means the percentage of our visitors who actually buy. We know that our customers have lots of questions, and we discovered that many people shop at night. So we extended our customer service hours. We answer the phones until 10:00 PM (EST). That increased our conversion rate significantly. We also added LivePerson software (**www.liveperson.com**), which lets you chat online with a customer service person.

What about your products?

More and more people want items personalized. We just bought an engraver. So, if the item itself isn't personalized, we can add a tag that is. This allows us to price a little higher and increases our profit because we have an in-house graphic designer and printer. We also use the engraver to personalize some of the items we import.

THE ADVICE

Where do you get your design ideas?

Mostly from the brides themselves and from trade shows. We also have an agent over in China now. Women tend to have a critical eye when it comes to knowing what appeals to brides.

THE PLAN TO FOLLOW

STEP 1

Go to Overture (**www.overture.com**), research what people are searching for online, and determine how many people have done so for the product you want to sell.

STEP 2

Create a website by using Yahoo! Merchant Solutions.

STEP 3

Visit AmericasMart in Atlanta, and experience the world's largest wholesale marketplace. Order direct from China, and go to the Canton Fair, which is a huge export commodities fair held twice annually in the spring and fall.

NOTE: Manufacturing quality varies.

STEP 4

Take photos of the products, and post them on your website. Write descriptions for each item.

NOTE: Nichols says the key ingredient to Internet sales is good photos.

STEP 5

Utilize the drop shipping business.

STEP 6

Bring customers to your website by using pay-per-click (PPC) advertising. To get a better conversion rate and increase the percentage of people who buy your product, consider extending your customer service hours. Add LivePerson software (**www.liveperson.com**).

NOTE: Nichols discovered that the longer you use PPC advertising, the more people click on your ad, the better your conversion rate is, and the lower your click fees are. "My advice to others is not to just start bidding. Pay for some kind of course on PPC before you try it. Even those cheesy sales letters have good information, and they always say, 'Money-back guarantee,'" she says.

STEP 7

Get your name out as a wholesaler.

STEP 8

Sell to your own retail site.

NOTE: Nichols suggests drop shipping with no minimums for free. "Helping our competition hasn't hurt our retail site because we never undercut other retailers," she says.

THE HIGHLIGHTS

- Do your footwork and research by going to trade shows and export commodities fairs.
- Get a reseller's license and a reseller's tax ID.
- Build solid outsourcing relationships with manufacturing companies in China.
- Learn all you possibly can to set up, manage, and promote your online store.
- Utilize online tutorials such as Yahoo! Merchant Solutions, and purchase customer service software such as LivePerson.
- Maximize pay-per-click (PPC) advertising to increase traffic to your website.
- Join industry associations such as the National Customs Brokers & Forwarders Association of America, Inc. (NCBFAA).
- Be a drop shipper, and use wholesalers to ship products directly to your customers.

THE RESOURCES

MORE INFORMATION ABOUT JENNIFER NICHOLS

My Wedding Favors
www.myweddingfavors.com
Jennifer Nichols' website.

Kate Aspen
www.kateaspen.com
Wholesale counterpart of My Wedding Favors.

Brad Fallon
www.bradfallon.com
Search engine optimization tips and books by Nichols' husband, Brad Fallon.

WHERE TO GO

AmericasMart-Atlanta
www.americasmart.com
With more than 300,000 annual visitors buying and selling apparel, decorations, gift items, and other products, AmericasMart claims to be the biggest wholesale marketplace in the world.

Bridal Expo
www.bridaltradeshows.com
This New Jersey firm hosts bridal trade shows in five eastern states with numerous exhibitors.

Canton Fair
www.cantonfair.biz
Held twice a year (spring and fall) in Guangzhou, China, this export commodities fair is considered the largest trade show for gifts in the world.

The National Bridal Market
www.mmart.com/nationalbridalmarket
Hosted by the Merchandise Mart, this October trade show in Chicago exhibits bridal apparel.

WHO TO KNOW

Association for Wedding Professionals International (AFWPI)
www.afwpi.com
The AFWPI is a trade organization and information resource for people who service weddings. The website also lists trade shows.

National Customs Brokers & Forwarders Association of America, Inc. (NCBFAA)
www.ncbfaa.org
The NCBFAA represents more than 800 trade facilitators. Its website is a useful source of links to related industry organizations and government agencies.

THINGS TO GET

DropshipDesign.com
www.dropshipdesign.com
This company specializes in fulfilling drop ship orders directly to your customers.

Yahoo! Merchant Solutions
http://smallbusiness.yahoo.com/ecommerce/
Everything you need for small business e-commerce.

Solid Cactus
www.solidcactus.com
This web design company specializes in Yahoo! Store development. Existing templates range anywhere from $900 to $3,300 for custom designs.

Google AdWords
https://adwords.google.com
A pay-per-click (PPC) advertising service from the popular search engine.

Bidvertiser
www.bidvertiser.com
An online service in which other companies bid to place PPC ads on your website.

Overture
www.overture.com
An online resource to see what people are searching for and how many are searching for a particular product or service.

WorldTariff
www.worldtariff.com
Operated by FedEx, WorldTariff is a fee-based service providing current information on customs duties in 118 countries. FedEx Trade Networks also serves as a customs brokerage.

DotComPhoto
www.dotcomphoto.com
You can mail product samples to this Florida company to produce photographs for use in catalogs and on websites. Its service starts at $25 per item.

Federal Tax ID
www.federaltaxid.us
For a small fee, use this website to sign up online for a Federal Tax Identification Number or an Employer Identification Number. (There are other similar sites on the Internet.)

SOFTWARE

Stone Edge Technologies, Inc.
www.stoneedge.com
Order manager software provides e-commerce functions such as shopping cart, inventory control, credit card processing, order fulfillment, and shipping features.

LivePerson
www.liveperson.com
This New York company's Timpani software enables real-time, online chats between service representatives and customers. It manages incoming e-mail traffic and web form requests.

Tariffic, Inc.
www.tariffic.com
This Canadian company produces software that enables users to access global trade rates and codes over the Internet.

HOW TO OUTSOURCE

The Outsourcing Network
www.outsourcingnetwork.net
This firm specializes in outsourcing manufacturing work to China, and it has offices in the major Chinese manufacturing regions.

Made-in-China.com
www.made-in-china.com
This website provides a directory of Chinese product suppliers in various categories.

WHAT TO READ

Yahoo! Store Profits
www.yahoo-store-builder.com.
Jenkins, Andy, and Audrey Kerwood. *Online Store Profits, A Step-By-Step Visual Training System.*
This downloadable e-book offers advice for setting up and managing a Yahoo! Online Store.

Millionaire Blueprints neither endorses nor recommends any of the companies listed in the resource section. Resources are intended as a starting point for your research.

Amanda
RAAB

This entrepreneur sells purely profitable pearls.

BUSINESS NAME:
PurePearls.com

TYPE OF BUSINESS:
Jewelry Products Online

LOCATION:
Shiner, TX

ADAPTED FROM:
Millionaire Blueprints magazine article,
"Purely Profitable Pearls,"
September/October 2006

The town of Shiner, Texas, is a long way from Asia's exotic pearl farms, but Amanda Raab travels between the two buying and selling those precious underwater gems. The Texas native owns PurePearls.com—an e-commerce business selling high-quality pearls at low prices.

She first learned about e-commerce as a graduate student while looking for a way to earn extra money. When she stumbled across an article about pearls on the Internet, the seed for her company was planted.

Now Raab works directly with pearl farmers and other experts to bring the best pearls to the online market. PurePearls.com competes with some of the best-known retail jewelers in the marketplace, and she has gained clients from all over the world.

THE BEGINNING

How did you start this company?

I started another company before PurePearls.com. It was a website based on gardening (**www.birdsandbeespatio.com**), and it was the stepping stone to where I am now. I did a lot of experimenting with it. I learned HTML and how to build a website.

How did you know where to start?

I really didn't know where to start because I was also working while going to graduate school. I had thoughts that I would really like to try this again with something that I could be passionate about—something that I could really put my whole heart into.

So I sold that company for just a couple hundred dollars, which wasn't a lot, but actually I made money on it. I sold it online at **www.buysellwebsite.com**. It was based on selling e-commerce stores, and I posted it on there for sale.

THE IDEA

Where did the idea of selling pearls come from?
I actually did a lot of my work from 10:00 PM until 4:00 AM when I was in graduate school. One night in early October 2003, I was researching online and looking at some jewelry items. I was reading articles on jewelry and gems, and I kind of fell into the ones about pearls. It clicked in my head that this could be something that I could really be passionate about.

Where did you find the articles you were reading about pearls?
The Gemological Institute of America's (GIA) website (**www.gia.edu**). I found them doing a Google search. I was reading on the GIA site, and I started typing in pearls to read more about them. I found all this interesting information. I knew it had to be e-commerce, so I thought, "How can I do this online?" The next day, I sought out suppliers, because I knew I couldn't sell pearls without the pearls.

THE INFORMATION

How did you find suppliers?
I contacted hundreds of people. I would find contacts in articles that I read, and I e-mailed them to find out how I could source pearls from them. I realized a lot of people who sell pearls don't sell wholesale, but I needed to start somewhere. My first step was in networking in the right direction. My e-mails read something like, "I am starting a pearl business, and I'm looking to find suppliers for my pearl company."

Do you think some of them viewed you as their competition?
That might be it, plus a lot of pearl companies didn't want to tell me anything unless I was going to buy from them. However, I slowly figured out that a lot of these companies were buying directly from pearl farms. I decided, hey, that's what I'm going to do, and so I actually joined up with another pearl company.

I found someone who would answer all my questions. He's actually my mentor. He explained to me how the business worked and that if I pooled money in with his sales, we could have this volume-based business, and we could pull a lot better pricing from the pearl farms.

How difficult would it have been for you without your mentor?
Extremely difficult. My mentor had those contacts for buying directly from pearl farms.

So basically, he helped you get the same contacts he had already set up dealing directly with the manufacturers and the pearl farms.
Exactly. He was already traveling to Asia, and he knew exactly where to go and which pearl farm doors to knock on, and he generously passed this information along to me.

THE PRODUCT

So how did you decide what products to sell?
When I started, my selection was much smaller than it is right now. I didn't have any of the customized pieces I do now. I had a price list from the farms that I went through and chose what I thought would be the staple products for the company—kind of as a test to see what would sell the best. So I got a pretty good assortment of pearls, but they were all mainly just freshwater Akoya pearls and Tahitians. South Seas is a very high-end pearl, so I didn't really carry any of those in the very beginning.

THE WEB

Once you started buying your pearls and built an inventory, how did you develop your website?
I was going to have a professional do it. I used a web design company called Lime Dot Webshop (**www.limedot.com**). I knew the color scheme I

wanted, and I knew that I wanted it to be very informative for my customers.

How do you market your company on the Internet?

The first thing I used was search engine optimization because I could afford it. I engineered my website so that it's highly readable by just different search engines like Google and Yahoo!. If you log on and type in "pearls," my website comes up number three. That's a natural ranking. I'm not paying for that. Google sees my website as a very valuable pearl website, and pulls it up really high when you type in "pearls." For that, I had to do a lot of research just trying to figure out what search engine optimization was, because those are very intimidating words. I bought a whole bunch of books on the subject, and I optimized my website myself.

Did it take you a long time to do that?

Yes, and it's an ongoing process. Still to this day, we optimize our website. We keep the site really clean and full of information, making sure that other websites are interested in our company so they will link to us. That is very helpful for our search engine optimization campaign. When other companies link to us, it shows that we're a good, valuable, credible company.

THE MARKETING

Most of your marketing has been done through the Internet. Have you done anything else?

I had some disposable income to build the business, so I looked into getting a public relations company, and I found one. I Googled pretty much every keyword I could in PR. I found a PR company in Houston, and I am paying a monthly retainer. PR costs between $1,000 and $10,000 per month, depending upon the experience of the company. I was paying in the mid-range.

So most of your marketing has been strictly through the Internet and PR?

Yes, and I do my own marketing. I market myself by talking about the company with different people. I have a huge return customer base, and a lot of my customers tell their friends. Also, we're trying to develop our website so it will provide more information to customers. We're constantly building out what we already have.

THE ADVICE

Has your company grown more because of your passion, or because of your hard work?

Starting a business is hard work. I think anybody can start a business if he or she has the initiative and the drive to do so. I think a lot of people think it's going to be overwhelming, and they just give up before they ever start to work on their idea. But the thing is, that's what separates people who actually capitalize on their ideas from others who just throw them out.

THE PLAN TO FOLLOW

STEP 1

Do your research! Learn everything you can about your possible products before you go searching for them.

NOTE: Raab found The Gemological Institute of America (**www.gia.edu**) to be full of information.

STEP 2

Start searching for, and contacting, suppliers.

NOTE: When you start contacting suppliers, make sure you do your research on the company. Unfortunately, you can run into a lot of frauds on the Internet.

STEP 3

Develop a website to sell your products online. Include information on your products, as well as your company's background.

NOTE: Raab used web design company, Lime Dot Webshop (**www.limedot.com**). She also does a lot of the website design herself, in addition to word-of-mouth marketing.

STEP 4

Market your company through a public relations representative or on the web.

NOTE: PR firms know who to contact to get your company and its products positive exposure. Always keep your website up to date with new features such as a customer rewards program or a refer-a-friend program.

THE HIGHLIGHTS

- Time spent researching your possible products should not be underestimated.
- Make sure your suppliers are legitimate. There can be a lot of fakes in the jewelry market.
- It is not crucial to have a formal business plan with this type of venture.
- Offer great service to encourage word-of-mouth marketing.
- Networking will play a major role in helping your business grow.

THE RESOURCES

MORE INFORMATION ABOUT AMANDA RAAB

PurePearls
www.purepearls.com
Amanda Raab's company sells high-end pearls.

Birds and Bees Patio
www.birdsandbeespatio.com
Raab's first website—the stepping stone to her creation of PurePearls. Birds and Bees Patio still sells birdhouses, canopies, and more in unique designs for outdoor comfort and endurance. Raab has since sold this website to **www.buysell website.com** and made a small profit.

JEWELRY EXPERTS

The Gemological Institute of America (GIA)
www.gia.edu
GIA is the world's largest and most respected nonprofit institute of gemological research and learning. GIA discovers, imparts, and applies gemological knowledge to ensure the public trust in gems and jewelry.

The JCK Show—Las Vegas
www.jckvegas2007.expoplanner.com
This annual show features more than 2,700 jewelry manufacturers and designers, representing a broad range of product categories. LUXURY by JCK is an invitation-only event offering an exclusive collection of the finest jewelry brands from the world's most-renowned designers and manufacturers.

The Hong Kong International Jewelry Show
www.hkjewellery.tdctrade.com
Held once a year in Hong Kong, this is an exclusive jewelry show for approximately 2,000 exhibitors.

SEARCH ENGINE OPTIMIZATION (SEO)

Wikipedia
http://en.wikipedia.org/wiki/SEO
Search engine optimization defined.

Digimedia
www.digimedia.com
This company owns and operates a portfolio of powerful, common generic domain names and corresponding websites. Its form of direct navigation (where users type in via their address bar) results in pure, highly qualified website traffic for e-commerce businesses.

E-COMMERCE AND SMALL BUSINESS OWNERS

U.S. Small Business Administration (SBA)
www.sba.gov
The SBA helps business owners start, finance, and manage their businesses. It offers an online women's business center to assist female entrepreneurs.

The National Association of Women Business Owners (NAWBO)
www.nawbo.org
This organization shares resources to help shape public policy for female business owners. It offers networking opportunities, training, and other resources through membership in its national organization and local chapters.

Texas Women Ventures Fund
www.texaswomenventures.com
This organization helps female entrepreneurs get to the next level in their businesses by providing growth capital, money, and mentoring.

WEB DESIGNER

Lime Dot Webshop
www.limedot.com

PUBLIC RELATIONS

All About Public Relations
www.aboutpublicrelations.net
A wealth of information explaining the benefits of proper public relations. This site is loaded with articles and tips.

PR Newswire
www.prnewswire.com
Offers electronic delivery of news releases and information directly from companies to the media and consumers.

ZeroMillion
www.zeromillion.com/marketing/public-relations.html
Do-it-yourself public relations tips and advice for businesses on a shoestring budget.

Millionaire Blueprints *neither endorses nor recommends any of the companies listed in the resource section. Resources are intended as a starting point for your research.*

Yanik
SILVER

Yanik Silver taps into the secrets of online success.

BUSINESS NAME:
Surefire Marketing, Inc.

BUSINESS TYPE:
Information Products Online

LOCATION:
Potomac, MD

ADAPTED FROM:
Millionaire Blueprints magazine article,
"A Web-Made Millionaire,"
September/October 2006

W hen Yanik Silver was only two, he and his family moved to the United States from Russia. With only $256 and little knowledge of the English language, Silver's father worked hard to build a multimillion-dollar business.

His work ethic and independent spirit were not lost on his son. While growing up, Silver worked for his dad's medical sales business, and, in turn, he developed his own entrepreneurial spirit.

Silver eventually launched his own business—a different take on Internet sales utilizing the most important commodity of all: information. Silver has since built a multimillion-dollar Internet business himself, marketing everything from e-books to how-to packages and self-improvement courses.

Today, Silver's Internet business allows he and his wife and young children to enjoy life at an unhurried and pleasant pace. But regardless of his success, Silver has never forgotten the basic values he learned as he followed in his father's footsteps.

His business isn't just about himself. "I'm a firm believer in helping others," he says. "I want to always give people something that has a value ten to a hundred times what they pay me."

THE BEGINNING

When did you start working for your father?

When I was about twelve years old. At fourteen years of age, I was doing telemarketing with all my own leads and follow-ups. When I was sixteen years old, I got my driver's license, and he said, "Hit the road. Make some sales for us."

What were you selling?

Very sophisticated medical equipment. I did fairly well, but quickly realized I didn't want to just knock on doors. One of my clients gave me a tape I listened to a dozen times. It opened my eyes to the possibilities of direct marketing where I didn't have to cold call doctors. I could simply send a marketing message to them and contact thousands of doctors at once.

How did you start working with direct-response marketing in your dad's business?

I wrote full-page ads with lots of text and classic direct response mail-order ads.

Why did you become interested in the Internet?

I could see people selling legitimate products online, such as e-books—products with no delivery cost and no product cost. People paid for them with their credit cards and downloaded the products. I became completely enamored with that business model.

THE IDEA

Your business launch was centered on a question. What was that question?

I asked myself, "How do I create a fully automatic website that provides an incredible value and makes money for me while I sleep?"

I wanted to create something that worked on autopilot and made money regardless of where I was in the world. I also wanted to provide incredible value. I knew it couldn't just be an e-book. An e-book is an easy way to get into the Internet business and start selling information, but I wanted it to be different—not the exact same thing anyone else had.

What is an e-book?

An e-book is an electronic book. Most of the time, it's delivered as a Portable Document File (PDF).

Why is an e-book a great product to sell?

The reason it's such a great product to sell is that you keep 97 percent of the money. The topics are endless.

THE PRODUCT

When did you discover your answer?

I woke at 3:00 in the morning, and the idea for instant sales letters just came to me. I could create a package that consisted of sales letters—fill-in-the-blank sales letter tools—for any kind of business. I jumped out of bed, registered the domain (**www.instantsalesletters.com**), and got to work.

What was your experience with this first Internet business?

After the first month, sales were very solid at $1,800. That wasn't too bad. Then it went up to about $3,600. Then it progressed to about $7,200 by the third month. By the fourth month, I was doing about $9,000 off this little $29 e-product.

THE WEBSITE

How do you create a successful website?

There are two components that must be in place. The first is to sell the product, and the second is to capture information, like an e-mail address, from the people who don't buy.

How do you write copy that sells successfully?

Present your entire sales message to somebody once you've got their attention with the headline. Then counter every objection. Explain your product in detail, provide testimonials, and give them a reason why they should make a purchase.

How do you get people to leave their contact information?

I give them an incentive (usually a free report or information) to leave their name and e-mail address. Then I use this information to build a mailing list.

THE INFORMATION

What is another means of generating content?
A great area I love is public domain.

What is public domain?
Public domain means it's fallen out of copyright. It literally means belonging to the public. Anything published in the United States before 1923 is public domain now, and anything published and copyrighted in the United States from 1923 to 1963—and not renewed in its twenty-eighth year—is public domain.

How can you use public domain works on your website?
You can do just about anything you want with public domain, which means you can even sell it! You can break it into pieces to use as a giveaway incentive for people's e-mails. You can have someone scan a public domain book and put it into an e-book to sell.

How can you apply your own copyright to a public domain work?
It's called a derivative work. And you can do this lots of different ways. You can add your own illustrations, comments, or thoughts to the public domain work. You can record it on audio CD. You can write your own foreword to it, and leave the rest alone. You cannot claim copyright on the material you left alone, but it becomes more unique. You can take pieces of it out, and retitle it. You can create a compilation where you own the order or selection. Finally, you can create video based on the content, and more.

How do you know if something is public domain?
You've got to do some searching. I have a course outlining how to do it at **www.publicdomainriches.com**. One place you can search is **www. alibris.com**. There's also a place called **www.gutenberg.org** with free public domain e-books. *The Public Domain* by Stephen Fishman is a good resource available on **www.amazon.com**.

THE MARKETING

Once you have a website, how do you get more people to visit?

Ways I've found that are really good and sustainable are pay-per-click, e-zine ads, articles, and affiliated programs. Pay-per-click is the easiest and quickest way to generate web traffic. These are sites such as Google AdWords and Yahoo! Search Marketing.

You mentioned ads in e-zines. How would you go about advertising there?

E-zines are e-mail newsletters. To find an e-zine on your topic, go to a search engine and type in your subject, plus "newsletter e-zine."

You mentioned that writing articles is another good method of advertising.

One of the very best! Write an article on the subject of whatever you're selling, and submit it to an article directory. The biggest one is **www.ezinearticles.com**. When they're looking for content for their e-zine, the publishers will look at that site. At the end of your article, add a resource box. Articles keep bringing traffic to your website forever. The more articles you get out there, the better.

THE AFFILIATE PROGRAM

What about your affiliate program?

This is how you can get hundreds, thousands, and even tens of thousands of people promoting your website for you, and you only pay them when they make a sale.

How did you get started with affiliate programs?

I searched the Internet for keywords and found the top people in the search engines. I went to **www.betterwhois.com**, and it gives you the identity of the person behind the website. I got their e-mail address, went to each site, wrote them a personal note, talked about their site and what I liked about it, and told them about my product—how well it had sold so far and what kind of affiliate commission I was offering. I offered 45 percent affiliate commission. This means that if they make a sale, no matter what the product sells for, they get 45 percent.

THE ADVICE

What are the different ways people can sell information on the Internet?
You can package information as e-books, membership sites, templates or tools, courses, or anything. Just be creative.

As Silver's business continues to grow, he keeps one of his basic motivations in mind—helping others. "I have great success stories," he says. "One is a guy who wanted to move back to his hometown, a tiny town in Mississippi. He hated the big city, and his Internet business let him move."

Helping others and having plenty of time to spend with his family are wonderful results of years of dedication and independent thinking. These are traits that Silver picked up from his hard-working father. Silver's father took a step of courage and moved to America, where he built his own multimillion-dollar business. Today, Silver is taking that same spirit and sharing it with people across the United States and around the world.

THE PLAN TO FOLLOW

STEP 1

Develop an information product, or use public domain.

NOTE: Silver says financial, self-improvement, and how-to are the most popular types of information sold on the Internet.

STEP 2

Develop a website to sell your products online, and capture contact information from visitors to build a database.

NOTE: Silver suggests that you keep your site simple. Add an attention-grabbing headline, present your entire sales message in detail, and provide testimonials. Add an incentive (a free report or information.)

STEP 3

Market your site with pay-per-click advertising, e-zine ads, and articles.

NOTE: Silver suggests you write a couple of 500- to 700-word pieces about your product and submit them to article directories. He says this is one of the very best ways to market your product.

STEP 4

Set up affiliate programs.

NOTE: Silver suggests that you search keywords online to find the top twenty companies, and look them up on **www.betterwhois.com** to find the identity of the people behind the websites. Contact them with your proposal for an affiliate program.

THE HIGHLIGHTS

- This is an excellent home-based business. It allows you the freedom to work from anywhere.
- E-books require no delivery cost and no product cost. People pay with credit cards and download products instantly.
- You can make money on one website for years without any additional work.
- You can launch this business with very little startup capital.
- This e-marketing business has a 97-percent profit margin.
- You can have other people promote your website through affiliate programs.

THE RESOURCES

MORE INFORMATIOJN ABOUT YANIK SILVER

Surefire Marketing, Inc.
www.surefiremarketing.com
Yanik Silver's online information products company.

Instant Sales Letters®
www.instantsalesletters.com
Silver's first e-commerce website that offers packages consisting of sales letters (fill-in-the-blank sales letter tools) for any kind of business.

SELLING INFORMATION ON THE INTERNET

Internet Association of Information Marketers
www.netaim.info
Dedicated to enhancing the success of Internet information marketers.

KnowThis.com
www.knowthis.com/Internet.htm
Detailed information on Internet marketing, including the basics of e-commerce, methods, and strategies.

PURCHASING DOMAIN NAMES

Go Daddy
www.godaddy.com
A great domain-purchasing site. Also offers hosting services and a do-it-yourself site application.

Yahoo! Small Business
http://smallbusiness.yahoo.com/domains
Purchase a domain name through Yahoo! Small Business.

WEBSITE AND GRAPHIC DESIGN

Quick Biz Builder
www.quickbizbuilder.com
This is a valuable resource for anyone wanting to build their own website.

Yahoo! Small Business
http://smallbusiness.yahoo.com/webhosting
Build your own website with one of the web's most trusted search engines.

Business.com
**www.business.com/directory/Internet_and_
online/web_design/freelance**
An extensive list of freelance web designers you
can hire.

iFreelance
www.ifreelance.com
An efficient and affordable way to connect with
talented freelance professionals.

E-Lance
www.elance.com
Global marketplace that matches buyers and
sellers of services.

E-MAIL LISTS

L.I.S.T. Incorporated
www.l-i-s-t.com
Full-service supplier of e-mail, mailing, and telemarketing lists.

E-MAIL AUTO-RESPONDERS

E-mail Auto-Responders
www.autoresponder-review.com
Discusses auto-responders and what to look for.

WRITING WEB SALES COPY

Yanik Silver's Copywriting Workshop
www.ultimatecopywritingworkshop.com
Silver's secrets to effective web copywriting.

Workz.com
**www.workz.com/content/view_content.
html?section_id=503**
This webpage features helpful tips on web copywriting, including secrets for an attention-grabbing
opening.

Lowery, Shelley. "Writing Effective Sales Copy."
www.websource.net/web_site_design8.htm
This short article gives a series of helpful hints to
get you started quickly.

PUBLIC DOMAIN

Public Domain Riches
www.publicdomainriches.com
Moneymaking online tutorial for finding,
repackaging, and selling public domain content.

Alibris
www.alibris.com
Similar to an online used bookstore. Search for
books and audiobooks by the publishing date
and topic.

Project Gutenberg Consortia Center
www.gutenberg.com
Distribution of free electronic books now in
public domain.

Fishman, Stephen. *The Public Domain.*
Available via www.amazon.com
An in-depth e-book about how to find works
now in public domain.

E-BOOK SOFTWARE

e-Book Edit
www.ebookedit.com
Software that will help you create your own
e-book.

e-Book Compiler
www.ebookcompiler.com
Software program to create e-books.

e-Book Power
www.ebookpower.com
Creating e-books with multimedia.

AFFILIATE PROGRAMS

Better-Whois.com
www.betterwhois.com
Research companies and then search this
domain registrar to find the identity of the person behind the website.

DW Solutions
www.dw-solutions.net
An Internet marketing firm that specializes in
affiliate marketing.

RECEIVING PAYMENTS ONLINE

PayPal
www.paypal.com
A useful service for receiving online payments by
credit cards or checks.

Chronopay
www.chronopay.com
An online merchant account provider. There are
many others as well. A search on Yahoo! for
"online merchant account provider" will reveal
numerous options.

Conley, Jim, and Matt Mickiewicz. "Guide to
Online Payment Acceptance."
**www.sitepoint.com/article/online-payment-
acceptance-1**
This article explores how to choose the merchant provider that is right for you.

GENERATING WEB TRAFFIC

Yahoo! Search Marketing
http://searchmarketing.yahoo.com
Provides many options for marketing your website.

Webmaster Forums
www.akamarketing.com/webmaster-forums
These forums cover many topics, including web
advertising and generating traffic.

PAY-PER-CLICK (PPC)

Google AdWords
www.adwords.google.com
A successful pay-per-click option.

E-ZINE ADS

Callan, David. "Advertising in Ezines."
www.akamarketing.com/advertising-in-ezines.html
An article discussing the pros of e-zine ads.

Submitting Articles Online
www.ezinearticles.com
Users can upload or download free expert content that can be used within e-mail newsletters or websites.

Millionaire Blueprints *neither endorses nor recommends any of the companies listed in the resource section. Resources are intended as a starting point for your research.*

Joseph
TANTILLO

How one nearly broke fraternity brother turned a waiting room idea into a thriving online company.

BUSINESS NAME:
GreekGear.com

TYPE OF BUSINESS:
Customized Greek Products Online

LOCATION:
Freeburg, IL

ADAPTED FROM:
Millionaire Blueprints magazine article,
"Going Greek,"
August 2005

Deeply in debt, and having just found out that his wife was pregnant, Joseph Tantillo needed a new source of income—and fast. Ever since his college fraternity days, Tantillo had been intrigued by the idea of selling merchandise bearing the Greek letters of sororities and fraternities.

While leafing through a waiting room magazine, he began to read an article about creating an online company. Suddenly an idea sparked Tantillo's imagination. That idea, combined with his knowledge, experience, and circumstances, formed a concept that would soon become Tantillo's lucrative GreekGear.com.

Now a thriving online company, GreekGear.com sells T-shirts, sweatshirts, and just about anything else college kids might want that can be customized with their Greek organizations' letters.

Tantillo shares how he went from operating out of a spare bedroom to his new state-of-the-art 10,000-square-foot facility—and how others could follow his example in building successful online stores.

THE BEGINNING

How long did it take to get the company up and running?

I went home from the doctor's office and started working on it that night. The website was up and running in a couple of weeks. Within days, I got the first order.

How did you create your website so quickly?

I used Yahoo! for everything. It only cost $80 to get up and running. Knowing graphic design made it a bit easier, especially when it came to adding the pictures and creating a good layout. They do have great templates that you can customize as little or as much as you want. Everything you need to get started is there—the shopping cart system and security for accepting credit cards—the whole bit.

Your niche is specializing in one-of-a-kind items with no minimums. How do you do that?

We have supplier relationships that allow us to order just one piece if we want. We carry little or no inventory on many items. We also keep blanks of the popular items in inventory, and then customize them one at a time. No one else customizes like that. We have all the machines here for screen printing, embroidery, tackle twill, pad-printing, engraving, sign and banner equipment, and we have a great art department.

THE WEBSITES

How many domain names do you own?

I think I own about twelve right now. The first domain name I bought was GreekGearExpress.com. I wanted GreekGear.com, but someone else owned it. They wouldn't sell. But since they weren't using it, I kept checking back. One day, it was available.

Was it easier to start the other online companies?

Once the template was up with GreekGear.com, the others were very easy to start. I use the same suppliers for the items that start as blanks, and I found additional suppliers by searching online for the rest of the merchandise.

How did you come up with those ideas?

I realized that people are passionate about their fraternities and sororities. So, when I was ready to create other businesses, I asked, "What other things are people passionate about?" That is where the ideas for all of the other businesses came from.

Who manages your websites now?

I still use Yahoo! for all of it. They take a percentage of every sale, but it works out great for the way we do business. I do hire graphic designers now and then to spiff up the design work.

THE PRODUCT

How did you fill those first orders?

I'd simply relay it to my suppliers. I wasn't holding any inventory. I knew several suppliers already, and I scouted around for the rest. Some I found online by searching for "Greek merchandise," and others I found by going to stores and checking the tags to see who manufactured them. Then I contacted the companies to find out if I could buy from them. Most of them had minimum order quantities, but I had to be able to order just one.

As you've expanded, how have your supplier relationships changed?

Since we now have the equipment to customize so many things so quickly, we decided to become a supplier too. We set up a new online store called WholesaleGreek.com that retailers can buy from. It's the same merchandise we sell to everyone else. The difference is that we have order minimums, usually six to twelve pieces, and we don't sell to end users like individual fraternities or sororities. We only sell to resellers.

We're on the verge of purchasing some items from China as well. I found a supplier online just by searching around. And we've also switched to making some of the items in-house, not just customizing them. For example, take our sweatshirt blankets. We couldn't find a supplier to make them in the colors we wanted, so we purchased the fabric and now we make them here.

THE LEGAL

Do you have to license your products?

Yes. I had my website online for a couple of days when I received a call from Affinity Marketing Consultants (**www.greeklicensing.com**) saying that I was infringing on licensing rights. Affinity was founded by Sigma Chi, but now represents lots of Greek organizations. I signed a licensing agreement to pay royalties and follow certain rules.

That must have taken you by surprise?

Yes, it did. I had to make the decision at that point to become licensed. I didn't know that so many of the Greek organizations required it. So it wasn't something I had planned on. We're now the leading supplier of Greek gear. And, because we're licensed, we can advertise anywhere. We get more business because we are up front.

THE MARKETING

How do you stay in touch with what is in style for the college crowd?

We look at magazines and catalogs, and pay attention to what our suppliers are offering. We go to the mall now and then to watch people. We also go to the Spirit Show (**www.thespiritshow.com**) each year to see what's new.

How did you advertise in the beginning to let people know you were out there?

I did a lot of e-mailing. I sent marketing e-mails to every fraternity. I also e-mailed friends to ask their advice about how the site looked and what products I should sell.

How do you advertise now?

Now we advertise exclusively online. We use pay-per-click advertising with Yahoo!, Google, and a few other companies. We spend nearly 10 percent of our revenue on advertising. We get lots of word-of-mouth advertising too.

THE PROFIT

What do you do to maximize profits?

I work on increasing profits by adding products and services. I added rush service once we had the blanks and the embroidery machine to customize them in-house. Now, for an extra $10 per shirt, people can have them shipped out within twenty-four hours. That adds directly to profit.

How did you buy the machines for customizing everything?

I bought the screen-printing equipment just before I started the business and paid cash for it. It was a whole getting-started kit for $2,500, and you can buy them on eBay. I financed the embroidery machine, but paid it off early. When we were ready, I bought the four-head (a machine that embroiders four items at once) on eBay for $24,000. I waited until we had enough orders to justify it—and the cash on hand to buy it.

THE ADVICE

What do you look for when you're buying a business?

I look for a good fit, and I want the deal to be fair for everyone. I also research the business and look at the financials. I think if you do right by everyone involved, it comes back to you.

What advice do you have for someone just starting out?

You win the Internet game by creating a niche and making one-of-a-kind items. You need to invest in yourself, believe in yourself, and be passionate. You're going to have ups and downs. Focus on the ups. When you're going through one of those down times, figure out what you can do to turn it around.

THE PLAN TO FOLLOW

STEP 1

Develop a website to sell your products online.

NOTE: Tantillo created his first website using Yahoo! Website Services (**http://website.yahoo.com**). A perfect solution for web hosting, Yahoo! provides the tools you need to successfully design a website, including design templates and security for credit card charges.

STEP 2

Contact and form relationships with suppliers for your product.

NOTE: Tantillo uses companies that supply GreekGear.com with blank items such as T-shirts and backpacks. GreekGear.com purchases these supplies and then customizes them for clients. To find a supplier, Tantillo suggests doing an Internet search for [your product here] merchandise.

STEP 3

Purchase additional domain names to direct more traffic to your chief website.

NOTE: Tantillo owns roughly twelve separate domain names such as MySpiritGear.com and CoEdGear.com, all of which direct back to his principal website, GreekGear.com. Look for domain names similar to your company and product by using a search engine on the Internet.

STEP 4

Get licensed.

NOTE: Tantillo reminds us that an online store is more than just selling merchandise. Make sure you have the proper rights and licenses to sell your product to keep your company 100 percent legal.

STEP 5

Focus your advertising directly toward your target audience.

NOTE: At the beginning, Tantillo says that advertising in a newspaper gave him no results. He changed his marketing plan and switched to e-mailing his target audience—every fraternity and sorority that he could find—to get the word out.

STEP 6

Consider expanding the type of products and services you offer to boost revenue.

THE HIGHLIGHTS

- An e-commerce business has very little startup capital.
- Web hosting sites, such as Yahoo!, make creating a website to sell your product an easy task.
- For niche products like those sold at GreekGear.com, word-of-mouth advertising is a great built-in marketing tool.
- Domain names cost as little as ten dollars per year, an inexpensive fee for growing your business.
- Don't forget that the Internet is a vast resource for finding the perfect companies to supply and license your product.

THE RESOURCES

MORE INFORMATION ABOUT JOSEPH TANTILLO

Featured Companies Owned by Joseph Tantillo:

Joseph Tantillo's domain names:

www.greekgear.com

www.myspiritgear.com

www.coedgear.com

www.greekgearexpress.com

www.wholesalegreek.com

The Spirit Show
www.thespiritshow.com
This is an open trade show dedicated to Greek, cheer, college, and recognition products.

Solid Cactus
www.solidcactus.com
This web design company specializes in Yahoo! Store development.

Affinity Marketing Consultants, Inc. (AMC)
www.greeklicensing.com
AMC manages licensing for travel, insurance, and other products for forty-seven national Greek organizations.

Yahoo! Merchant Solutions
http://smallbusiness.yahoo.com/ecommerce/
Everything you need for small business e-commerce.

Google AdWords
http://adwords.google.com
A pay-per-click advertising service from the popular search engine.

Yahoo! Website Services
http://website.yahoo.com
A perfect solution for web hosting, Yahoo! provides the tools you need to successfully design a website, including design templates and security for credit card charges.

TRADE ASSOCIATIONS AND SHOWS

Camex
www.camex.org
The National Association of College Stores operates this annual collegiate retailing trade show, with nearly 700 exhibitors showing a huge range of products from sweatshirts to pencils.

The National Association of College Stores
www.nacs.org
An organization representing campus stores across America.

Specialty Graphic Imaging Association
www.sgia.org
A trade group for screen-printing, digital printing, embroidery, and pad-printing professionals.
Embroidery Trade Association
www.EmbroideryTrade.org
The professional organization for those in the embroidery business.

NBM Shows
www.nbmshows.com
NBM organizes apparel decorating trade shows.

GOVERNMENT AGENCIES

U.S. Department of Labor—Office of Small Business Programs
www.dol.gov/osbp
Offers information and some financial support programs for small business owners.

U.S. Small Business Administration
www.sba.gov

U.S. Patent and Trademark Office
www.uspto.gov

THE PARTS TO BUILD THE BUSINESS

Affinity Internet, Inc.
www.affinity.com
Web hosting for small- to medium-sized businesses with e-commerce options, including site design and online payments.

Bidvertiser
www.bidvertiser.com
Bidvertiser runs an online service in which other companies bid to place pay-per-click ads on your website.

ClientReady
www.clientready.com
Custom e-commerce website design and hosting, including shopping cart functions.

Ecommerce-guide.com
www.ecommerce-guide.com
News, case studies, product guides, and more for online businesses.

Pay-Per-Click Analyst
www.payperclickanalyst.com
This site reviews pay-per-click advertising search engines.

We Build Pages
www.webuildpages.com
An Internet marketing firm that offers pay-per-click ad services.

EQUIPMENT AND SUPPLIES

Able Engravers, Inc.
www.able-engravers.com
This company offers engraving machines and materials for all levels.
All-About-Fabrics.com
www.all-about-fabrics.com
Offers information on numerous fabric suppliers.

Beacon Graphic Systems
www.beacongraphics.com
Offers sign making supplies and equipment.

Blank Shirts, Inc.
www.blankshirts.com
A supplier of unadorned clothing suitable for imprinting.

Brother, Inc.
www.brother-usa.com
Huge line of business appliances, including industrial sewing and embroidery equipment.

Chase Plastic Services, Inc.
www.chaseplastics.com
A wholesale supplier of plastic materials with no minimum orders.

Cuda Apparel
www.cudaapparel.com
Professional apparel services including screen printing, embroidery, and custom tackle twill.

Epilog Laser
www.epiloglaser.com
Sells laser engraving and cutting systems.

ITW Trans Tech
www.itwtranstech.com
ITW specializes in pad-printing inks, plates, and machines for nonfabric items.

M&R
www.mrprint.com
M&R says it is the world's largest manufacturer of screen printing equipment.

NES Clothing Company
www.nesclothing.com
A blank apparel supply company.

Service Tectonics, Inc.
www.padprinting.net
Their Pad-Printing Network has information on the process, equipment, and supplies.

SWF Mesa Distributors
www.swfmesa.com/machines/embroidery_machine.htm
The product line includes single- and multi-head embroidery machines.

Singer, Inc.
www.singerco.com
The Singer name is an old, and trusted, brand of sewing and embroidery machines.

Stahls, Inc.
www.stahls.com
Stahls has a wide range of graphic systems and equipment for screen printing and embroidery.

DIRECTORIES

Thomas Register Directory
www.thomasregisterdirectory.com
This vast website has valuable information about a number of industries, including clothing materials and plastics.

Millionaire Blueprints *neither endorses nor recommends any of the companies listed in the resource section. Resources are intended as a starting point for your research.*

2

True Stories of
REAL ESTATE
Millionaires

Robert G.
ALLEN

Robert G. Allen uses job rejections and bankruptcy to become a stronger entrepreneur.

BUSINESS NAME:
BookWise™ & Company

TYPE OF BUSINESS:
Real Estate, Publishing, and Marketing as an Entrepreneur

LOCATION:
San Diego, CA

ADAPTED FROM:
Millionaire Blueprints magazine article,
"Setbacks Become Stepping Stones,"
July/August 2007

R obert G. Allen was at the height of his career in 1986 when a freak accident took everything he owned. That year, an avalanche struck his mountain home. Not only did this act of nature obliterate Allen's home; it wiped out his bank account as well.

A decade earlier, he had achieved phenomenal success and was nearing millionaire status with the realty business he had launched in 1974. Four years later, he left the company to share his experience with the world. The result became one of America's most popular realty books titled, Nothing Down: How to Buy Real Estate With Little or No Money Down.

The situation was devastating, to say the least. So Allen and his wife decided to make a clean break and start completely over in California. There, he and a friend started teaching seminars on financial success.

"We had ninety-three people who paid $1,000 apiece for a seminar," he recalls. "I felt guilty trying to teach people how to be financially successful. So I stopped in the middle of that first seminar and said, 'I'm sorry. I'm not the guy you think I am. I've got more debt than all of you combined.'"

That was the most difficult speech Allen had ever made. When he finished, he expected everyone to demand a refund. The actual response floored him.

"They came up to me and said, 'Wow. Just tell us the truth. We love it,'" Allen recalls. "I was stunned," he says.

That moment transformed Allen's life. He discovered that many people suffer through bankruptcy just as he did.

Allen's career began when he couldn't find a job after college. After thirty rejections, he realized he was meant to take a different path. Today, his advice and business tips are highly sought after across the country.

THE BEGINNING

How did you buy your first property?

When I went into business for myself, my first property was a little duplex about a block and a half off the BYU campus. I was reading ads in the newspaper when I saw this one. I had $1,500 from graduation that my dad had given me, and that was all the money I had. My income was very spotty, but I gave them everything! I put all my down payment into that duplex, and I negotiated for a balloon payment in three months, and another three months after that. I totally risked myself.

You put $1,500 down on your first property, which was all the money you had. That was pretty risky.

It was totally risky. I don't know what I was thinking! Really, I just have very strong intuition. I knew I could pull it out somehow. When I went in and fixed up the place, cleaned out all the garbage, and worked really hard, I was able to sell it a week later.

You sold it a week later?

Yes. The neighbor wanted to buy the property when it came available, but he had been in Mexico. When he came back and found out I had bought it, he made me an offer I couldn't refuse. It tripled my money or something like that. He took over my balloon payments. I never had to make even one, and I walked away with some nice cash.

THE BUSINESS

How did your book, Nothing Down, *come about?*

I was doing investing from 1974 to 1978, but I just didn't want to be a commissioned salesperson anymore. I had this hunch that I should write a book. I thought of the title, *Nothing Down: How to Buy Real Estate with Little or No Money Down.* So I walked over to my manager on January 1, 1978, and said, "I'm never going to collect another commission." He said, "What are you going to do?" I said, "Well, I'm going to write a book."

Do you remember what your proposal was?

It contained chapter titles, a proposal letter, a sample chapter, and a silk screen cover of what I thought the book should look like. I handed my proposal to fifteen or twenty publishers at the American Booksellers convention (now called BookExpo America), and it was well received. I came away very encouraged. But I wanted Simon & Schuster, and they weren't calling me back yet.

THE MONEY

What did you do to get Simon & Schuster's attention?

I finally called them again and said, "Hey, I'm getting offers. Do you want it, or don't you?" And they said, "Yes. We'll give you a $7,500 advance, half now and half upon delivery of the manuscript." As they say, the rest is history.

THE NEED

What's in the future for you?

I recently joined a business venture with Richard Paul Evans, a famous author. The company is called BookWise (**www.bookwise.com**). It costs $35 a month. Not only is it a book club, but it also teaches you how to become financially independent. We've designed BookWise to be the most intelligent home-based business in the world. People are signing up like crazy.

What comes with the $35 monthly fee?

A hardcover bestseller, or one of the major book classics, an e-book, and an audio book. But it's more than that. We teach financial teleseminars every week, plus monthly tax classes. Just imagine the benefits of being coached weekly on the phone by successful entrepreneurs like myself and Richard Paul Evans.

THE PROFIT

Do you still buy and sell property, or are you focused on books and speaking?

I still have my finger in the pie—you bet. But in terms of my major focus, it's on my trainings, seminars, books, and other business ventures.

THE MARKETING

Didn't you accept a challenge that someone could drop you in a city with just $100, and you would have properties bought and sold within seventy-two hours?

That's exactly right. *The Los Angeles Times* took me to San Francisco in January 1981, and took away my wallet. The headline for the article was: *Buying Homes Without Cash, Boastful Investor Accepts Times' Challenge and Wins.* I bought seven properties in fifty-seven hours and gave the reporter $20 back in change.

That must have been worth millions in publicity.

Oh boy, was it ever. That pushed my book, *Nothing Down,* back up *The New York Times* bestseller list, and it stayed there for forty-six weeks. Today, it's sold over 1 million copies. And it's still selling, and it's still in hardcover. It's never seen paperback in twenty-five years.

So why is it that the first thing you do for people is to send them something free?

That's usually the best way to get people to raise their hands and say, "I'm interested in that." If you ask for money up front, then your ad has to be really good because people don't send money from a one-step ad very often. They want a two-step process. Raise my hand, let me taste it and see if the cookie is good, and then I'll buy it.

THE LEGAL

Does the same idea work with licensing?

Licensing is either renting someone else's success or renting out your own. Let's say American Greetings wants to use the name "Chicken Soup for the Soul" on some of their cards. They license the name "Chicken Soup for the Soul." In this case, American Greetings is doing all the work, the marketing and retailing, etc. Chicken Soup for the Soul Enterprises, Inc., gets a licensing fee and maybe 10 percent of what the wholesale price might be, and they don't have to do any selling or any printing. They just receive money. The Walt Disney Company makes enormous money this way. That's licensing: renting someone else's fame to help sell your product easier, or making money by renting out your already successful name.

THE ADVICE

"If anyone who reads this might learn anything, it's that you can survive and come back better from bankruptcy. No matter what setbacks you suffer, or what obstacles are put in your way, you can do better than you've ever done if you just continue to pursue your dream," Allen says.

THE PLAN TO FOLLOW

STEP 1

Recognize the truth about wealth. Wealth is expensive. Wealth takes hard, hard work.

STEP 2

Be honest, and be willing to take risks.

STEP 3

Be willing to learn.

STEP 4

Look for ways to create a relationship with a mentor who is passionate about the information he or she is willing to offer.

STEP 5

Do your homework. Read books by the experts, like Allen's *Nothing Down.*

THE HIGHLIGHTS

- You don't have to reinvent the process; just learn the system.
- Use job rejections and financial instabilities to become a stronger entrepreneur.
- Be bold, maintain self-confidence, set lofty goals, and never give up.
- Follow your intuition—even when it goes against standard practice.
- Don't be afraid to start over—even against all odds.
- Network with friends, colleagues at industry conventions, and professional mentors.

THE RESOURCES

MORE INFORMATION ABOUT ROBERT G. ALLEN

Robert G. Allen's website.
http://www.robertgallen.com

BookWise™ & Company
http://www.bookwise.com
Robert G. Allen's newest business venture.

SELECTED LIST OF BOOKS BY ROBERT G. ALLEN

Nothing Down: How to Buy Real Estate With Little or No Money Down [self-published in 1980; republished in 1984]

Nothing Down for the 2000s: Dynamic New Wealth Strategies in Real Estate [2004]

Creating Wealth: Retire in Ten Years Using Allen's Seven Principles of Wealth [2006]

Multiple Streams of Income: How to Generate a Lifetime of Unlimited Wealth! [2005]

Multiple Streams of Internet Income: How Ordinary People Make Extraordinary Money Online [2006]

The One Minute Millionaire: The Enlightened Way to Wealth by Mark Victor Hansen and Robert G. Allen [2002]

Cracking the Millionaire Code: Your Key to Enlightened Wealth by Mark Victor Hansen and Robert G. Allen [2005]

Nothing Down for Women: The Smart Woman's Quick-Start Guide to Real Estate Investing by Robert G. Allen and Karen Nelson Bell [2007]

TRAINING

Multiple Streams of Income
www.multiplestreamsofincome.com
Visit this site to enroll in free teleconferences with Robert G. Allen.

The Enlightened Wealth Institute™
http://ewitraining.com
801-852-8700 (Robert G. Allen's office phone.)

The 5-Minute Mentor™ Solutions For A Busy World
www.nothingdownforwomen.com
Here, you can sign up for The 5-Minute Mentor, as well as for a year-long interactive mentoring program with daily phone support from multi-millionaire real estate coaches.

Nothing Down for Women
www.nd4w.com
Visit this site, and sign up for a free teleseminar with Robert G. Allen and Karen Nelson Bell.

GENERAL REAL ESTATE TIPS

Real Estate Investing Depot
www.reidepot.com
An Internet resource for real estate investors.

FINDING REALTORS OR HOMES FOR SALE ONLINE

RealtyTrac
www.realtytrac.com

Lead to Realty
www.leadtorealty.com

FINDING MOTIVATED SELLERS

"The Recipe for Real Estate Success . . . Finding Motivated Sellers"
LegalWiz
www.legalwiz.com/freearticles/finding-motivated-sellers.shtml
A good article about locating motivated sellers.

MORTGAGES

Mortgage 101.com
www.mortgage101.com
Everything you need to know about the mortgage process.

"Borrowing Tricks"
The Note Investors Group
www.noteinvestors.com/borrowing-tricks.htm
A simple article about lowering your mortgage payments.

GENERAL INFORMATION ON TAX LIEN CERTIFICATES

Creating Wealth Without Risk
www.professorprofits.com/clickbank/index.php#
Robert G. Allen's site includes this link to information about tax lien certificates.

TAX ROLLS

Most tax rolls can be found by doing an Internet search on "tax roll" with the name of your county or city.

INFOPRENEURING

HighSpot, Inc.
www.juicedconsulting.com/ezine.php
A monthly e-zine for infopreneuring strategies.

Women's Business Gallery
www.womens-business-gallery.com/infopreneuring-101.html
A free e-course called Infopreneuring 101.

BOOKSELLERS CONVENTIONS

BookExpo America (BEA)
www.bookexpoamerica.com
BEA is a dynamic environment for networking, sourcing, and relationship building.

Maui Writers Conference
www.mauiwriters.com
A great conference for learning about writing.

FINDING A PUBLISHER OR AGENT

WritersMarket.com
www.writersmarket.com
This in-depth website helps you locate new, up-to-date markets for publishing your work, get insider advice, and track your manuscript submissions and publishing contracts. It includes information on the *Writer's Market,* a highly recommended book.

WRITING A PROPOSAL

Adler & Robin Books, Inc.
www.adlerbooks.com/howto.html
Information on writing book proposals.

Millionaire Blueprints neither endorses nor recommends any of the companies listed in the resource section. Resources are intended as a starting point for your research.

Karen
NELSON BELL

Karen Nelson Bell shares million-dollar lessons with fellow female entrepreneurs.

BUSINESS NAME:
Karen Nelson Bell

TYPE OF BUSINESS:
Real Estate Investing With Nothing Down

LOCATION:
Las Vegas, NV

ADAPTED FROM:
Millionaire Blueprints magazine article,
"Nothing Down,"
May/June 2007

K*aren Nelson Bell was facing an uncertain future after a devastating job loss in late 2000, and she wasn't sure how to proceed. She had been an accomplished musician in Las Vegas, touring the country and producing a show that was growing in popularity. Then one day, everything came to a crashing halt. The show was sold, and the new owners no longer saw a need to have her on the staff. To make matters worse, the savings she and her husband had accumulated were gone within a month of her unemployment.*

She had to do something and fast. So she began reading a book by Robert G. Allen, called Multiple Streams of Income: How to Generate a Lifetime of Unlimited Wealth. *At the end of his book, Allen included a paragraph that extended an invitation for individuals to become "guinea pigs" in a new protégé program. Bell read the invitation, and called the office immediately.*

She was accepted and plunged headfirst into the mentoring program, devouring information on real estate, information marketing, and how to purchase homes with no money down. She learned how to use other people's funding and credit to negotiate great deals and resell homes for a sizeable profit.

Four months and nine days after starting the mentoring program, Bell became an equity millionaire.

THE BEGINNING

What caused you to leave the music business and begin working in real estate?

The show I had been hired to produce was making millions. We featured it in theaters worldwide. When the company decided to sell, I wanted to buy it. But I couldn't raise $5 million. The people who bought it looked at the bottom line and said, "Why are we paying her to do something that we do?" When I gave my resignation, they said, "Well, that's good, because we were going to fire you anyway."

After you resigned, what happened?

Around the time we found out the show was going to be sold, I read a book by Robert G. Allen called *Multiple Streams of Income*. It was as if he had written it straight to me because it talked about what happens when the one source of income you depend on comes to a screeching halt.

What did you do after reading Robert Allen's book?

A paragraph at the end of his book, *Multiple Streams of Income*, noted that he was looking for people to take part in his Protégé Program. So I called his office and demanded, begged, and pleaded to be mentored in these real estate strategies! I studied real estate with Robert Allen and two of his favorite mentors for ninety minutes every week. I would listen to what they suggested, and then I'd go do it. Our homework is what helped me become a millionaire so quickly.

How did the Protégé Program work?

The Protégé Program teaches you how to buy and sell real estate without putting any money down—without using your own money.

THE PROFIT

After you started participating in the Protégé Program, how long was it before you became a millionaire?

I became an equity millionaire in four months and nine days.

What is an equity millionaire?

"Equity" refers to the difference between the value of your home and the loans on it.

THE BUSINESS

Can you remember what steps you took to become an equity millionaire?

First, you have to find a deal by looking for people who have a reason to sell. The deal that put me over the equity millionaire mark was a gal who had a $1 million mansion and moved into a $5 million mansion. She was tired of two payments.

THE PROPERTIES

Why are you looking for people who have a reason to sell their homes?

If they have a reason, they will be motivated to give you one of two things: a really great discount or financing where you don't have to use your own credit.

How do you find sellers who are motivated?

Think about what makes a person motivated to sell, and then start looking in those places. In the newspaper, I look for classified ads that say, "Vacant." If an ad says, "Immediate occupancy," the homeowner probably had a transfer, or maybe they've moved to a new home and haven't been able to sell the other one. I look for an ad that says, "Or best offer." This means the price isn't firm, and they're willing to negotiate.

Once you find a vacant home, what do you do?

I find out who owns it. If it has a sign in front, it's not difficult to find out. If it's vacant and doesn't have a sign, I go to the county records.

Tell me more about the mansion that put you over the million-dollar mark.

It was worth $1.2 million, and I decided to make her a very low offer and come back with a more reasonable offer later. She'd already turned down $950,000 from someone else, and I was hoping she'd sell it to me for about $960,000. But we wanted her to have the consideration in her mind that the house was not going to get high offers. So we offered her $805,000, expecting to negotiate, and she said yes. That means we were going to make $400,000 off that mansion.

How did you find her?

I found her through a realtor. A lot of real estate investing gurus will tell you not to use realtors because they think you should only deal with the sellers themselves. But at least half the house deals I've developed came from working with realtors.

THE MONEY

Take me back to when you offered $805,000. After she said yes, what was your next step?

She required a large amount of earnest money—$40,000. So I borrowed what I needed from a bank.

If you had run across the same deal and had bad credit, what would you have done?

I would have brought in a partner. I would have used somebody else's credit and given them a piece of it. When you've got $400,000 staring at you, you can easily find somebody to work with you.

You needed $40,000 in earnest money—or a down payment—on the house, which you borrowed from the bank. Did you need the rest of the $805,000, or was that money you paid the seller later after you sold the house again?

The $40,000 earnest money went toward the $805,000, and I got a regular bank mortgage for the balance.

So basically, you made the deal to buy the house before you had the money.

Yes, and this is where some people get confused. They think they have to get the money first, but that's not the case. If you've got a good deal, good money will flow to it. If you have a great deal, great money will flow to it. Everybody wants a piece of a great deal.

Where would you suggest people go to find funding partners?

Start personal. Start with your friends, family, and people you do business with like your chiropractor, dentist, doctor, attorney, or CPA.

After you borrowed the $40,000, was the mansion ready to sell?

No, she had really let it go. I had to borrow money to fix it up. I put an ad in the paper stating that I needed some money to fix up a house. It read, "If you'll lend me the money, I'll give you a second trust deed." That meant I would use the property itself as collateral so, if I didn't pay them back, they would be able to foreclose on me. I was surprised at how many people wanted to lend me money!

How much money did you borrow to fix up the house?

I had to borrow another $100,000. I figured it was going to take about $40,000 to fix up, and I didn't know how long I was going to have to sit on it and make big payments. I got my payments down from $8,000 a month to $3,500 a month.

Wow. How did you do that?

Just through refinancing. She had a loan that wasn't as good as what I could get.

THE BOOK

You wrote a book with Robert Allen titled **Nothing Down for Women.** *What sparked your idea?*

After I became a millionaire so quickly, I started teaching for his Protégé Program. After a couple of years, I started to notice a pattern in how women absorbed the materials. They absorbed them differently than men did. I got the notion of testing the idea, and I started writing my view of his materials, and tweaked them to suit me as a woman. Women perceive differently; they are able to read between the lines.

THE PLAN TO FOLLOW

STEP 1

First, you have to find a great deal by looking for people who have a reason to sell. Look in the newspaper for motivated sellers. Look for classified ads that say, "Vacant," "Immediate occupancy," and "Or best offer." You can also drive around and look for vacant houses, then search county records to find the owner.

NOTE: Bell says that you can also work with a realtor to find motivated sellers.

STEP 2

Contact the seller, and make an offer on the property.

NOTE: Bell suggests that you make a lower offer than what you are willing to pay to give yourself room to negotiate.

STEP 3

After you have secured a great deal, find an investor to put up the money for the down payment, repairs, expenses, and a cushion to cover mortgage payments until the property sells.

NOTE: Bell suggests that you first ask your friends, family, and people you do business with like your chiropractor, dentist, doctor, attorney, or CPA. She then suggests you run an ad in the paper offering the property as collateral to motivate lenders.

STEP 4

Take care of repairs and remodeling projects to help the house sell quickly and help you obtain the best possible price. Then, put the house on the market.

THE HIGHLIGHTS

- You can start this business with no money.
- Find a great deal first, and then find the money.
- Work with motivated sellers to give you one of two things: a really great discount or financing where you don't have to use your own credit.
- You can work with a realtor to find motivated sellers.
- You can save a lot of money by refinancing a mortgage.

THE RESOURCES

MORE INFORMATION ABOUT KAREN NELSON BELL

www.nothingdownforwomen.com
Sign up to receive free chapters from the book *Nothing Down for Women: The Smart Woman's Guide to Real Estate Investing* by Robert G. Allen and Karen Nelson Bell. A link will take you to a page where you can sign up for the 5-Minute Mentor™ Solutions for a Busy World. You can then decide if the interactive training is right for you.

NOTHING DOWN IN REALTY

Allen, Robert G., and Bell, Karen Nelson. *Nothing Down for Women: The Smart Woman's Guide to Real Estate Investing.*

Allen, Robert G. *Nothing Down for the 2000s: Dynamic New Wealth Strategies in Real Estate.*

NO MONEY DOWN TRAINING

www.nothingdownforwomen.com/affiliate
You can sign up to become an affiliate and earn $300 for every friend you refer to the program.

Robert Allen Protégé Program
www.enlightenedwealthinstitute.com

GENERAL REAL ESTATE TIPS

Real Estate Investing Depot
www.reidepot.com
This is an Internet resource for real estate investors and one that contains a wealth of information.

FINDING REALTORS OR HOMES FOR SALE ONLINE

RealtyTrac
www.realtytrac.com

Lead to Realty
www.leadtorealty.com

FINDING MOTIVATED SELLERS

Allen, Robert G. "Finding Motivated Sellers."
www.articlefinders.com/business/1294
This is a good article with a list of tips on how to tell if a homeowner is motivated to sell.

Bronchick, William. "The Recipe for Real Estate Success . . . Finding Motivated Sellers."
www.legalwiz.com/freearticles/finding-motivated-sellers.shtml
This is another good article about locating motivated sellers.

COUNTY RECORDS

County Records.com
www.countyrecords.com
This is an online resource for finding county records in a number of states, including a list of affiliated websites. To search for county records in a particular area, run an Internet search on "county records" and your county's name.

FINDING MONEY FOR YOUR BUSINESS

America's Home Business Funding Directory
www.businessfinance.com
This is where you can search for business loans and capital sources.

U.S. Small Business Administration
www.sba.gov
This website offers tips on starting, expanding, and financing your small business.

FINDING INVESTORS

Allen, Scott. "About: Entrepreneurs: Finding Funding for Your New Small Business."
http://entrepreneurs.about.com/od/financing/a/startupfunding.htm
This article explains the basics and includes links to help you further explore the topic.

MORTGAGES

Mortgage 101.com
www.mortgage101.com
Everything you need to know about the mortgage process.

Richards, Jon. "The Note Investors Group Borrowing Tricks."
www.noteinvestors.com/borrowing-tricks.htm
This is a simple article about lowering your mortgage payments.

IMPROVING YOUR CREDIT

TransUnion. *Improve Your Credit.*
www.bellco.org/ImproveCredit.asp
Here are five simple steps to get you started.

Millionaire Blueprints *neither endorses nor recommends any of the companies listed in the resource section. Resources are intended as a starting point for your research.*

Linda
COUGHLIN

Learn how Manhattan's Metro-Home millionaire, Linda Coughlin, created her own niche in the innkeeping industry without a single real estate purchase.

BUSINESS NAME:
Metro-Home NYC LLC

TYPE OF BUSINESS:
Short-Term and Extended-Stay Housing Solutions

LOCATION:
New York City, NY

ADAPTED FROM:
Millionaire Blueprints magazine article,
"Subletting in the City,"
January/February 2006

L inda Coughlin was barely into her marketing career in the fashion industry when she realized that she would rather be an entrepreneur than an employee. She was a buyer for a major department store in California when her grandmother passed away, and she was shocked when her supervisor refused to allow her time off to attend the funeral. When another boss prevented her from spending Christmas with her family, Coughlin knew she'd have to find a better way to make a living.

She had discovered, however, that while she was traveling for business, she could make a little extra money by renting out her apartment through a bed-and-breakfast (B&B) service. In fact, she often covered her entire month's rent in just a few days. "Sometimes, just to make ends meet, I moved out whenever they had a client. It was better than selling my blood!"

This seemingly simple, but clever cost-cutting technique turned out to be the spark of genius that has now parlayed itself into a multimillion-dollar success story for Linda Coughlin.

A few years later, in 1996, Coughlin was married and living in New York City with her husband and children, and she remembered her earlier rental trick. So she again rented a small portion of her townhouse out as a studio and one-bedroom unit to a B&B service. But this time, she didn't stop there. She got a job at a rental agency, earning a commission while she learned the ropes of the B&B business in her city. She learned that, since she was a rental agent, she could earn a finder's fee equal to a month's rent just by matching tenants with apartments. Then she began buying apartment leases and renting them on her own.

Once she discovered this niche, Coughlin suddenly found that she was making $12,000 in just a few weeks, and she was on her way to becoming a millionaire. Today, her company, Metro-Home, owns the leases on more than 170 apartments across Manhattan. She ensures that they are spotlessly clean, well-furnished, and secure. She rents them by the night, week, or month to business and vacation travelers, Broadway show cast members, student interns, and even the entire staff of the Republican National Convention.

THE BEGINNING

How did you begin your business?

Using $3,000 I'd earned in commissions, I rented a desk at a small rental agency in Manhattan and invested in advertising to get my own business started. I used their inventory for my clients, and I developed my own inventory at the same time I was developing my own clients. I was a client myself, but I was also an agent. I had business cards made, and I ran an ad in *The New York Times* that read, "Do you want to sublet your apartment? We take sublet listings." I also advertised the apartments I had for rent. When I got a call from someone who needed a studio for three months, I would rent the agency's inventory and take my commission—a little over 10 percent per month on each property—which I built into the rental price. Then, as I added my own inventories—the sublets I bought on my own—it kind of snowballed. At that point, in 1997, I was still a little ten- to twelve-unit business.

THE CUSTOMERS

So how do you get your high-level customers?

I network among the top-level companies to find contacts to serve those companies' corporate housing needs. To get these contacts, I just call the company and ask who handles all their corporate relocations. Then I call that person, introduce myself, and explain my services. Once that initial contact is made, I stay in touch with them regularly. When a need arises, they call me. Stay in touch with them. It is a very effective strategy, and one that costs nothing but time and attention.

THE PRICING

How do you decide how to price the rental units?
Price is based on what the market will bear, and that is linked back to
local hotel prices. I always do costing on the basis of at least a 20-percent
savings. If a hotel is $99 a night, you want to rent a one-bedroom apart-
ment at $79 to make it attractive.

THE PROCESS

How does the process work? Walk us through a sample transaction.
Potential customers might see our brochure, or they might have found
us online through eBay, or by doing a search for "hotel alternative
Manhattan," which could lead them to our website where they can look
over our inventory and see our price ranges. They can e-mail us, or we may
receive a call requesting an apartment, or a block of apartments, in a specific area. We let them know what the price is, then e-mail them pictures
and a property profile. The client gets back to us about whether it works
for them or not. If it does, we quote a price. If everything is still agreeable,
we draw up a sublease contract with all the important elements and have
them sign it, subject to credit approval if it's a personal customer. Or, we'll
do monthly billing if it's a corporate client. Sometimes it takes as little as a
few hours; sometimes it takes a few weeks.

THE LEGAL

What kinds of regulations do you have to worry about?
Now, as I'm growing bigger, and as I have bigger deals to negotiate, I am
careful to have an attorney look over my contracts. Make time to develop
a relationship with an attorney who will charge you fairly to look over a
contract.

You've advised us about what to look for in the contract when you rent an apartment. What do you need in a contract between your company and the tenant?

You need to have a cancellation policy and access clauses so you can show the property, if necessary, during the tenant's stay. You have to be sure you are covered for any liability, establish the length or term of the stay, set the price, and establish what that price includes such as housekeeping, HBO, or cable TV.

THE MARKETING

Marketing is key to business development. How do you market your company?

I work with an outside marketing firm to develop an Internet marketing strategy, which includes virtual tours, pricing with comparisons to hotels, and a reservation form. The firm also creates brochures for distribution by the salespeople. When I thought it would be interesting to be on eBay, they posted a weekend getaway for bidders. It gave us a lot of exposure. The web is the best form of advertising. By having Internet strategy people for placements, we get between 9 million and 10 million hits per year.

Who do you register with on the Internet?

We have registered with Expedia (**www.expedia.com**) and Condo Savers (**www.condosavers.com**). You have to contact the sales agent from those companies for your area, and they have to build a profile of your services. It's a two-week process.

THE EXPANSION

Tell us about the other ways your business has grown.

In 2002, I got a call from one of my colleagues who had to retire for personal reasons. He owned the company that I worked with when I first started out. He asked if I would like to absorb his business into mine. It was a huge expansion, but I took it on, adding his staff and assets. His business was doing $15,000 a day, so I knew if we added the right elements, like more inside sales and outside sales, the rest would follow. It was a business growth move. That first month, January 2003, was one of my best months. I think we did $30,000 the first day. All of these sales came in over the Internet, twenty or thirty of them, some for whole months at a time. Having so much more inventory made a huge difference.

THE ADVICE

Although you started this business alone, today you have fifteen employees. Do you have any special advice on selecting staff?
    It's so important to hire good people. I'm lucky, and I have a very dedicated staff. A good way to find people is through word of mouth among friends and colleagues. I have inside salespeople who handle incoming calls and e-mail inquiries, outside salespeople who make cold calls all day long to companies that may need corporate housing, a general office manager, a customer service director, a housekeeping director, and office staff.

THE PLAN TO FOLLOW

STEP 1

    Work for a rental agency so you can earn a commission while you learn the B&B business in your city. As a rental agent, you could earn a finder's fee equal to a month's rent just by matching tenants with apartments. Then you can begin buying apartment leases and renting them on your own.

STEP 2

    Build a reputation for top quality by providing spotlessly clean, well-furnished, and secure properties. Then be diligent in maintaining that trusted reputation.

STEP 3

Network among top-level companies, and establish relationships with contacts there so that they will come to you to serve their corporate housing needs. It is a very effective strategy, one that costs nothing but time and attention. When they have a need, they will call you.

STEP 4

Marketing is key. Work with an outside marketing firm to create brochures and to develop an Internet marketing strategy including virtual tours, pricing with comparisons to hotels, and a reservation form.

STEP 5

Make time to develop a relationship with an attorney who will charge you fairly to look over a contract. He can also write contracts that cover you for any liability, that will establish the length or term of the stay, that set the price, and that explain what amenities the price includes.

THE HIGHLIGHTS

- You can start this business with very little working capital.
- Learn the business by working for a rental agency so you can earn a commission while learning the ropes.
- Build a reputation for top quality by providing spotlessly clean, well-furnished, and secure properties.
- Network among top-level companies to establish contacts that will come to you for their corporate housing needs.
- Work with a marketing firm to develop an Internet marketing strategy that includes virtual tours, pricing, and a reservation form.
- Develop a relationship with an attorney who will charge you fairly to look over and write contracts for your business.

THE RESOURCES

MORE INFORMATION ABOUT LINDA COUGHLIN

www.metro-home.com

www.enterprisingwomen.com/EW2006_women
oftheyear-Over5Upto10Million.htm

www.wipp.org/nfp_details.asp?nfp_id=62

www.hotel-online.com/News/PR2006_2nd/
Apr06_LCoughlin.html

COMPANIES TO REGISTER WITH ON THE INTERNET

www.expedia.com

www.condosavers.com

BUSINESS INFORMATION AND CONTACTS

www.ebay.com
A great resource for Internet referrals.

Women Impacting Public Policy (WIPP)
www.wipp.org
WIPP is a national bipartisan public policy organization of 505,000 women. The organization
advocates for women in business in the legisla-
ture in an effort to increase women's participation, influence, and economic opportunities.
Another important goal is to help build alliances
between businesses.

Women Presidents' Organization (WPO)
www.womenpresidentsorg.com
WPO is a peer advisory group of women presidents and entrepreneurs of women-owned companies that are valued at $2 million or more. The
organization's mission is to enhance the success
of member-owned businesses. Members meet at
an annual national conference, and on a monthly
basis, in cities across the country to discuss issues
they're facing in individual businesses from
financing and investment information to employee
or growth issues.

Women's Business Enterprise National Council
www.wbenc.org
The council certifies women-owned businesses
and facilitates third-party connections to generate business for women-owned businesses.

U.S. Small Business Administration
www.sba.gov
This organization provides financing assistance,
training, and networking to new and prospective business owners.

LOCATING BED-AND-BREAKFAST INNS FOR SALE

www.bedandbreakfastforsale.com

www.bb-4-sale.com

FINDING BED-AND-BREAKFAST PROPERTY LISTINGS

www.bedandbreakfast.com

www.bbonline.com
Sales and additional information is offered here,
including many resources for furnishing rooms
and reservation services.

www.corporatehousing.com
Agencies provide corporate housing to companies whose employees travel for training or
other purposes. If they need additional units,
they will contact smaller rental companies. Linda
Coughlin says this third-party contracting is common. Look for other agencies by searching the
Internet for "corporate housing," or by visiting
this website.

Millionaire Blueprints *neither endorses nor
recommends any of the companies listed in the
resource section. Resources are intended as a
starting point for your research.*

Kirk
LANCASTER

The road to wealth could start with a ridiculous offer.

BUSINESS NAME:
Lancaster/Crowley Investments LLC

TYPE OF BUSINESS:
Real Estate Investing

LOCATION:
Fort Worth, TX

ADAPTED FROM:
Millionaire Blueprints magazine articles,
"The Road to Wealth Could Start with a
Ridiculous Offer," Spring 2005,
and "Buy It Right," June 2005

W hen it comes to buying, selling, and leasing residential real estate, Fort Worth, Texas, investor Kirk Lancaster says that his guiding principle of real estate investing is: *You make your money when you buy.* In other words, he means to say that buying residential property at below-market value gives you instant equity. Keep it as rental property, he says, and let your tenants pay off the note for you while your investment continues to gain value while costing you nothing. Thus, you gain equity from both ends.

"Do this ten times over, and you will be very pleased with how much equity you will gain just on a monthly rate," he says.

And he should know. Since his first rental house purchase, when he was just two years out of high school, Lancaster has bought, sold, and leased enough properties that he is now able to live independently on his own schedule. Effectively, he says, he retired in his early thirties. His properties provide investment income that allows him to live comfortably, travel, and spend his days as he chooses. He is quick to add that it's hard work. Setting up a real estate career as he and his business partner, Kyle Crowley, have done is a design for the long haul—to get your investments working for you to provide living income for now and investment income for the future.

This is quite a contrast, Lancaster says, from the "get it, spend it, and be rich for a day" mentality hyped by real estate infomercials. Setting up a real estate business is just that—a business—and all the rules of good business apply. That includes working hard, being persistent, honest, and having the courage and discipline to keep reinvesting your profits in your business to build for a long-term gain. If you aspire to follow a similar path to real estate success, take a cue from Kirk Lancaster's nod to that famous Nike tagline—and "just do it."

THE BEGINNING

Tell us how you got started.

I bought my first property when I was about twenty years old. The purchase price was $12,000, and my father cosigned a note at the bank for me. Then I put an ad in the paper, put a sign in the yard, and someone came and rented it. To figure out how much to charge, I just asked around. In this business, it really boils down to what the market will allow you to charge. I knew nothing about the rental business, and not too much about real estate, but I knew what I wanted to do, and I figured the only way to learn was just to do it. I have learned something on each one, and I am still learning!

THE GOAL

What was your goal when you started out, and how did you go about finding and purchasing residential properties?

When I started out, I had a goal of owning ten houses. As I began to buy more and more houses, banks would loan me more than 100 percent of the note. Today, our goals remain the same—to add properties that will benefit our business; to sell properties that are not working well for our business; to keep a low vacancy rate on our rental properties; and to reduce any debts against our properties. We are also creating notes through owner financing, which is beneficial to us, as well as to our loyal renters who are interested in purchasing. These notes average yields of up to 23 to 30 percent.

THE PROFIT

What do you think is the key to making money in this business?

The most important thing to remember is that you make your money when you buy the property. If they're asking $50,000, don't be afraid to offer $25,000 or less. You just never know what circumstances might make someone take a much lower offer. I once offered $12,000 on a piece of property for which they were asking $24,000. The realtor said, "She won't take it," and she didn't. I said, "I'll go back in three months and offer it again, and she'll take it." And sure enough, she did. We painted the house and resold it for $24,000.

THE MARKETING

Where do you look for investment properties that can be bought at below-market value?

We look for vacant houses for sale, unkempt, overgrown yards, or houses in obvious need of repair. We also put out signs in high-traffic locations and run ads that read, "We pay cash for houses." We add our phone number as well. That way, most of our sellers come to us. In addition, I recommend that you become acquainted with bank asset managers, real estate brokers, and attorneys who handle the processing of wills for estates in your area. These people hear first about properties for sale. If you do this right, you'll have a never-ending supply of properties to buy.

THE MINERAL RIGHTS

If the property you find happens to be raw land, is there something we should ask about?

Make sure that you're getting the mineral rights along with it. Most people don't even ask about this, but it can make a huge difference to the value of the property. If it isn't specified otherwise, mineral rights automatically pass with the land. I never buy land without making sure I get at least a percentage of the mineral rights.

THE PROCESS

You talked about "buying notes." What does that mean, and why would I want to do it?

The term "buying notes" simply means finding an owner-financed mortgage and paying the owner the cash equity he or she has in the property, and then taking over the note to get a higher yield of return on your money. If you buy a $100,000 note for $100,000—full face value—at

9 percent, you're getting a much better return on your money than the 2 percent you'd get with a Certificate of Deposit (CD). Unlike buying a property and renting it out, buying a note means you're no longer responsible for taxes, insurance, repairs, and vacancy rates. You're just holding the note and collecting the monthly payments.

THE STRATEGIES

What other strategies can you share with us?

Our favorite way to maximize our yield—but it's a long-term investment—is to combine all these concepts. Buy that $100,000 house for $45,000, but get a 100-percent loan, or more, if they'll let you. Some banks will loan up to 110 percent on a note if your credit is good. Then, rent the property out, and let your tenant pay the note off for you, as well as the taxes and insurance. Then, once the note is paid off, create your own note, and sell the property for $100,000 at 10 percent interest over thirty years. The monthly note payment at that amount would be $877.58, and the thirty-year life of the note would add up to $292,168.80. Now think about it—if you don't have any of your own money in it, and you never did, what would the rate of return be?

Once you find a note you want to buy, then what do you do?

First you go to a title company. That is how you can make sure the title is clear, and confirm who the property really belongs to. Just make sure that it is a deed of trust and not a contract deed. This is very important, because a contract deed means the original owner still holds the deed to the house.

THE ADVICE

What do you advise if what once appeared to be a good deal turns out to be a bad one?

If the market takes a dip, and you realize that your property will no longer bring what you paid for it, just stay with the program, keep it rented, and keep paying toward the note. This happened to us when a $30,000 investment dropped to $10,000. We continued to rent it for the same amount of money, which paid for the expenses and the note. This same property today is worth $69,000, and it still brings in $800 per month in rental income.

Lancaster says that although you may have heard the phrase, "cash is king," when it comes to investments, he believes that is just not so. His advice, he says, quoting Oklahoma humorist Will Rogers, is, "Buy land, and never sell—they're not making any more of it."

THE PLAN TO FOLLOW

STEP 1

Look for investment properties that can be bought at below-market value. Then buy houses by getting a 100-percent loan, or more, if your credit is good.

NOTE: Success in real estate investing requires working hard, persistence, honesty, and the courage and discipline to keep reinvesting and building for the future.

STEP 2

Then rent the properties out, and let your tenants pay the note off for you, as well as the taxes and insurance.

STEP 3

Then, once the notes are paid off, create your own notes, and sell the properties at 10 percent interest over thirty years.

STEP 4

Keep a low vacancy rate on your rental properties, and reduce any debts against your properties.

STEP 5

Create notes through owner financing, which is beneficial to you, as well as to your loyal renters who are interested in purchasing. These notes average yields of up to 23 to 30 percent.

THE HIGHLIGHTS

- Buy investment properties at below-market value by getting a 100-percent loan, or more, if your credit is good.
- Rent the properties out and let your tenants pay the note, taxes, and insurance for you.
- Pay off the notes, then create your own, and sell the properties at 10-percent interest over thirty years.
- Keep a low vacancy rate on your rental properties and reduce any debts against your properties.
- Create notes through owner financing. These notes average yields of up to 23 to 30 percent.

THE RESOURCES

MORE INFORMATION ABOUT KIRK LANCASTER
www.realestatecoachingbykirk.com

CALCULATING MORTGAGES
HP12C at Office Depot is a mortgage calculator that will figure your yields.

KEEP UP WITH YOUR NOTES
www.notesmith.com
Visit this website to find several good programs for keeping up with your notes.

Millionaire Blueprints *neither endorses nor recommends any of the companies listed in the resource section. Resources are intended as a starting point for your research.*

Stacey
SANTOS

Entrepreneur makes millions by providing a "home away from home."

BUSINESS NAME:
A Suite For You, Inc.

TYPE OF BUSINESS:
Relocation Housing

LOCATION:
Albuquerque, NM

ADAPTED FROM:
Millionaire Blueprints magazine article,
"A Suite Destination,"
May/June 2007

S tacey Santos and two business partners launched A Suite for You, Inc., in October 2000, in Albuquerque, New Mexico, with only $9,000 on two credit cards. Santos had never run her own business before, and she was learning day by day.

Santos found her niche in corporate housing and relocation. She discovered that companies often use uncomfortable extended-stay hotels for employees. She wanted to provide a better solution.

A Suite for You, Inc., offers fully furnished apartments and homes with short-term leases as brief as seven days or a few months. With Santos' help, clients spend their transition time in a spacious living area where they can relax, cook their own meals, and save money. It's a win-win situation.

When she started the business a little over six years ago, Santos did not know much about how to run her own company. But with a little footwork, some research, and a lot of motivation and drive, she turned $9,000 into a million-dollar venture.

THE BEGINNING

When did you get involved in realty?

At the beginning of 1994, when I was about twenty-five, I went to work for a top realtor here in Albuquerque.

How did you learn about relocation and corporate housing?

In the process of working with the real estate company, I came in contact with a company that did corporate housing. I went to work for them in 1999 to find out if I really liked it.

Can you explain exactly what relocation is?

When you are speaking of "people relocating," you are referring to people who are looking for a shorter-term lease. These people may be waiting for their home to be built. Or they want to get to know the area before they purchase a home. Or they are in town on a short-term basis for business training. Apartment communities don't want to rent something for just one, two, or three months. So I take the longer-term lease and sublet it for a short period of time.

THE BUSINESS

What caused you to decide to start your own business?
I wanted to become an independent business owner.

Did you start your business on your own, or did you have partners?
I had two business partners.

THE MONEY

How much money did you need to start your business?
We started the company with $9,000 in credit cards.

Do you remember how you used the $9,000? Was it for rent?
We used the $9,000 to front the rents. We took a cash advance and paid the rents on the apartments that we were taking on.

THE NEED

How did you go about finding these apartments and getting leases?
First, we talked to our potential clients before we signed long-term leases with apartment complexes. We found out what our clients' needs were, how many bedrooms they needed, how long they were going to stay, and specifics such as phone service, cable television, and things of that nature. After that, we would go and find it.

So you approached the complexes personally?
We would go there, ask them what their availability was, tell them what our needs were, and then sign a lease accordingly.

THE PROFIT

How do you decide on rates for your clients?

I have to figure my expenses for rent, furniture, utilities, cable, and phone for a certain period of time, and add $200 to $400 a month for profit.

What is another way to make profit besides subletting an apartment?

Sometimes we arrange with homeowners to let us use their properties, and then they go into corporate housing short term, and make a decent profit. If you have access to private properties, you can purchase properties once you start gaining a bit of capital. Then you can use those properties in your inventory.

THE HOUSING

You mentioned that your properties are already furnished. Where do you get the furniture?

We rent the furniture from Aaron Rents, Inc. Renting furniture is a great way to get started. You can go to a furniture company and say, "I want this furniture, and I want to purchase it over a period of time." By the time your lease is up, you own that furniture. If you continue to keep that lease, then you no longer pay the bill for the furniture but you do include that in your rent price.

What is the estimated rental payment for a furniture package for a two-bedroom apartment?

Mine is anywhere from $250 to $300 a month for an upgraded furniture package. That's on a rental basis, not a purchase basis. If you want to purchase it, it will cost a bit more. That's kind of a double-edged sword. If, for some reason, it's destroyed, and you own it, you have to make arrangements to replace it and dispose of it. If it's rented, you just call them, charge the renter for damages, and it's replaced for you.

THE MARKETING

How did you market your company?

I've done some knocking on doors. But once somebody uses your service, if you do a good job, they'll tell a few people. My philosophy was to do a good job, and if they told a couple of people, that was a great source.

Most of your marketing is done by word of mouth?

Yes. They've either dealt with somebody who has worked with us, or who has gone on the Internet and found us. Some of them find us through the phone book. In the very beginning, we ran commercials on the WB Television Network because the vice president of the WB's New Mexico area stayed with us. In exchange for a couple of months of free rent, they produced and ran a commercial for us.

Are you in the Yellow Pages?

We are. I don't recommend that you do a big ad in the beginning. Just get your name in there. It's important to make sure you're under the correct directory. You might want to put your name under the apartment heading, or under a relocation or corporate housing section.

Would you suggest using the Internet to get the word out?

Get a website together. People are visual, so take pictures. If you don't have a furnished apartment, go to your furniture rental company, pick out a furniture package, and have them stage it, and take a photo for you. They're going to be appreciative to have your business, so they will want to help you.

THE LEGAL

Do you need a license to run this type of company?

Yes, you need a business license and, in some states, you may be required to have a real estate license.

THE ADVICE

If someone came to you and said, "I'm going to try to do this in my city." Is there anything else you would tell them?

This is a business you can start with a credit card and just $10,000 or $15,000 of working capital. Don't get yourself in so much debt that you are buried under it.

It is also very important to treat every person as though they're the most important person, and provide a product that you are going to have little to no issues with. When your clients move in, they're not seeing all the things that could have been better. They're seeing how their experience was better.

THE PLAN TO FOLLOW

STEP 1

First, contact your local chamber of commerce, and find out if they have any businesses that do this particular relocation service and, on the average, how many relocation packages are requested. You might also check out the visitor's bureau in your city.

STEP 2

Scout the area and see what properties are available for rent. Look at apartment complexes, maybe condominiums, and small homes. What's the rental market like? Is it as expensive to rent a home as it is an apartment? See what is out there that you can make the best use of for your clients.

NOTE: The apartment communities can be a great source for referrals. They may be contacted by people who will ask, "Hey, will you do a one-month lease for me, or do you have furnished apartments I can use?" The communities can be a phenomenal source of business for you.

STEP 3

See what companies are in the surrounding area, within twenty to thirty minutes. Then find out how often they might be hiring and how often they bring people in to train. Look specifically for large companies with a high transition period.

NOTE: Contact a company's human resources department, and find out what they currently use for corporate housing and relocation. Find out if it's an extended-stay hotel, or if it's just a hotel. Find out how frequently they bring people out and for how long.

STEP 4

Once you've established that there is a need, you'll need to get your business license. Santos suggests that you get your company incorporated. Either do a limited liability corporation, an actual S corporation, or a C corporation. Find out what you need, and if you need a real estate license.

NOTE: Contact your state's corporation commission. Ask them exactly what you need to run that type of business in your state.

STEP 5

You need to solicit clients. Go to companies and businesses that might need your services. Join your local chamber of commerce and the visitor's bureau. They know when companies are coming in, and people request information from them about the area and housing. If you start putting your advertising there, it can be really helpful.

NOTE: Santos suggests that you get a commitment from a company to try your services first, before you find apartments to rent. You don't want to take on a bunch of properties and just hope you'll have the clients to sell them. You really want to get a commitment from somebody. It really doesn't make sense to put a product out there and just hope that people like it.

THE HIGHLIGHTS

- You can start this business with very little working capital.
- Find the clients first, and then find housing to suit their needs.
- Contact your local chamber of commerce and larger businesses to gauge the relocation market in your area.
- Offer great service to encourage word-of-mouth marketing.
- Contact apartment complexes in your area for referrals.

THE RESOURCES

MORE INFORMATION ABOUT STACEY SANTOS

A Suite Destination
www.asuitedestination.com

**GENERAL INFORMATION ABOUT
CORPORATE HOUSING AND RELOCATION**

Corporate Housing Providers Association
www.chpaonline.org

Realty Times
http://realtytimes.com/
This is a leading real estate news source.

Real Estate Investing Depot
www.reidepot.com

FOR BUSINESS LICENSE INFORMATION

Business Licenses Online
www.businesslicenses.com/prequal.php?track
code=bizcom

WHERE TO OBTAIN BUSINESS LICENSES

www.sba.gov/hotlist/license.html
This is a list of websites that provide business
license information for each state.

Real Estate Express
www.realestateexpress.com
This website offers online preparation for real
estate exams.

**FINDING CORPORATE HOUSING
AND RELOCATION COMPANIES**

Larger corporate housing companies often want
to work with smaller companies located on the
outskirts of major cities. Check with these corporations to see if they are looking for someone
in your location.
Oakwood Corporate Housing
www.oakwood.com

Amber Lodging Company
www.amberlodging.com

Crye-Leike
www.crye-leike.com

Prudential Relocation Services
http://relocation.prudential.com/

BUSINESS CREDIT CARDS

Compare Credit Cards
www.e-wisdom.com/credit_cards/business.
html?y

NEGOTIATING LEASES

Lease Negotiation
http://apartments.about.com/od/leases/a/
negotiation_tip.htm?once=true&
This website contains tips from About.com.

Negotiating a Lease
www.bankrate.com/brm/news/advice/1999040
6a.asp

Negotiating Apartment Leases
www.mattmurph.com/MyBlog/?blogid=129
This blog offers insight about apartment negoti-ations that are based on personal experiences.

ADDITIONAL INFORMATION ABOUT LEASING YOUR PROPERTY ASSOCIATIONS

National Real Estate Investors Association
www.nationalreia.com

ECONOMIC DEVELOPMENT GROUPS, VISITOR'S BUREAUS, AND CORPORATION COMMISSIONS

To find any of these groups in your area, simply run an Internet search on your city's name, and run a search on the name of the group you are seeking.

U.S. Chamber of Commerce
www.uschamber.com
Local Chamber of Commerce
http://www.uschamber.com/chambers/directory/default.htm?d=false
Use this directory to find your local chamber of commerce, or run an Internet search with your city's name.

Millionaire Blueprints *neither endorses nor recommends any of the companies listed in the resource section. Resources are intended as a starting point for your research.*

3

True Stories of
INVENTOR
Millionaires

George
BOUDREAUX

How a small-town pharmacist's compound with a funny name became a best-selling topical ointment—and attracted the loyalty of national retailers.

BUSINESS NAME:
Boudreaux's Butt Paste

TYPE OF BUSINESS:
Healthcare Products

LOCATION:
Columbus, IN

ADAPTED FROM:
Millionaire Blueprints magazine article,
"From the Bottom Up,"
June 2005

The product? Boudreaux's Butt Paste. The story of its rise from a simple pharmacist's compound to a national multimillion-dollar phenomenon is one of marketing genius, perseverance, and relentless energy and imagination. George Boudreaux, the man behind the paste, is truly one of a kind, and Millionaire Blueprints decided to see what this icon of marketing might share with our readers to help them see beyond the possible, imagine past the expected, and reach for the success that may be waiting for them just outside the proverbial box.

THE PRODUCT

Tell us about the origin of Butt Paste.

I was working as an intern in a pharmacy in Covington, Louisiana. I had finished pharmacy school and, in those days, there were all sorts of compounds pharmacists made up. Today, this must be done with a doctor's prescription. So that was when I learned to compound and prepare a few basic recipes. Later, as a licensed pharmacist and owner of the pharmacy, I continued to build on what I had learned. I tweaked the ingredients and percentages until I came up with this thick ointment that had pediatricians from miles around sending their patients to me to buy it for diaper rash.

How did the name "Butt Paste" come about?

One of my referring doctors was about to write a prescription for another diaper rash ointment, but the young patient's mother said, "Oh, no, I'll just go get some of Dr. Boudreaux's butt paste. It'll take care of this rash." The doctor called me, laughing as he told me this story, and then he asked, "So when are you going to market this butt paste of yours, anyway?" After that, the name just sort of stuck.

THE IDEA

What made you decide to take that plunge and try to sell it?

Again, it was the urging of the doctors who kept referring and recommending it to their patients. People were beginning to discover the paste's other uses by then, including how fast it healed cuts and scrapes, as well as split, bleeding cuticles and jock itch—even though the product isn't clinically indicated for these uses.

THE FUNDING

How did you get your startup money?

We saved every penny we could because I knew my future at my first job was limited. The chance to make the break came when a guy offered to let me run his drugstore and be a 50-percent partner. Shortly after that, an opportunity came my way to open a store. We were quite small, but filled seventy-eight prescriptions the first day we were open. In 1980, a friend who was a realtor was putting together a proposal for a commercial development. He wanted to sell in 5,000-square-foot parcels for $50,000 each. I told him I'd take one of the parcels. Then I called a friend of mine, a doctor, and asked if he would like to take the parcel adjacent to mine and let me buy it back from him in a year for $75,000. And he did, plus one more. A year and a half later, we bought the one next to us. The property had always been interesting to me because there were two hospitals on the same street, so a steady traffic line of people needing a pharmacy was virtually guaranteed.

THE MANUFACTURING

Tell us about your production facility in those early days.

When we were still making the product in the pharmacy, we had a very small prep area. We made ten pounds at a time and sold it one to two ounces at a time. But in order to sell it commercially, we knew we had to get a licensed manufacturer to make it for us on a much bigger scale. I wanted to find one nearby, but there weren't many people in Louisiana who make this type of product.

What challenges did you face in finding someone to manufacture your Butt Paste?

There were really no manufacturers in Louisiana who could create what we needed. And when you ask someone to do contract manufacturing for you, they have to have enough volume of product to make it worthwhile. I found an old company in New Orleans called Dr. Tichenor's Antiseptic that made products like it. Then a friend told me there was a plant called Old Hickory Medicine in Andalusia that made old-fashioned pharmaceuticals. We signed a contract, and they came up with the product that was exactly as I needed it. Our orders grew, and we finally had to go to a bigger facility. We continued to grow and had to get a secondary manufacturer.

Tell us how your inventory system works. What deal did you make with your manufacturer?

Our manufacturer, Dr. Tichenor's, makes antiseptic, antiseptic gel, and toothpaste. The only custom-manufactured product they make is Butt Paste, and we have half the plant now. We ask them to keep a certain amount of product on hand. We always tell them in advance about trade shows. With our track record, they know how much to increase production to make sure we're covered. We actually buy the product from the manufacturer when it's sold. It costs us a few extra dollars, but in the long run it's much better than having inventory sitting on the floor. Nowadays, we keep 50,000 tubes on hand, so if we get a big order we have enough to advance it to the stores. Most manufacturers expect you to pay for your inventory, but we negotiated. The inventory's still yours, but this way it feels different than going into so much debt for your inventory.

INFORMATION

What approvals, licenses, and other formalities did you need to have in place before you started actual production?

We had to get FDA approval. Since we were having a product manufactured outside of our pharmacy, we needed product liability insurance. We found out that to sell a product to national retailers, you have to supply the insurance. You have to have $5 million of product liability insurance before they'll even talk to you.

THE MARKETING

Once you got all of that in place, where did you go first?

We went to a pharmaceutical trade show in Florida. We gave away 288 T-shirts and did not make one sale. But I knew we were planting seeds, and if we kept at it long enough, it would grow.

How else did you build your following in those early days?

At that point, we had so much invested, we knew we had to get out and sell the product to someone. So we contacted some of the wholesalers who attended the trade show in Florida. One guy, who was a representative from one of the largest drug companies in the country, said, "If you can get some of my customers to want it, we'll stock it for you." So I started knocking on doors and offering samples. And, from the beginning, we guaranteed the product. We were able to get in with many of the wholesalers from that meeting, and today we are in all the major wholesale outlets throughout the country.

You're obviously a marketing genius. Tell us some of your favorite trade show strategies.

You've got to have some kind of little gimmick. In one case, it was the year the Super Bowl was going to be played in New Orleans, so we had a raffle for two tickets. We had people lined up as far as you could see. And we were giving out Butt Paste T-shirts, ball caps, and a bobble-head baby figurine we had made up.

Besides the trade shows, how else do you market Boudreaux's Butt Paste?

We do a lot of the national association shows such as the Advanced Wound Care, the American Society of Consultant Pharmacists, the American Society of Healthcare Professionals, and many others. We have also received a great deal of exposure through our involvement with NASCAR. We sponsor a Busch series car, and the response has been phenomenal.

THE CONCLUSION

Could you ever have imagined how far your Butt Paste would take you beyond your pharmacy?

My life has changed quite a bit since I first decided to market my now famous Butt Paste to the 100-mile radius surrounding my Covington pharmacy. But it's been a ride I've enjoyed—far beyond my wildest dreams of owning my own pharmacy. I used to be on the road a lot, but now I'm also in the air a lot. I'm now traveling all over the country. I go somewhere every week. We have been truly blessed.

THE PLAN TO FOLLOW

STEP 1

Learn everything you can about the healthcare market you want to start your business in, and work as an employee for a successful company in this market.

NOTE: This will help you gain experience and develop a list of contacts.

STEP 2

Look into your market for problems that need solutions, and then develop products that will solve the problems.

STEP 3

Lock in your startup funding, and then find a manufacturer that will re-create your product precisely how you want it.

STEP 4

Demonstrate your product at trade shows specific to your industry.

NOTE: Allow customers to place orders for your product at the trade shows.

STEP 5

Begin large-scale manufacturing and commercial sales.

THE HIGHLIGHTS

- If the need is there, unique healthcare products can produce large profits.
- Before you manufacture and sell your product, gain some experience in that particular field.
- Be prepared to spend a good amount of time perfecting your product.
- Come up with a strong business plan to secure funding and a strong marketing strategy.

THE RESOURCES

International Academy of Compounding Pharmacists (IACP)
www.iacprx.org
This nonprofit organization represents and serves more than 1,300 compounding pharmacists. Here, you can register for IACP's annual meetings, learn about trade shows, access the Task Force webpage, obtain state updates, get information on pharmacy employment opportunities, and read the Code of Ethics, the newsletter, and legislative updates.

The International Journal of Pharmaceutical Compounding
www.compoundingtoday.com
This website provides compounding professionals with an extensive journal database to access scientific information.

American Association of Colleges of Pharmacy
www.aacp.org

Drug Topics
www.drugtopics.com
This website is an online news magazine for pharmacists.

Professional Compounding Centers of America (PCCA)
www.pccarx.com
This website provides independent pharmacists with a complete support system for compounding unique dosage forms. It is owned and operated principally by pharmacists. The PCCA provides the bulk pharmaceuticals, equipment, devices, flavors, American Council on Pharmaceutical Education (ACPE)-accredited training classes and seminars, marketing support, and the technical consulting assistance needed to help pharmacists build successful compounding practices.

U.S. Pharmacopedia
www.usp.org
This website teaches drug standards, education, and distribution.

U.S. Food and Drug Administration Center for Drug Evaluation and Research Pharmacy Compounding
www.fda.gov/cder/pharmcomp
This comprehensive website is where pharmacy readers can follow the agency's activities on pharmacy compounding.

www.rxshowcase.com
This website provides information about pharmacy compounding suppliers, management and training, and pharmaceutical chemical providers.

TRADE SHOWS

www.medtrade.com

DISTRIBUTORS

http://rxinsider.com/distribution_pharmaceutical_distributors_wholesalers.htm

www.tjpcompany.com/distributionpharmaceuticalwholesale

LICENSING

www.pharmacist.com/articles/l_t_0001.cfm

PHARMACEUTICAL INFORMATION

www.rxinsider.com

www.eventseye.com

Millionaire Blueprints *neither endorses nor recommends any of the companies listed in the resource section. Resources are intended as a starting point for your research.*

Shawn
DONEGAN

A simple question sparks a million-dollar idea.

BUSINESS NAME:
Speed Rollers®

TYPE OF BUSINESS:
Painting Supplies

LOCATION:
Palm Harbor, FL

ADAPTED FROM:
Millionaire Blueprints magazine article,
"The 'Rolls' of the Paint World,"
May/June 2007

*S*hawn Donegan had become a success in the real estate world, as well as in the coating and painting industry. One sleepless night, he pondered how to increase his business. If only he could finish his paint jobs faster, he would be more successful in growing a stronger and healthier business. A simple answer came to mind. Using two paint rollers instead of one just might do the trick. And with that idea, Speed Rollers® was born. Donegan teamed up with a friend, Mike Puczkowski, and they engineered the new paint roller through trial and error. In March 2004, Donegan took the prototype to a Las Vegas convention. It was an immediate hit. Orders were pouring in for a tool that he wasn't even ready to mass-produce yet.

Today, Donegan sells his tool in Sherwin-Williams stores, on his website, and through other stores. The simple question Donegan posed to himself on that sleepless night has ultimately resulted in a million-dollar business.

THE IDEA

How did you come up with the idea for a different type of paint roller?

One night in 2003, I was lying in bed and asked myself, "What's the quickest way to paint?" And I said to myself, "Multiple rollers." In painting, you have to dip, fill the roller up, then lay it off, and back roll it. If the top roller could do the application and the bottom roller could lay it off, you'd be painting two to three times faster.

THE DESIGN

Did you work on the design with a partner?

Mike Puczkowski was working for me as a painter. The first idea he showed me was two eighteen-inch rollers side by side, which made a thirty-six-inch roller that was really too large. So we came up with the "printing press" idea. We put a couple of dual rollers together and put different feeds to it.

After you completed the basic idea, what did you do next?

Once we had the raw, crude item put together, I went to a friend who was in the manufacturing business of stamping. This is the metal forming business. It's when the various parts of a tool are created from a premade die. This means the product can be mass-produced by just setting up a machine and "stamping out" the pieces.

What happened when you saw your friend in the stamping business?

He said, "You need a design engineer to draw your tool." So we needed a firm to start creating engineering drawings from the prototype model.

What was your next step?

We drew up the very first Speed Rollers. Then I saw my attorney about applying for a patent.

THE TESTING

Did you do a focus group test on the Speed Rollers?

Yes. My father did a focus group to see the reaction we would receive by putting it in front of the common consumer. It was very, very positive.

How was he able to do a focus group?

He sat on the board of an industrial concrete form company called EFCO. They had carpenters, painters, and other tradesmen. He ran it in front of the average consumer and anybody with a contractor background.

THE PROTOTYPE

When did you build the prototype?

We started building the prototype in November 2003 when we submitted a provisional patent. We set a goal that, by the middle of March 2004, we were going to introduce this company at the Paint and Coatings Expo (PACE) annual convention in Las Vegas.

How did you develop the prototype for the convention?

I contracted it to different vendors. Everything from the H-frame (the plastic part that holds the two roller covers) to the chrome shields—all the parts of the tool, including about fourteen major components—were sent to vendors.

THE MONEY

How much did you spend on the prototype?

I had approximately $175,000 into it by the time we got to the show.

And how much did you spend on a booth for the convention?

I spent $10,000 on my booth design, and $3,000 for the space at the convention. We had six prototypes built for the show. They were about $30,000 each.

Were you still dabbling in real estate?

I sold it all. I took that money and invested it into the Speed Rollers company.

THE CONVENTION

Was your product well received at the Las Vegas convention?

People wanted the product right away. But I didn't have anything to give them at the time. I hadn't even built my tooling—the production line you use for mass production.

Did you have any actual orders from the convention?

Yes, but we said it would be six to eight weeks out before any deliveries could be made. We also started the price really high. Our first units were selling for $389. I could sell them for that price because I explained that the product saved a "man day." They would buy the tool based on that.

After you saw that people wanted your product, what was your next step?

The next step was to get the tooling going, and to start an Internet website. We also wanted to get in with Sherwin-Williams.

THE PRODUCTION

Who did you contact to get your tooling produced?

I went to a good friend, Fred Montag, president of Allied Tool, Inc., who was in the stamping business for metal, automotive, lawn, and garden products. He lined me up with a lot of good vendors.

Did you also get tubing and other parts through the same vendors?

For tubing and other like materials, I was going into home centers such as The Home Depot, and looking at major distributors who handled tubing. We were looking for a cost-effective, reliable tube for mass production. The one that ended up being the best was from a company called Saint-Gobain.

When was your tooling completed?

The actual tooling was delivered in late 2004. We made some initial runs on it and stamped out five of the major parts.

THE PRODUCT

What was your new "home center" model?

Our current industrial and commercial tool is based out of high-grade aircraft aluminum and nylon composites. The home center tool would be an all-plastic tool. A complete painting system is composed of the pump, line, inline gun, valve, heavy-duty extension rolling pole, and the Speed Rollers frame, which is a two-roller painting system.

Where would the home center model be sold, as opposed to the higher-grade version?

There are two different channels for paint and coatings sales. Approximately 70 percent of the paint sold in the United States is sold by paint store chains. That includes Sherwin-Williams. The places that sell home center models are stores such as The Home Depot and Lowe's.

THE DEAL

What has been the toughest thing you've faced in bringing your product to the market?

Getting in with Sherwin-Williams has been the toughest. It's taken us two years. They are the largest buyer in the country of airless paint spray equipment.

Did you go to Sherwin-Williams personally?

No. You have to get rep groups to go to them. I had an equipment rep group talking to them for eighteen months.

How did you find the rep group?

I found them through associations with other sales reps. I picked up a rep who had Ohio, West Virginia, Kentucky, Indiana, and Michigan. I also got a sales rep from my contacts in the early 1990s.

When did you start working with Sherwin-Williams?

Interestingly, we'd met with buyers of Sherwin-Williams when I was at $389 and wholesaling the product for $190. They didn't like that price. I told them I was selling value. We sold about fifty units with them at that price. We are now in Sherwin-Williams' distribution service center. The offshore manufacturing cost and volume has lowered the price.

THE EVIDENCE

Was there a defining moment when you thought to yourself that you were going to make it?

When we went to the convention in Las Vegas and received such a strong, positive response, I knew there was validity in the product, and that I hadn't made a mistake on the dollars I had put into it. That was a big find.

THE PLAN TO FOLLOW

STEP 1

Locate a stamping company, if needed, in order to mass-produce your invention.

NOTE: Donegan used his connections with a friend in the business to secure a stamping company. He suggests hiring a design engineer to draw your "tool" to create your first prototype.

STEP 2

Patent your invention by contacting the United States Patent and Trademark Office.

STEP 3

Conduct focus groups to gather feedback about the marketability of your product.

NOTE: Donegan suggests holding a focus group with members of your target audience so they can test your invention and give you their feedback.

STEP 4

Rent a booth at conventions and trade shows to display your product and boost awareness.

STEP 5

To mass-produce your product, invest in a tooling system.

NOTE: Donegan found vendors for each and every piece that was a part of his product. Once his tooling was complete, he was able to mass-produce the product.

STEP 6

Promote your invention to chain stores to expand your company.

NOTE: Donegan worked for two years before making a deal with the largest seller in his respective industry. For an open door, contact representatives who will act as the middle men between you and the corporate decision makers.

THE HIGHLIGHTS

- If you have an idea for an invention, do not assume that it has been done before.
- Networking through friends and family can save you a lot of time and effort.
- For an unknown product, attending conventions is a great way to get your name out there.
- If your product is for commercial use, consider expanding into home models for the public.
- Don't be afraid to go for the big fish—the companies that will sell your product.

THE RESOURCES

MORE INFORMATION ABOUT SHAWN DONEGAN

Speed Rollers
www.speedrollers.com

INFORMATION ABOUT PATENTS

Thrasher Associates, LLC
www.thrasherassociates.com
Steven Thrasher, a registered patent attorney, can help you through all the stages of your invention process.

Thrasher, Steven. "The Top Ten Reasons Not to Even Think of Patenting It Yourself."
www.thrasherassociates.com/topten

America Invents
www.americainvents.com
Kris Hudgens, Executive VP, Licensing, and the America Invents team specialize in helping new inventors.

Fay Sharpe LLP
www.faysharpe.com
Shawn Donegan recommends this intellectual property law firm. Note: The patent application process can take four years or more. Don't wait for the patent to issue before you move on to the next steps.

United States Patent and Trademark Office
www.uspto.gov

JOIN INVENTOR CONVENTIONS

When you're feeling inventor's fatigue, Steven Thrasher says it can be helpful to talk with other inventors who can offer advice. He recommends the following conventions:

Independent Inventors Conference at the United States Patent and Trademark Office
www.invent.org/iic/

Minnesota Inventors Congress
www.inventhelper.org

Yankee Invention Exposition
www.yankeeinventionexpo.org
These expos take place every October in Connecticut.

DEVELOP A BUSINESS PLAN

Develop a business plan with a professional. Steven Thrasher suggests the following resources:

Small Business Development Centers
To find a development center in your region, do an Internet search using your state name.

Service Corps of Retired Executives
www.score.org
This organization will pair you with a retired executive from your industry.

BizPlanBuilder
www.jian.com
Visit this website, and click on Business Plan, BizPlanBuilder. This business-planning software helps you create a professional plan that can be purchased online.

FIND FINANCIAL RESOURCES

If the inventor already has funding, he can move on to the next step in his business plan. Otherwise, inventors should meet with a business consultant to evaluate options. If financial resources are a serious issue, consider licensing the invention.

BUSINESS CONSULTANTS

R. Todd Lazenby, WP Capital Partners, L.P.
www.wpcapitalpartners.com

Payne Harrison, WP Capital Partners, L.P.
www.wpcapitalpartners.com

Bryan Scott, Sun Capital Management
bryanascott@gmail.com

POSSIBLE FUNDING OPTIONS

Some funding options are friends and family, credit cards, and hedge funds. For promising inventions protected by an issued patent, some hedge funds will give you a loan if you pledge the patent as collateral. They are typically for millions of dollars, but are also high interest (up to 30 percent.)

The following websites provide additional information about hedge funds:

www.hedgeworld.com

www.hedgeco.net

www.thehfa.org

EMERGENT TECHNOLOGY FUNDS

Texas and Michigan are among the states that offer funding to inventors who partner with universities. Investments of between $200,000 and $2 million can be made. To see if this is available in your region, contact one of your state universities.

ANGEL INVESTORS

Angel investors are wealthy individuals who like to risk money in new ventures. Beware that some angels demand a great deal of control for what may be a very small investment of as little as $10,000 to as much as $500,000 in the long run.

The InvestIn Forum
http://theinvestinforum.com/
This is an angel investor group.

INCUBATORS

This is a great resource for inventors who want to raise money, but not manage the ins and outs of their own company. An incubator will often manage the company for the inventor, make an angel-sized cash investment, and then locate an additional round of funding—$500,000 to $2 million.

STARTech Early Ventures
www.startechev.com/
An incubator located in Richardson (Dallas), Texas.

DEVELOP A PROTOTYPE

Find a design engineer to draw your prototype and coordinate its development. The following resources may help:

CADTutor
www.cadtutor.net
Some inventors use computer-assisted drafting/design software to aid in the prototype process. This website provides a tutorial for the software.

1.800.CONTRACTOR.com
www.1800contractor.com
This website may be helpful in finding design engineers in your area.

COMPANIES THAT CONDUCT FOCUS GROUPS

e-FocusGroups
www.e-focusgroups.com

The Focus Group
www.focusgroupmarketing.com

Group Dimensions International
www.focusgroupdimensions.com

DEVELOP TOOLING FOR MASS PRODUCTION

When considering mass production, remember that tooling is expensive. Make sure you have all the kinks worked out before producing your tooling.

TOOLING COMPANIES ONLINE

Tooling Technologies Incorporated
www.toolingtec.com

Tyco Electronics
www.tycoelectronics.com

UGS Solid Edge
www.solidedge.com/industry/tooling.htm

Tooling Press Release
www.tooling-press-release.com
This website is for people who buy or produce tooling.

Saint-Gobain
www.saint-gobain.com
Shawn Donegan recommends this tubing distributor.

FINDING A RETAILER

STAR.com
www.star.com/cfm/?go=retailerLocator.retailerSearch&
This search engine is specifically designed for finding retailers.

TRADE SHOWS

Trade shows are a great way to test the demand for your product and to meet buyers and sales reps. You can find additional websites by running an Internet search on "trade show directories."

The American Tradeshow Directory
www.tradeshowbiz.com

Tradeshow Week
www.tradeshowweek.com

DIRECTORY OF BUYERS

DiversityBusiness.com
www.diversitybusiness.com/Directories/Buyer/corporationreport.asp
For a small yearly fee, you can use this website to search for buyers from specific retail stores in your region.

WEBSITE CREATION

QuickBizBuilder.com
www.quickbizbuilder.com
This is a great web page for creating your business website.

AKA Marketing.com
www.akamarketing.com/webmaster-forums
These webmaster forums cover many topics, including web advertising and generating traffic.

MARKETING PIECES

VistaPrint
www.vistaprint.com
This is an inexpensive resource for creating business cards, postcards, flyers, and more.

Proforma
www.proforma.com
This website offers custom promotional products, business forms, commercial print solutions, and more.

PUBLIC RELATIONS

Crain's Business
www.crain.com
Shawn Donegan recommends this business publication. Visit this website to locate Crain's Business in your region, or run an Internet search on "Crain's" with the name of your city or state.

LICENSING

If you are considering the licensing route, the following resource may help:

The Stirling Group
www.stirlinggroupusa.com

ADDITIONAL ASSOCIATIONS

Building Owners & Managers Association (BOMA) International
www.boma.org

Painting & Decorator Contractors of America
www.pdca.org

U.S. Small Business Administration
www.sba.gov

Millionaire Blueprints *neither endorses nor recommends any of the companies listed in the resource section. Resources are intended as a starting point for your research.*

Patrick
DORI

Forget suntans and sandcastles—Patrick Dori went to the Jersey shore and created a revolutionary advertising medium.

BUSINESS NAME:
Beach'n Billboard, Inc.

TYPE OF BUSINESS:
Advertising

LOCATION:
Leonia, NJ

ADAPTED FROM:
Millionaire Blueprints magazine article,
"King of the Beach,"
September/October 2006

S kippy Peanut Butter thought Patrick Dori was nuts. That's what the publicity director of CPC Best Foods told Dori when he heard his idea about placing Skippy ads in the creamy beige sand of New Jersey's beaches. Dori said, "You're right, but the first advertiser who gets this is going to walk away with a ton of publicity." That thought was enough to convince Skippy to take a chance on the inventor and become his first client.

Dori's company, Beach'n Billboard, Inc., has been contracted by seaside cities in his home state of New Jersey, along with advertisers that include Skippy, Snapple, 7-Up, Sobe, Yellow Book, and Volvo. It's also gone international, selling franchises in the Netherlands, Puerto Rico, and Portugal. The company that began as a dream in 1994 now makes 3,000 to 5,000 imprints daily for advertisers, on more than 600,000 square feet of each of its growing list of high-traffic beaches in the United States and abroad.

THE BEGINNING

How did the idea for Beach'n Billboard come about?

I believe my father placed this idea in my head. In 1994, almost one year to the day of his passing, I woke from a dream. The entire vision of Beach'n Billboard was dancing in my head. I went to my drafting table and drew out my vision.

What did you do with the idea?

I had a patent attorney already. The patent process was very difficult. They rejected us three times over four years. We had to do a patent search and submit anything similar. What we do is called "grooming and impressing on compliant ground" like sand or snow.

THE BUSINESS

How does the program work?

Municipalities clean the beaches every day, and our machine hooks up behind their equipment. Depending on the amount of people and the size of the beach, the advertisers pay us for the service, and then we pay the municipalities $100 to $200 per day. That reimburses the municipality for gas and offsets the cost of their beach-cleaning equipment and the salaries. The pattern on the mat leaves impressions. At the end of the day, the impressions are virtually gone from the foot traffic.

How does it actually work?

The machine had an imprint area of roughly 12-by-4 feet. I devised a way to make two machines in one—a trailer with retractable wheels and an imprinting machine—so the mats didn't touch the ground on the way to and from the beach.

Were there other technical issues?

We had problems figuring out the electrical system and the retractable wheel motor. The rubber mats got stretched out, which created a situation where a 200-pound imprint mat could whack somebody if it broke. Engraving the mat was another challenge. We experimented with a CNC machine. It worked, but we had to find special bits for cutting the mats and a computer program to convert the graphics. We went with PageMaker. For the drum, I subcontracted a basket manufacturer that made wire garbage pails.

THE MONEY

How much did the prototype cost?

It cost about $25,000 for all the experimentation, plus another $25,000 for the patent. So I was in the hole $50,000—but it was all my money.

How did you find the first client?

I left a voicemail with CPC Best Foods saying, "This is the weirdest phone call you've ever gotten in your entire life. I've invented a machine that puts advertising in the sand on beaches. Imagine 5,000 Skippy Peanut Butter jars imprinted all over a beach along with the words, 'Please Don't Litter.' The publicity value alone is astronomical." Fifteen minutes later the publicity director called and said, "Yes, that was the weirdest phone call." I explained it and offered to show him the videotape of our testing. Eventually, they gave me the go-ahead and $25,000.

How did you come up with that figure?

I based it on a full-page, black and white newspaper ad. I also found prices for aerial advertising, and I calculated how many people were on the beaches daily using demographic information. We factored in production costs and estimated the fair market value of the advertising with a beach season of only two or three months. They sent a check for $25,000.

THE NEED

How did you communicate your benefit to towns to get them to contract to use your service?

Our machine had an unexpected benefit. Cleaning a beach usually resulted in three full loads of trash every day, but after our machine started printing an anti-litter message, there were only two loads. The city manager gave us a letter stating they experienced a 20-percent litter reduction, and we used that to solicit other municipalities.

THE PROFIT

Why did you decide to franchise internationally?

We are expanding faster internationally. Right now, we have four beaches—plus Miami Beach—that allow nonprofit or public announcements, but not commercial advertising. We'll consider partnering with people to grow, but we feel it isn't the right time to sell a United States franchise outright. The first year, we sold international licenses for Puerto Rico and the Netherlands. In June 2005, we sold the rights to all of Portugal; the investors bought six machines and six imprint mats for utility and telephone companies to advertise there.

THE EXPANSION

How did you expand?

The makers of Coppertone called me with a list of beaches they wanted to advertise on: South Padre Island, Fort Lauderdale, and other places. So we shipped a machine down and drove the entire Florida coastline doing demonstrations. We were only able to open a couple of beaches, though. We needed someone locally pushing in our favor. To get them on board, you have to contact the city council and the mayor's office. Once you get a proponent on your side, they can walk you through the municipal red tape. Each municipality has its own rules and regulations. You have to spend a lot of time dancing with politics. The key to success is to stay focused.

THE MARKETING

How did you market to advertisers?

I generated a beautiful brochure with a fictional advertiser called Wave Cola. On the bottom I put, "Please Don't Litter." I thought a public service announcement would make it a soft sell. I bought lists of companies in the area and sent hundreds of mailers, but I got no response from any of those. I tried to think of every commercial product that would be appropriately advertised on a beach—suntan lotion, beverages, movies, and cars—and I spent hours on the phone cold calling as many of those as I could think of.

Who bought into your idea?

Some municipalities liked it and wanted to sign on, so my lawyer drew up an eleven-page contract for them. Today, we're down to a two-page agreement, which outlines what is expected of us and what we expect from the municipalities.

How do you find advertisers now?

They usually contact us. We get a fifty-fifty success rate, because a lot of people are looking for specific beaches that we're not handling. I could be booked solid if I had California and Florida beaches. We've gotten about $8 million in publicity and have a lot of credibility now. That's because people have seen it and realize that it's an effective medium.

THE LEGAL

So, what happened with the patent?

The whole thing with all the rejections and the attorney fees ended up costing more than $25,000. If they had approved it the first time, it would have only cost $4,000 to $5,000. Anybody with a patent-worthy idea should ask people they discuss it with to sign a nondisclosure, noncompete agreement. It's for your protection. Also, make sure your patent attorney is certified and, preferably, has worked in the United States Patent Office. Make sure he knows the criteria for the patent he is filing. For example, if you have an electronics product, make sure he is fluent in that area.

How did you handle this?

My attorney, who worked at the patent office, said we had to request a hearing with three senior patent officials, and go to court over it. I didn't wait for the patent though. By this time, I had already put tons of money into it and built the machines. The day we launched with Skippy Peanut Butter, my attorney called to say the patent was approved.

THE ADVICE

What would you say to someone who has a groundbreaking dream?

I would tell a fellow entrepreneur to listen to his dreams, and then be willing to do the legwork to make them happen. The dream might happen overnight, but seeing it come to life will take hard work, research, and time.

THE PLAN TO FOLLOW

STEP 1

Patent your idea. This can be a costly process, but you have to protect your intellectual property. Consider nondisclosure agreements with people who you share your vision with.

STEP 2

You need a prototype. People want to see what they are buying into. Show them what you can do, even if it's through photographs and printed materials.

STEP 3

Test and retest your idea. Be willing to alter your product until it works best for the most people.

STEP 4

Contact city officials when you have an idea that can benefit the community. Don't get derailed by the red tape. Be diligent in getting your word out.

STEP 5

Franchising internationally might be your next step. Beach'n Billboards, Inc., has international licensing deals in place and is expanding faster internationally than domestically. They sell each country the right to purchase an international licensing agreement. Consider requiring specific training before relinquishing the license. To determine the cost of a franchise, do market studies of comparative franchises and expected revenue per year.

THE HIGHLIGHTS

- You can make your dream a reality with time, research, and money.
- Businesses that help other businesses, as well as the community, are mutually beneficial.
- Contact your local chamber of commerce and larger businesses to gauge the market in your area.
- Provide quality services to ensure repeat customers and word-of-mouth referrals.
- Look for franchising opportunities that don't infringe on your own desires.

THE RESOURCES

MORE INFORMATION ABOUT PATRICK DORI

Beach'n Billboard
www.beachnbillboard.com

www.spiritsalespromo.com

INVENTION RESOURCES

Academy of Applied Science
www.aas-world.org
This is an organization created to promote creativity, promotion, and scientific achievement. Members include inventors, entrepreneurs, attorneys, business people, and others interested in innovation.

United Inventors Association
www.uiausa.org
This organization is aimed at providing educational resources for inventors. Under "Help Resources," click on "Inventor Organizations" to find a local inventors' group near you.

Inventor's Bookstore
www.inventorhelp.com
This website is run by the United Inventors Association. It offers the Inventor's Resource Guide, which is a good resource for the beginner.

Invent Now—National Inventors Hall of Fame
www.invent.org
This national organization sponsors conferences, programs, workshops, and a summer camp for kids.

ADVERTISING

Outdoor Advertising Association of America
www.oaaa.org
This is the lead trade association for outdoor advertising such as billboards, street furniture, and transit media. It represents 90 percent of industry revenues.

American Advertising Federation (AAF)
www.aaf.org
This organization represents 50,000 advertising professionals. The AAF brings members together and strives to educate, promote, and protect advertising.

Fedstats
www.fedstats.gov
This is an online guide to U.S. demographics.

Millionaire Blueprints *neither endorses nor recommends any of the companies listed in the resource section. Resources are intended as a starting point for your research.*

Rebecca
FINELL
and
Ryan
FERNANDEZ

For Rebecca Finell and Ryan Fernandez, good things come in "green" packages.

BUSINESS NAME:
Boon Inc.

TYPE OF BUSINESS:
Juvenile Products

LOCATION:
Tempe, AZ

ADAPTED FROM:
Millionaire Blueprints article,
"Leapfrogging to Success,"
May/June 2007

*I*f opportunity knocks, sometimes it's best not to answer the door. When Rebecca Finell won first place in the 2004 Juvenile Products Manufacturers Association (JPMA) Student Design Competition, she knew she was on to something big. Not only did her entry earn Finell an all-expense-paid exhibit in the prestigious International JPMA Trade Show, but, suddenly, many heads in the infant products industry were turning in her direction. Everyone was raving over her innovative Frog Pod, a scoop, drain, and storage unit that looks like a frog and attaches to the bathtub wall to provide a place to store children's bath toys.

Finell was overwhelmed. She had something every entrepreneur dreams of— a patent, a prototype for a product, and a demand beyond her wildest expectations. All she had to do was choose which door she wanted to open.

But behind every door, she found the same thing—manufacturers telling her they'd change her frog creation to fit their own product lines. Finell wanted none of that. She had an endless list of other products she wanted to manufacture, and she knew it would be painful to watch somebody else do it their way. So she began to consider manufacturing it herself. But she had a limited understanding of starting a business, running the sales and distribution aspects, and entering into a very difficult market to penetrate. She was on the verge of signing a licensing contract when fate stepped in and brought her in contact with Ryan Fernandez.

It started as a casual meeting at church outside the nursery where their kids played. Finell discovered that Fernandez was looking for an opportunity to start his own business. Intrigued, she secretly began to interview him. To her delight, Fernandez had all the missing pieces—an MBA in Entrepreneurship and more than ten years of experience at Intel Corp., where he worked in a myriad of sales and marketing positions. He understood Finell, her designs, her style, and where she wanted to go with her crazy green frog idea, and he was willing to sacrifice everything to make it happen. It was the perfect union of art and business. Soon afterward, Boon Inc., was born, and Finell's innovative Frog Pod began leaping into stores around the world.

THE PARTNERSHIP

What was your first task as new partners?

REBECCA: The first thing we did was sit down and ask ourselves, "How do we build this, and build it the right way?" We felt that, in order to know exactly where we stood and what kind of company we wanted to have, we needed to understand what our goals were.

How is your business partnership structured?

REBECCA: It's a fifty-fifty partnership. We spent a great deal of time with legal counsel to make sure we answered all the questions about what would happen in the event of various situations such as death, divorce, if one of us became disenfranchised, or if someone got sick.

Does one person have more decision-making power than the other?

REBECCA: No. We decided that most of the big decisions involving the company had to be a super majority, not just a majority. A super majority means it takes both of us to be in total agreement for anything to take place. We did this because, when we started out, we gave a very small amount of equity ownership in the company to some outside investors. Because of that, if we had kept with the typical bylaws that are associated with an S corporation, we could have been in trouble with certain decisions.

THE PRODUCT

Did you have any product to sell when you first started the company?

REBECCA: No. All we had was the Frog Pod prototype that had been entered in the JPMA contest.

What was the first thing you did once the company was created?

REBECCA: The first thing we did was to take the working prototype and create computer-modeled files that could be used to obtain manufacturing quotes. We ended up making five plastic prototypes at $500 each to show at the next JPMA Trade Show.

How did you find a manufacturer for the Frog Pod?

REBECCA: We searched the Internet, we asked different consultants and industrial design firms we were working with, and we met with key people from the JPMA Trade Show.

THE MANUFACTURING

Once you had choices, how did you select your manufacturer?

REBECCA: If you're going overseas for your manufacturing needs, definitely start by interviewing prospects on the phone or by e-mail. But once you've whittled it down to a select group, always pay them a visit, and meet the owner and managers of the plant. Know who you're working with because it's very hard to change factories.

Is there a safe way to find an overseas manufacturer?

REBECCA: Hire a sourcing agent. A sourcing agent is a company or person who acts as a middleman. They'll help you find factories overseas and help you interface with them. You'll still go there and visit these factories, but your sourcing agent will help you by being your eyes and ears on the ground.

How did you find your sourcing agent?

REBECCA: We were at the 2005 JPMA Trade Show, and he was there checking out the show. He came up to us and said, "If you need any help finding factories in China, I'd be willing to do that for you." So we told him we were going to China in a few weeks to check things out, and he agreed to meet us there and help us visit several factories.

How did you get your product to the United States?

RYAN: I quickly found out, when working directly with ocean carriers, that our rates were far too high. So, through the JPMA trade network, we took advantage of TOYSA (Toy Shippers Association), a freight buying group that works for toy and juvenile manufacturers to secure competitive freight rates and vessel space. This really helped to reduce the headache of finding our own freight carriers, and it gave us a much more affordable rate.

Where did you store the product once it arrived in the United States?
RYAN: We hired a 3PL (third-party logistics) company with facilities near the major ports of call where our products arrived. I chose a 3PL company with warehouse capabilities on both the East and West coasts. By warehousing product in two locations, we could cut down on ground freight costs for all of our customers nationwide.

Where did you learn how to deal with the issues of overseas manufacturing?
REBECCA: We had some fantastic guidance from our board of directors. In his book, *The Art of the Start,* Guy Kawasaki drives home the point that, if you're going to have a board of directors, you have to put together a group of people that can help you be successful.

THE MARKETING

How did you initially build interest in the Frog Pod?
REBECCA: We started by exhibiting at the 2005 JPMA Trade Show. That was the show where all the major players would be, and we didn't want to approach them quietly. Our little frog prototype was the reigning champion from the year before, so we wanted something spectacular. We decided to spend a fairly large amount of money on a great booth presence.

Did you take any orders?
REBECCA: We had hundreds of orders! Large chains, small boutiques from all over the country, and international distributors all seemed equally excited about the Frog Pod.

What kind of marketing do you do now?
REBECCA: Well, we do a lot of online marketing, some limited print

advertising, and we exhibit at the major industry trade shows. We have also been fortunate to get quite a bit of editorial coverage in the parenting magazines. As a matter of fact, an editorial is what really launched the Frog Pod into the mass market. It was a full-page photo of the Frog Pod in a magazine called *American Baby*. Since then, our products have been featured in many other parenting magazines.

How do you get in the magazines?

REBECCA: Most of the time, they call us and say, "We love the product; please send it to us. We're going to feature it in an editorial." Our marketing director, Kate Benjamin, has relationships with all of the parenting magazine editors, and she sends out press releases every time we launch a new product.

THE NEED

How did you decide what to do next?

REBECCA: Most of the buyers wanted other bathroom items so that our products could be together in the same aisle of their stores. So, I researched some of the issues that parents have with their kids' bathrooms and developed some innovative new solutions.

How do you know what does and doesn't work?

REBECCA: Since I'm a parent, I come across the same issues as any other parent. So, most Boon products are based on these common issues with products, or with a lack of products. But I also conduct mom research groups, where I bring a group of moms together and test out new ideas.

THE LEGAL

Do you patent your products?

REBECCA: Definitely. We patent them all and will continue to file more patents on each one after the first patents issue.

THE PLAN TO FOLLOW

STEP 1

Create a working prototype of your invention and have it patented.

STEP 2

Have computer-modeled files of your invention created so that you can use them to obtain manufacturing quotes.

STEP 3

Find a manufacturer that can re-create your invention exactly the way you want it.

NOTE: Finell and Fernandez suggest that you hire a sourcing agent to help you find an overseas manufacturer.

STEP 4

Find a carrier to import your product into the United States.

NOTE: Finell and Fernandez suggest that when first starting out, you do some research to find a freight-buying group in your industry. This will significantly cut your freight costs.

STEP 5

Show and demonstrate your product at trade shows specific to your industry. Take orders for your product.

NOTE: Finell and Fernandez also suggest that you send press releases for new products to various media that would be interested in a new product in your industry.

THE HIGHLIGHTS

- If you plan to venture into a partnership, seek legal counsel to clearly define details before you go into business.
- Hire a sourcing agent to help you find an overseas manufacturer.
- Carefully select a board of directors that can help you be successful.
- Educate yourself or hire experts to help with issues that you are not familiar with.
- Once you've established your brand, create products that fill other needs in your industry.

THE RESOURCES

MORE INFORMATION ABOUT REBECCA FINELL AND RYAN FERNANDEZ

Boon Inc.
www.booninc.com
Check out the website for Rebecca Finell and Ryan Fernandez and their business.

HOW TO GET STARTED

The Art of the Start by Guy Kawasaki
www.guykawasaki.com

INCORPORATING YOUR BUSINESS

S Corporation
www.scorporationsexplained.com
This website provides a thorough definition of an S corporation and of its benefits.

The Company Corporation
www.corporate.com
This website features all the advice and know-how you'll need to start and run your company.

PROTOTYPE CONSTRUCTION

Schmit Prototypes
www.schmitprototypes.com
This company will build a model, or working prototype, of your product for a very reasonable fee.

Davison Inventegration
www.davison54.com
Look here for information about how to turn your product idea into a fully working product sample that you can manufacture yourself, or sell to corporations for licensing rights.

Stanley I. Mason. "How to Make a Prototype."
www.morebusiness.com/running_your_business/businessbits/d1020642502.brc
This informative article provides some valuable insight about how to create your own prototype.

PATENTS AND LICENSING

United States Patent and Trademark Office
www.uspto.gov
This website provides comprehensive information on current patent rules and regulations, as well as guidelines for filing a patent on a product or idea.

Nolo
www.nolo.com
This website provides a detailed "how-to" guide about acquiring a patent without using an attorney.

INFANT PRODUCTS TRADE SHOWS

International Juvenile Products Manufacturers Association (JPMA) Trade Show
www.jpma.org
Known as "the show" in infant products circles, this is the one to attend if you want to put your

product in front of the major industry players. Buyers from all over the world come to this show looking for innovative new products to sell in their retail stores.

Toy Industry Association—American International Toy Fair 2007
www.toyfairny.com
This is the largest toy trade show in the Western Hemisphere. It attracts more than 20,000 buyers and industry professionals from more than ninety countries.

Trade Show Center
http://tradeshow.globalsources.com
This search portal provides a diverse listing of upcoming trade shows for importers of Asian-made products.

TRADE SHOW EXHIBITS

Skyline Exhibits
www.skyline.com
This website provides a total package solution for your trade show exhibit needs from concept and design to full-scale production.

The Trade Group
www.tradegroup.com
This is another great option for creating a trade show exhibit.

PRODUCT SOURCING AGENTS

TradeConsult
www.export-expert.net
This company offers product sourcing and supplier solutions for people looking to outsource to foreign markets.

Built In China
www.builtinchina.com
This is a one-stop website that can help you find a manufacturer for your product in China.

Alibaba.com Corporation
www.alibaba.com
This website brings buyers and sellers together from all over the world. It also includes a concise listing of upcoming trade shows in just about every industry imaginable.

The Federation of International Trade Associations
http://fita.org
This global trade portal provides an excellent source of trade leads, events, and links to more than 8,000 international trade sites.

INTERNATIONAL SHIPPING

MOL Logistics USA
www.mol-logistics.com
This is one of the world's largest international shipping companies with ports in America, Europe, Japan, and Asia.

Maersk Logistics USA
www.maersklogistics.com/sw32842.asp
This is another worldwide shipping company with ports all over the world.

Menlo Worldwide
www.menloworldwide.com
This website provides a variety of overseas transportation and warehousing options, as well as product sourcing and manufacturing.

Phoenix International
www.phoenixintl.com
This is the largest privately owned, full-service international freight forwarders and customs brokers headquartered in the United States.

HomeShipping.com
www.homeshipping.com
This website provides access to more than 250 different shipping vendors around the world. It is a great place to obtain a shipping quote instantly, book a shipment, and pay for it.

CUSTOMS BROKERS

World Class Shipping Cleared and Delivered
www.clearedanddelivered.com
This site helps you quicken the import and customs process by providing fast and easy customs clearance through all ports in the United States.

National Customs Brokers & Forwarders Association of America, Inc. (NCBFAA)
www.ncbfaa.org
This site helps you find a U.S. Customs broker quickly and easily.

THIRD-PARTY WAREHOUSING

Jacobson Companies
www.jacobsonco.com
This is a third-party logistics (3PL), third-party warehousing company with fifty-five facilities across the United States.

Logistic Edge
www.logisticedge.com
This full-service warehousing company provides assembly, fulfillment warehousing, labeling, packaging, shipping, and transportation services.

Seaboard Warehouse Terminals
www.seaboardwarehouse.com
This public warehouse provider and distributor serves clients from the East Coast to the Midwest.

SOCIAL RESPONSIBILITY

Cal Safety Compliance Corporation
www.cscc-online.com
This company monitors safe working conditions around the globe. If you are in doubt about the working conditions of an overseas factory and want to check its status as a humane, safe working environment, contact this company for a report before you conduct business.

Millionaire Blueprints *neither endorses nor recommends any of the companies listed in the resource section. Resources are intended as a starting point for your research.*

J. J.
MATIS

This lifelong fan found the perfect fashion accessory to pitch to the big leagues.

BUSINESS NAME:
J. J. Creations, Inc.

TYPE OF BUSINESS:
Customized Bags

LOCATION:
Sherman Oaks, CA

ADAPTED FROM:
Millionaire Blueprints magazine article,
"Making It in the Majors,"
May/June 2006

J. J.

Matis launched her business from a seat in Dodgers Stadium— the same one she's watched games from since she was a little girl. What began as the creative efforts of a devoted fan, quickly showed real marketing potential. Encouraged by the many compliments she received for her custom-made Dodgers bag, she presented her idea to the Dodgers in September 1999. By the following May—two weeks after she graduated with an MBA—she received a letter of approval from Major League Baseball (MLB) Properties. Starting with $30,000 of her own savings and one bag she sewed herself, Matis has added many more products to her line. She sells to all thirty Major League Baseball (MLB) teams. Matis has come a long way, but she is steadily increasing her list of buyers.

THE INITIATION

How did you get the Major League Baseball license?

My father has had season tickets since I was little, so I go to a lot of games. I made my first bag as a fan. I've always been a sewer. It was a baseball bag, and I took it around town and to games. Everywhere I went, people were asking, "Where did you get that adorable bag?" I realized I might be on to something, so I told our usher, whom I had known for years, about it. I said, "Sara, I'm getting inundated by people who love my bag. What should I do?" She told me to take it to Mike Nygren, who was the director of Dodger merchandise.

How did you approach him?

I was very naïve about the whole process. I wrote a little one-page letter, took a Polaroid of the bag, paper-clipped it to the letter, and sent it to him at the stadium. The next day, he called me and asked, "J. J., are you the girl with the bag everyone keeps asking about?" I told him I was, and he said, "If you get an application from Major League Baseball, get the official prototype done, and work on the details in your graduate school program, I'll endorse it when you send it in."

Where did you get an MLB application?

I contacted them and let them know that I was a prospective licensee, and that I would like an application. They mailed it to me in a packet, and it was a huge questionnaire. It was like submitting two business plans because you need your own official business plan, but then you're also filling out pages of questions as well.

THE PREPARATION

Who helped you with your business plan?

I worked on pieces of it in my classes in grad school. I also bought the book called *How to Write a Business Plan,* and I went to the Small Business Development Center (SBDC). They had an outline course about how to write one. I worked on each section bit by bit, and all of a sudden, it became a little book. I put a copy of the business plan with the application and the first product sample, and I sent it in. Within about six weeks, I got a letter from Major League Baseball saying I had become an official Major League Baseball licensee. Then I received the contract, which is literally a book about what I can and cannot do, and what products I am licensed for. I signed the papers saying I had received it, and sent them back.

THE MANUFACTURING

What about the challenges of being a small supplier?

Most buyers like to deal with the big companies like Nike or Adidas because they don't have to think about order minimums. The larger companies can order 10,000 hats and then split up the quantities among several retail avenues. A thousand might go to the stadium, and another thousand might go to a little mom-and-pop store. But if the stadiums are not willing to meet my minimums, I sit on inventory until they're comfortable with the sales, and then they take the rest of it.

Are you still using the same contract sewer?

No. I came to a point where everything was growing, but my cash flow and my working capital were suffering. I needed to lower my production costs. I had chosen a company called Industrial Stitchtech, which produced great quality products for me, but if I didn't lower my costs, I would go out of business. Something that costs me thirty-five dollars here in Los Angeles now costs me ten dollars from overseas.

How did you find a manufacturer in China?

I researched on the Internet, and I put the word out that I was looking for a reliable factory overseas. I found out I needed a specific type called a soft goods factory. I looked at other sport licensees to find out who they used. I went to their websites to try to figure out if they were manufacturing in China, and I bought merchandise and looked at the labels.

What did you say when you contacted a manufacturer?

I called and said, "I was referred to you by so-and-so, and I am looking to outsource. Please feel free to review my current collections at **www. jjmatis.com**. I am looking to increase my unit quantities, and lower manufacturing costs." If you say you make products for Major League Baseball, the NBA, or the NHL, people respond to that.

Once a manufacturer was interested, what did you do?

I set up meetings to see if my product could be replicated at their factory. I met with more than a dozen companies and individuals. In August 2003, my father was talking to one of his student's parents. He said I was looking for overseas production. The parent told my father I should call King Power Enterprises. They have a local office here in Los Angeles (Chino, California), and their factory is in the province of Guangdong in China.

How did things proceed with King Power?

At the initial meeting, I only showed them three of my product lines for the Dodgers and the Lakers. They were very receptive because they could see the potential for future growth. I gave them a dozen bags, which they took apart to see exactly how they were made.

THE PRODUCT

Who made the bags for you?

The prototype I sent in with the application had to be exactly what I intended to license—not a mock-up. I went back to the SBDC and used their resources to find local contract sewers. The SBDC gave me a list, and I called each of them and explained what I was doing. Then I met with the manufacturing facilities that sounded interested and that were receptive to working with a sports licensee. I interviewed maybe five to eight of them. That's when I chose Industrial Stitchtech.

What was your approach when you met with Industrial Stitchtech?

I showed the president and owner, Ed Perez, the bag I made. He wasn't that impressed, but when I explained that it was being considered for licensing by Major League Baseball, he became excited because, potentially, you could put every team logo on it and have a very successful licensed sports product.

How many bags did you order that first time?

We just started with a Dodgers baseball-shaped backpack, and I think we made a couple thousand of them. My initial order from the Dodgers was small. They were concerned about the price. My wholesale price was high; therefore the retail price was high.

What did you pay for them?

With embroidery and everything, they were almost twenty dollars each. I think I was making maybe five dollars a bag, if that. I think they were retailing for fifty-five to sixty dollars, but that's a pretty standard markup for retail. The prices have all come down now though.

THE MARKETING

How did you advertise?

The first bag I offered was a fourteen-inch baseball-shaped backpack licensed to the Dodgers. I didn't have an advertising or marketing budget. It was all word of mouth.

Once you're approved, how do you get other teams to order from you?

When you become a licensee, you get a list from MLB of all the buyers and merchandise directors at the team stadiums. Once they saw the sales record for the first month, Major League Baseball Properties (MLBP) wanted all the teams to carry my bags. They told me if I could get other teams to buy from me, they'd extend my license to include the other twenty-nine teams.

Do you have any other marketing strategies?

I also do charity work with the team foundations. For the teams, I'll donate products, and we'll have a player sign the product. Or I'll put a package together for an event, and they auction it off at their silent auction or game, and the proceeds go to the foundation.

THE CONCLUSION

So what makes you so tenacious?

I love the feedback I get—and the smiles. People write me, call me, stop me in the streets, and talk to me at games. I love the enthusiasm of being a fan and following the standings each season. For me, being a part of something positive by creating and designing team souvenirs that fans can bring home to remind them of their experience makes it all worthwhile.

THE PLAN TO FOLLOW

STEP 1

Create a demo of your product. Figure out its pros and cons, and then redevelop it.

STEP 2

Create a solid business plan and submit your request to obtain a license.

NOTE: Matis suggests reading the book, *How to Write a Business Plan,* and utilizing the SBDC.

STEP 3

Collect your startup funding, and then find a manufacturer that will re-create your product exactly how you want it.

NOTE: Be prepared to work with overseas companies.

STEP 4

Develop a marketing strategy and get publicity for your product.

NOTE: Word of mouth can play a huge role.

THE HIGHLIGHTS

- This can be a discouraging, yet profitable, business.
- Submit a strong business plan to the SBDC.
- Take your time in finding the right manufacturer for yourself, and for your product.
- Once you've developed a line, create other products you think will fill a need for consumers.

THE RESOURCES

MORE INFORMATION ABOUT J. J. MATIS
J. J. Matis' website.
www.jjmatis.com

HOW TO WRITE A BUSINESS PLAN
Small Business Development Center (SBDC)
www.sba.gov/sbdc/

ASSOCIATIONS
Travel Goods Association
www.travel-goods.org
This website represents the travel goods industry, including manufacturers, distributors, and retailers.

SPORTS LEAGUES
Stadiums
(From Wikipedia, the free encyclopedia)
www.wikipedia.org
For a fairly complete list of stadiums in the United States and worldwide, go to Wikipedia and type in "list of stadiums" in the search box. Each listing is also linked to information about the stadium.

Major League Baseball Properties (MLBP)
www.mlb.com
This is the official site of the MLB. Click on "Official Info" to get information about licensing.

National Basketball Association (NBA)
www.nba.com

National Football League (NFL)
www.nfl.com

National Hockey League (NHL)
www.nhl.com

Professional Golfers Association (PGA)
www.pga.com

MAJOR LICENSEES THAT PERFORM BUYING SERVICES
SportService
www.delawarenorth.com/aboutdnc/sportservice.asp

Aramark
www.aramark.com

Sports Avenue
www.sportsavenue.com

MANUFACTURERS
King Power Enterprise, Inc.
www.kingpower.com
This is the overseas manufacturer that J. J. Matis uses to produce her bags.

Industrial Stitchtech
www.industrialstitchtech.com
This U.S. manufacturer produced J. J. Matis' first products. Though the costs may be somewhat higher than overseas manufacturers, there are less transportation issues.

B2B Manufacturers.com
www.manufacturers.com.tw
This portal can help you search for manufacturers in Taiwan and China.

Global Sources
www.globalsources.com
This portal can help you search for manufacturers in China. It also lists sourcing fairs in China.

Ohio Travel Bag
www.ohiotravelbag.com
This company has a large selection of components, fasteners, and hand tools for the luggage, handbag, and shoe industry.

Millionaire Blueprints *neither endorses nor recommends any of the companies listed in the resource section. Resources are intended as a starting point for your research.*

Tamara
MONOSOFF

How an inventive mom turned her creative household solution into a resource for others like herself—and created a multimillion-dollar, family-centered business in the process.

BUSINESS NAME:
Mom Inventors, Inc.

TYPE OF BUSINESS:
Web-based Resource for Community of Mom Inventors

LOCATION:
Walnut Creek, CA

ADAPTED FROM:
Millionaire Blueprints magazine article,
"Mom Invented-Millions Sold,"
October 2005

The day her ten-month-old daughter, Sophia, pulled all the toilet paper off the roll and clogged the toilet, Tamara Monosoff knew she needed to design a better solution than simply keeping the bathroom door perpetually closed. This design, she reasoned, would stop her young toilet paper "bandit"—and countless others like her. So she sketched it out and matched the dimensions to a standard toilet paper roll. She called it TP Saver.

Not only did her TP Saver become a million-dollar item, it also paved the way for Monosoff to unite other mom inventors and form the company now known as Mom Inventors, Inc., a web-based collaborative resource for an entire community of moms and others who invent quality products dedicated to improving family life. In addition to creating an amazing online support community, Mom Inventors also provides education on the process of transforming great ideas into marketable products. Since she launched the TP Saver nationally in the fall of 2003, Monosoff's vision has led to the launch and encouragement of countless other inventor careers among stay-at-home moms, which has helped recognize the untapped potential of this creative, resourceful, and practical segment of the population.

THE BEGINNING

Once you knew what the prototype for the TP Saver should look like, what did you do?

I found a local machinist and described what I wanted over the phone. He wanted to see it, so I went over to the industrial side of town. He made it, but it took about eight renditions until we were sure we had the bugs out. And while he was working on that, I was figuring out how to get it to market.

What was the first step?

I started by calling patent attorneys, both from the phone book and on recommendations of other people I talked to along the way. I asked everyone I called for advice. I bought books on inventing, but nothing I found took me through the "getting to market" process, step by step.

When did creating this collaboration of mom inventors occur to you?

Along the way, I met other moms like me who had great ideas, but who didn't know how to get them out there. As we compared notes, I realized I wanted to create an online community to share the information I found with other moms. I wanted to give moms who invent things the support they need to go forward with their ideas—a road map to market that they could really use.

THE BUSINESS

So what did you do to make that happen?

I had a website created that contained all the information I discovered while marketing my TP Saver to serve as a resource for sharing ideas and information. I realized that the best ideas for new inventions came from my target market—other moms—but they are generally busy being moms and rarely have the time, or incentive, to research this stuff on their own.

What do you do to educate moms about how to move forward with their inventions and ideas?

One thing I did was teach Saturday morning seminars—with childcare. Moms could even dial in and participate from home. Everyone asked questions. We get some amazing feedback in these seminars, and it gives the mom inventors an opportunity to talk about what they're doing with others like themselves. We recorded the seminars on CDs. The eight-CD set (ten hours of content) is called the *Product Development Blueprint* and is available on the Mom Inventors website under "CD Seminars."

THE MONEY

What market research strategies work best if you don't have a lot of money?

I'm a big advocate of focus groups called primary research. Early on, I spent money for this kind of research, and then realized I could get the same information for free by using the message boards on various parenting websites. I also sent mass e-mails requesting opinions from a list of people I compiled who had expressed interest in our products.

When you spent money for market research, what did you get for your money?

When I created TP Saver, I wanted to hear from moms firsthand, so I hired a marketing company and had them conduct a special focus group. The feedback from the group was phenomenal. It is important to understand that the negative feedback is the most valuable. People don't want to hear it, but it is how you turn your product into something that will sell. Listen to every single word.

THE NEED

Tell us about secondary research. What were your best sources for that?

My secondary research was gathering information about my market generated by others, including Internet trade organizations, the U.S. Census Bureau, and surveys of all the popular trend information out there—learning everything I could about the people buying products in a certain category.

THE PROFIT

How do you know if you have a million-dollar idea, and how can you make the most of it?

Everyone thinks he or she has a million-dollar idea—and some people really do. But realistically, they may have a $10,000 idea or a $20,000 idea. The good news is that once you get in the inventor's mind-set, you tend to keep thinking that way—and royalties add up quickly. The royalty income you can receive from simply licensing your idea is amazing. So just keep thinking—and consider all the possible extensions of your original product. For example, retailers (large and small) prefer product lines rather than working with single product companies.

THE INTERNET

Do you charge anything for providing this information—like a membership or enrollment fee?

No. All the information on my website is free, like "The 10 Steps to Inventing, Licensing and Manufacturing." People can't believe I am giving this information away. We also feature a mom every month to inspire others. We had half a million hits last month.

THE MARKETING

How do you do market research?

It's common sense, really. Just figure out who will buy your product and how large the market is. The U.S. Census Bureau has information about how many people fit your demographic profile. I did that with the first product and decided a fraction of that number was a big enough market for me. It's good to be unique, but if your product is too specific, just let it go and move on.

THE LEGAL

Now, getting back to patents, how can people protect themselves from having their ideas stolen?

Be smart. If you go to an engineer or a machinist before your idea is patented, have them sign a nondisclosure agreement. This means they agree not to discuss your product with an outside party. That doesn't mean that they won't steal your idea, but it may dissuade them. Most people will not follow through. There are so many things to do to steal an idea. Find reputable people to help you and get recommendations through word of mouth. Create your own referral network.

THE ADVICE

What is your advice to other would-be inventors?

Attend all of the industry events you can. When attending a trade show, find the names of representatives of companies by making a simple phone call to the company, and asking who is attending the upcoming show to look for new products. Then invite them to your booth.

THE PLAN TO FOLLOW

STEP 1

If you can't afford a logo design, search your community for graphic design programs in universities. Find students in industrial programs at local or nearby colleges to make your prototype. They don't have to be pretty; you can refine it from there. Or think of it as an art project for yourself. Look around your house. If you need wire, plastic, whatever kind of material you envision being right for your product, use something you have. I've cut up packaging containers and used the material. You probably have what you need in your own house to design your packaging. Be creative.

STEP 2

What most people need to know is that getting a patent is not a roadblock. Save your money. Don't rush out and get a patent until you know your product will sell. Some very aggressive patent attorneys may tell you otherwise. But the truth is, the first thing you need to know is if people will buy it. It is important to note that many successful products are sold without patents.

STEP 3

You need to do market research.

STEP 4

Speak to buyers in local stores. Take a sample of your product to the store and ask to speak to the owner. Say things like, "I have a prototype for a new product. Can I ask you for some feedback? What would you have me change in order for you to buy it from me? How would it need to be packaged? How much would you pay? How much do you need to sell this for?" Then you'll be able to work backward to determine your pricing.

STEP 5

You can offer your product idea for licensing to a company. Licensing is a great solution for a mom who wants to have passive income from her ideas without the risk or hassle of doing it all herself. Understand that this takes time, and patience is the key.

THE HIGHLIGHTS

- You can have a successful home-based business with the right information.
- A website is a crucial element to any business.
- If you're sitting on a large number of units of an invention, consider having an eBay store.
- Don't get a patent until you know your product is the best it can be.
- Make sure your product's appeal is broad enough.

THE RESOURCES

eBay store
www.ebay.com

PRODUCT SUBMITTAL INFORMATION

www.qvcproductsearch.com

www.onestepahead.com

www.inventiveparent.com

www.mommyshop.com

TRADE SHOWS

Juvenile Products Manufacturing Association (JPMA)
www.jpma.org

All Baby Product Expo (ABC)
www.abckidsexpo.com

DEMOGRAPHIC INFORMATION

The U.S. Census Bureau
www.census.gov

Margin calendar
www.mominventors.com

Millionaire Blueprints *neither endorses nor recommends any of the companies listed in the resource section. Resources are intended as a starting point for your research.*

Peter
VON DYCK

Peter M. von Dyck's early career decision was later reinforced by a sad twist of fate that caused him to put his heart, as well as his mind, into this breakthrough business.

BUSINESS NAME:
Zassi® Medical Evolutions, Inc.

TYPE OF BUSINES:
Medical Devices

LOCATION:
Fernandina Beach, FL

ADAPTED FROM:
Millionaire Blueprints article,
"Pioneer on the Medical Frontier,"
May/June 2007

Peter M. von Dyck spends his days working on things that most people don't like to talk about. Inventing better medical devices for the gastrointestinal tract might seem like a thankless task, but patients all over the world are silently applauding his efforts. Though the rewards in this industry can be high, the risks are even higher. Fortunately, von Dyck's company has persevered and it is developing breakthrough devices that are dramatically changing health care.

When he began work in his father's company at age eighteen, von Dyck taught himself to read engineering blueprints. He devoured medical textbooks and journals so he could create his own medical product designs. After assisting his father's company in the transition to a new area of the market, he went off to learn more about the business world from a large multinational company. He then started his own company, Zassi Medical Evolutions, Inc. (**www.zassimedical.com**).

Peter von Dyck and a team of employees and partners managed to design the world's first solution to a simple problem that had been eluding the health-care industry for years. After winning the U.S. Food and Drug Administration's (FDA) clearance to commercialize the new technology in the U.S. market, he went on to sell it in more than twenty other countries. They later sold the assets and intellectual property to a large corporation, and have now moved on to their next opportunity.

THE BEGINNING

What got you started in this industry?

My father was a biochemical engineer who was recruited from Germany to work for a cardiovascular company in Florida. After many years of working on product development, he started his own company in the specialty plastic polymer arena. He eventually joined up with some doctors who had a new concept in medical devices and began producing new types of catheters that delivered nutrition to patients who were unable to swallow due to complications from strokes or other traumas.

And you worked at his company?

Yes. At first, I was just sweeping floors and such. But I watched the machine shop guys, and eventually they started giving me small assignments. The first thing they gave me was a blueprint of a very simple structure, but I couldn't read it. I was embarrassed because I knew they had given me something that was extremely simple.

What did you do?

I just kept looking at it and began deconstructing it, piece by piece, for many days. Then, all of a sudden, it made sense. When I could finally see it, I uncovered an appetite to learn like never before. The next day I began building that simple structure. That was a huge turning point for me. I knew I needed to find a unique niche for myself, and the life sciences market was highly attractive to me. So, while I was going to college at night and studying business administration, I was also "eating" medical books for breakfast. Over a period of a year or two, I became the resident expert in a new area of surgery and gastroenterology.

THE EXPERIENCE

When did you leave that company?

In 1994, when the company decided to sell certain products and assets to get funding to move in new directions. The buyer saw that I was one of the chief project managers and key inventors, so they made me an offer. I wanted to start my own company someday, and I thought this opportunity might be like getting my MBA to go from a small organization and experience to a much larger billion-dollar company.

What did you do for that company?

My main job was to take products they acquired and integrate them into its worldwide operations like sales, marketing, manufacturing, distribution, and quality control. I ended up inventing several other products for them during my tenure. During that time, I was developing my business plan at night for what is now my company.

How long did you work there?

For three years. In that time, I worked in Japan, Europe, South America, and all across the United States. I learned a lot and met great people. Many have elected to follow me and become part of my company.

THE MONEY

Where did your seed capital come from?

From one of the distributors I set up for my father's company. They liked my style and passion. I told them I was going to start my own company someday. They said, "When you do, we'd be happy to back you." In 1997, I told them I was ready if their offer was still good. On just a verbal agreement that was sealed with a handshake, I quit my job and moved to Florida to start my company.

They would be what are called "angel investors" in the capital world. They became shareholders and provided the initial funding of a couple hundred thousand dollars. The money had to be infused on a monthly level in small pieces. That was my only working capital at that time, other than my own, for about two years.

THE BUSINESS

What did you spend that money on?

I did patent searches and worked on developing solid patents. I spent money on product design and business plan development so I could begin traveling to build a network of clinical advisers who would be supportive of my designs, and validate them to financiers and strategic players. That way, I could raise more money.

So that initial funding just got your company off the ground?

Yes. It typically costs several million dollars to bring even one medical device from napkin sketch to market. So you usually have to undergo multiple rounds of funding.

THE PRODUCT DEVELOPMENT

What are the basic steps of getting a device to market?
After the initial invention is derived, you have to conduct design activities that capture global customer requirements and specifications. Simultaneously, you need to manipulate the design so that it works in harmony with the target anatomy and physiology of the body system you are interfacing with. This can take several years of work that involves tests in labs, or on cadavers or on animals, before the FDA (www.fda.gov) will allow you to try it on people. Once they give you the go-ahead, you use it on small groups of people—anywhere from ten to a hundred. Then, if all that works out well, you can apply for full approval from the FDA. The process is very similar in Europe, which is something you usually pursue concurrently. Once you satisfy these regulatory agencies, you can move to large-scale manufacturing and begin commercial sales.

How much risk is there in this market?
There's no doubt it's a high-stakes market, but the reward quotient is very high.

Take us through the creation of one of your products.
Having worked on things like feeding tubes for those people who can't chew or swallow food on their own, I was helping to create tons of human waste. This is not a problem for most of us because we can get up and use the toilet. But if you're stuck in bed, you can't get up. It's not a subject people like to talk about, but people all around the world are stooling on themselves. They're infecting themselves, and many are even dying from secondary infections.

In many cases, bacteria and organisms harbored in stool are the source of hospital-acquired infections (HAI). A lot of the pathogens that cause infections are from stool. Ironically, there were catheters so people wouldn't urinate on themselves, but there was nothing for stool. So it was very clear that this product needed to exist. That is why we developed the world's first bowel management system. It's called the Zassi Bowel Management System™, and it has a whole series of patents. I'm a cocreator and a coinventor on that system with a few other people. We formed a partnership, developed the product, and took it through the FDA to get clearance for sale. Then, over the last three years, we built a sales force. We used specialty distributors. I also employed some direct salespeople. We sold it throughout the United States and in about twenty other countries around the world until September 2006, when we sold that group of assets to a large, multinational company.

THE ADVICE

Knowing what you know now, would you do anything differently?
Not much. I believe that you learn so much from mistakes. I probably would have gone after higher caliber pharmacoeconomic clinical data on our first commercial device. I focused more on safety data. I think it would have been more efficient to place greater focus on cost-saving elements so that hospitals and doctors would have an easier time recognizing that the use of this new system doesn't just save lives—it saves money. More cost data might have led to more rapid adoption of this new technology, which would have increased our sales in the beginning.

THE PLAN TO FOLLOW

STEP 1

Learn everything you can about the medical market you want to start your business in, and work as an employee for a successful company in this market.

STEP 2

Look in your medical market for problems that need solutions, and develop inventions to solve these problems.

NOTE: von Dyck says that your device design must work in harmony with the target anatomy and physiology of the body system you are interfacing with.

STEP 3

Secure startup capital to set up the basic elements of business, patent your designs, develop prototypes, and create a solid business plan to raise more money.

NOTE: von Dyck suggests that you build a network of clinical advisers who will be supportive of your designs and validate them to financiers and strategic players.

STEP 4

Seek FDA approval.

NOTE: von Dyck says it takes several years of work that involves tests in labs and on cadavers before the FDA will allow you to try it on people. Once they give you the go-ahead, clinical trials involve small groups of people. Then you can apply for full approval from the FDA.

STEP 5

Upon receiving FDA approval, you can begin large-scale manufacturing and commercial sales.

THE HIGHLIGHTS

- Medical inventions are high risk, but yield high returns.
- Gain experience, and build relationships with industry experts before starting a business in the medical industry.
- Have a solid business plan in place. This type of business usually requires multiple rounds of funding.
- Be prepared to spend several years developing and testing your product before you apply for FDA approval.
- Study the process of clinical trials, relate lab test results to human physiology, and learn from mistakes.

THE RESOURCES

This is a complex and complicated industry where invention is merely the beginning. You'll need lots of help to successfully navigate your way through patents and federal regulations, not to mention selling your device through the proper channels, once you receive the go-ahead. But don't let that deter you. Following is a collection of websites to get you on your way.

MORE INFORMATION ABOUT PETER M. VON DYCK

Zassi Medical Evolutions, Inc.
www.zassimedical.com
Peter M. von Dyck's company website.

ORGANIZATIONS AND ASSOCIATIONS

Don't know where to begin? Contact the association most closely aligned with your product and goals, and let them steer you in the right direction. They're usually staffed with professionals, many of them volunteers, who know a lot about the industry and who are eager to help.

The Medical Device Manufacturers Association
www.medicaldevices.org
Trade association that represents independent manufacturers in the industry.

AdvaMed Advanced Medical Technology Association
www.advamed.org
Trade association for those transforming health care through technology.

Medical Device Link
www.devicelink.com
Online information source for the industry that contains news, a searchable directory for connecting with suppliers and manufacturers, and links to publications and trade shows.

Association for the Advancement of Medical Instrumentation
www.aami.org
Association dedicated to education and promotion of the safe and effective use of medical instruments.

GOVERNMENT OFFICES

You won't get permission to start selling your great idea without winning over the government. The Internet is a great place to dive in and start your research. Since this is an area that benefits public health, some agencies may even be able to help you with funding, research, and more.

U.S. Food and Drug Administration
www.fda.gov
Look down the left side under "Products FDA Regulates," and you'll see a heading for "Medical Devices." Click on that link, and you'll be taken to a page full of information and numerous links on the topic.

Advanced Technology Program
www.atp.nist.gov
This arm of the National Institute of Standards and Technology (**www.nist.gov**) helps innovative companies develop their high-risk research projects through funding, partnerships, and knowledge sharing.

The Office of Health and Consumer Goods—Health Industries
www.ita.doc.gov/mdequip
This agency is dedicated to advancing the U.S. health industry, both at home and abroad. It focuses on trade issues, policies, and increasing exports.

Small Business Funding Opportunities—National Institutes of Health
www.nih.gov/grants/funding/sbir.htm

Agency for Healthcare Research and Quality
www.ahrq.gov

United States Patent and Trademark Office
www.uspto.gov

TRADE MAGAZINES

Peter von Dyck read every medical book he could get his hands on when he got started, and you can be sure he stays up-to-date on the latest advances in his field. One of the quickest ways to do that is by reading the magazines that focus on your industry.

Medical Devices News
www.medicalnewstoday.com/sections/medical_devices/

Medical Design Technology
www.mdtmag.com

Medical Product Outsourcing
www.mpo-mag.com

Today's Medical Developments
www.jmdpublications.com

Medical Device Link
www.devicelink.com
Links to several trade publications are available via this website. Click on "search," and enter these titles: *Medical Device and Diagnostic Industry, Medical Product Manufacturing News,* and *Medical Device Technology.*

MANUFACTURERS, SUPPLIERS, AND DISTRIBUTORS

While you're in the development process, you may need some supplies and assistance in building prototypes. Once you have your device approved and ready to go, you'll probably need someone else to manufacture and sell it for you. The following sites may help in wading through the sea of options.

MDRWeb.com
www.mdrweb.com
Subscription-based site with detailed information and search capabilities on more than 17,000 medical device manufacturers and 82,000 products within the United States and abroad. This site states that it has "long been considered the official directory of medical suppliers."

Health Industry Distributors Association
www.hida.org
Provides support and education for distributors in the health industry.

Emergo Group
www.emergogroup.com
Consultant to medical device companies. Assists in regulatory areas, such as obtaining approval from the FDA or international markets. Also assists in the search for medical distributors in Europe.

Medical-Equip-Guide.com
www.medical-equip-guide.com
Need medical equipment for testing or research? Visit this directory of new and used medical equipment sites.

TRADE SHOWS

Canon Communications LLC
www.cancom.com
Specializes in publications and trade shows for the design industry, including medical devices. (Look on the left side of their site for links to each.) This company sponsors several trade shows nationwide.

Millionaire Blueprints neither endorses nor recommends any of the companies listed in the resource section. Resources are intended as a starting point for your research.

4

True Stories of PRODUCT-DRIVEN Millionaires

Terri
BOWERSOCK

Terri Bowersock overcomes obstacles and tragedy to forge a million-dollar success.

BUSINESS NAMES:
Terri's Consign & Design Furnishings and Still N Style

TYPE OF BUSINESS:
Furniture, Fashion, and Home Décor Consignment

LOCATION:
Tempe, AZ

ADAPTED FROM:
Millionaire Blueprints magazine article,
"Consign by Design,"
September/October 2006

Terri Bowersock has always been unconventional. When she was only nineteen, Bowersock drew up a business plan for a furniture consignment store with crayons and colored pencils.

Twenty-six years later, everything she envisioned in that plan has come true. From an initial $2,000, Bowersock built sixteen stores across the country and made $36 million—without ever taking out a loan. Today, she runs the number-one woman-owned business in Arizona, and it is only growing from there.

Bowersock has never done things the "regular way." She has dyslexia, so by definition, "the regular way" is simply not possible for her.

Her way of thinking, coupled with a dogged perseverance and a thread of hope despite the most difficult of circumstances, has helped Bowersock build her business into a multimillion-dollar success. To think, it all began with that one-page plan drawn with crayons.

Bowersock has done amazing things with her initial dream, even through the most tragic times. In 2004, Bowersock's mother—who also served as her business partner—was murdered. After a yearlong heart-wrenching search, Bowersock finally located her body, and was able to put her mother to rest. She then set out to build a legacy to her mother, by creating a second type of store focused on fashion and home furnishings in her mother's memory. Today, the first of many Still N Style stores stands next to a Terri's Consign & Design Furnishings—a tribute to her mother's life and wonderful influence.

THE IDEA

How did you come up with the idea for a consignment store?

I went to visit my father in Kansas in 1979, and he introduced me to a group of lawyers' wives who had started a little clearinghouse where they sold things on consignment and sent the money to charity. I really studied it. I don't even know why. My brain just started going boom, boom, boom. Dyslexics see in big pictures.

What exactly is a consignment store?

It's like a rich man's thrift shop. People give you their high-end items to sell, and you price them, frequently selling the pieces for half of what they were originally purchased for. Usually, you split the proceeds fifty-fifty with the people who bring in the items.

THE BUSINESS PLAN

After you watched this business and decided you wanted to do something similar, what did you do next?

I got out my crayons and colored pencils, started drawing a business plan, and, by midnight, I knew how to do it. I knew it was going to be across the country. I knew how much money it was going to make. I had drawn all the concepts on one big piece of paper.

Your business plan was quite unconventional. Do you attribute that to being dyslexic?

Yes. Dyslexics think and store information on the right side of their brains, rather than on the left. So we are natural out-of-the-box thinkers.

THE MONEY

After you drew this unconventional business plan, what was your next step?

I borrowed $2,000 from my grandmother. Then I found a little 2,000-square-foot house in Phoenix, Arizona, for the store, and I moved in. I called the store Terri's Consign & Design.

THE STORE

Where did you get your first items to sell?

I got my mother's living room furniture and my bedroom furniture. I put it in the store, opened the doors, and said to anyone and everyone who came through the doors, "Hi, this is a consignment store. If you have something to sell, bring it in, and I'll sell it for you."

Was your mom your first employee?

Yes. It's a cute story. I called my mother and said, "You're going to get skin cancer! I read it in a newspaper. If you stay in the sun and keep teaching tennis, you're going to get skin cancer. You've got to come into the furniture business. It's going to be big." I talked her into coming into the business.

THE FURNITURE

Did you sell new furniture pieces, too?

Over time, we started adding some new things to the store. Now we have 60 percent consigned and 40 percent new.

How did you deliver furniture?

In the early days, my mom and I would pick up furniture in the morning, sell during the day, and deliver at night. Today, we have a fleet of trucks in Phoenix.

How did you price the furniture?

The client and I set the price. I would ask how much she paid for it, and we'd price it from there. Over time, I had to change my tactics to something more efficient. So I invented "Terri's Blue Book," the only one of its kind.

What is "Terri's Blue Book?"

It's a blue book for furniture—the same method they use for pricing used cars. First, you look the furniture up by category, then you look up the type of furniture. The next line you look at is the brand, and if it is high, medium, or low quality, and the price. Next you look at the add-ons. At the end, you total the pluses and minuses, just like you would a car, and it gives you the price.

THE MARKETING

You have an interesting ad campaign theme, correct?

I focused ad campaigns on a mother-and-daughter furniture store. I started this energy around moms and daughters in business, and the women poured in. So word spread. Women would tell other women, and they'd bring each other to the store and have lunch with me and my mom.

Your first bit of publicity was from a rather different idea, wasn't it?

Yes! At the time, my mom had her tennis shop. It was in a high-traffic area, so I set up furniture on the side of the road by her shop, and I put a mannequin by the furniture. And one day a truck hit the mannequin! I called the newspaper and said, "There's been a mannequin accident." They came running over. I told the whole story and ended up with a half-page article in the *Tribune*. I learned that by sharing your life with the media, you get publicity.

Then you made television commercials?

I made my first commercial in 1983. They came out and brought the cameras. My mother kept worrying that they were going to see dirt. She kept saying, "Clean that; clean this." So the cameraman suggested that for the commercial, I hand Mom a duster at the end, and say, "Thanks, Mom," in a loving but kind of an: "I cleaned my room again" sort of way. And that became the signature for the first ten years of business—"Thanks, Mom."

THE LICENSING

Did you ever do franchises?
Yes, I did. But, now I do licensing.

Do you teach classes for the people who buy licenses?
I teach my own people about two times a year how to run their stores, or whenever someone needs it. They get all the manuals and books. After the initial signup fee, they pay $10,000 a year to use the name.

How much does it cost to start one of your stores?
I can put you in the furniture business with only $200,000 out the door.

What are the advantages of licensing with you rather than starting from scratch?
My blue book alone is worth the price! Pricing is where a lot of people mess up. I also bring licensees here to take a training course. Plus, I put them to work in my store. To me, there is no better place to learn. Licensees also get as much free-calling time as they need.

THE GROWTH

You recently started a new type of consignment store—fashion and home accessories. But, from what I understand, this new store started from a tragedy in your life.
Yes. I started the new store after my mother was murdered in 2004. My mother had gorgeous clothes and collected many accessories and other items. And you know, when you miss somebody, you want to do things that remind you of them. So I got to thinking, "What if someone started a store that was similar to a gently used Dillard's?" I opened Still N Style Fashion and Home Décor.

Have you gotten much publicity for the store?

The character of the store draws publicity. It's kind of like a big garage sale in one of those big mansions in Texas. Wouldn't you want to go?

THE ADVICE

If a person wanted to start their own store from scratch, what should they do?

It's simple. Find a building, and take everybody's furniture that you know. Seed the store with your own furniture, your friend's furniture, your parents' furniture—everybody. Put it in the store, and as quickly as you can, do publicity, advertising, or word of mouth. Tell people, "It's a consignment store. Bring your furniture. I'll sell it for you. You get 50 percent, and I get 50 percent, and when it's sold, I will write you a check."

THE PLAN TO FOLLOW

STEP 1

Find a location for your consignment store. Then, make arrangements to have furniture picked up and delivered.

NOTE: Bowersock started her store in a 2,000-square-foot house.

STEP 2

Talk to everyone you know about what you are doing, and ask if they have furniture that they would like to sell on consignment.

NOTE: Bowersock started her store with just her bedroom furniture and her mother's living room furniture. She suggests that you ask everyone who walks through the door if they have furniture they would like to sell on consignment.

STEP 3

Price the furniture according to style, brand, age, and quality level. Develop a mark-down system to get the furniture out the door.

NOTE: Bowersock suggests that the price starting point should be about half of the new price, and that you should adjust the price from there according to the condition of the furniture. She also suggests that items that don't sell quickly should be marked down after a specific period of time.

STEP 4

Encourage word-of-mouth marketing and try to get as much publicity as you can for the store.

STEP 5

Sell the furniture, and write the owner a check for 50 percent of the sale price.

THE HIGHLIGHTS

- You can launch this business with very little startup capital.
- In your marketing efforts, focus on what makes you different.
- By sharing your information with the media, you'll get free publicity.
- A business plan does not have to follow a set of conventional rules to be successful.
- Things we sometimes view as weaknesses, such as dyslexia, can end up being a source of great strength.

THE RESOURCES

MORE INFORMATION ABOUT
TERRI BOWERSOCK

www.terrisinc.com
To learn about purchasing a license with Terri's Consign & Design, call Terri Bowersock at 408-969-1121, ext. 1900, or e-mail her at **terrib@eterris.com.**

DYSLEXIA

The International Dyslexia Association
www.interdys.org
A nonprofit organization dedicated to helping individuals with dyslexia and their families. Its goal is to provide comprehensive forums for parents, educators, and researchers to share their experiences and knowledge.

Dyslexia.com
www.dyslexia.com
A website dedicated to the positive aspects of dyslexia. It offers information and training methods, a networking forum, articles, and reports.

Levinson Medical Center for Learning Disabilities
www.levinsonmedical.com
A website maintained by Dr. Harold Levinson, who is dedicated to resolving misconceptions about dyslexia and related disorders.

BUSINESS PLANS

Yahoo! Small Business
http://smallbusiness.yahoo.com/
This website contains a wealth of information about creating business plans, including multiple links to articles about starting your own business. You can also find this page by visiting the "Getting Started" section of Yahoo! Small Business.

TELEVISION COMMERCIALS

Marcus Productions
www.marcusproductions.com
A film company located in Hollywood, Florida, that specializes in creating high-end commercials.

Millionaire Blueprints *neither endorses nor recommends any of the companies listed in the resource section. Resources are intended as a starting point for your research.*

Marion
BREM

Marion Brem's successful journey as a multi-million-dollar car saleswoman began with her "scrapbook," which raised $800,000.

BUSINESS NAME:
Love Chrysler, Inc.

TYPE OF BUSINESS:
Car Dealership

LOCATION:
Corpus Christi, TX

ADAPTED FROM:
Millionaire Blueprints magazine article,
"Ladies, Start Your Engines,"
March/April 2006

Y ou're a homemaker diagnosed with cancer, and your marriage ends. You have no medical insurance, no job, and you don't even have a résumé. What do you do? If you're Marion Brem, you put on a wig to hide the ravages of chemotherapy, and you go from one automobile dealer to another until you hear these words: "I've been thinking of hiring a broad." You might not have wanted to hear those exact words, but you are, nonetheless, thrilled with the opportunity. So, you let the race begin.

Facing the most impossible odds led Brem to a sales job she never envisioned for herself. Becoming the top car salesperson was a good first goal, but she wanted more. She wanted her own dealership. She noticed everything, not just what worked for her, but what was and wasn't working for other people in the business.

Brem knows how to build and sustain relationships with customers. She focused on what she knew. Using the same techniques that she used to sell cars, she convinced a business partner to invest $800,000. After all she'd been through, that was the easy part.

THE STARTING POINT

In a very short time, you lost your life as you knew it. So how did you begin again?

I realized that homemakers do a lot. I recognized that I was an expert in friendships, management, budgeting, prioritizing, and negotiation. So I put a résumé together that highlighted all those skills, and I went out and shopped for a job.

I got sixteen rejections. And on the seventeenth try, the sales manager said he thought I was nervy enough to succeed, and he hired me.

So once you got the job, what happened to put you on the path to having your own dealership?

I sold cars for the first two years and then, by selling and performing well, I was promoted into management. Soon after, I started expressing an interest to others in the business about having my own dealership.

THE BUSINESS PLAN

When you first started, what inspired you to continue pursuing your dream?

In my first job with a car dealership, I answered the phone. I overheard lots of salesmen trying to sell cars, and the one thing I consistently noticed was how they ignored the women and sold only to the men. I realized that, although it might have been the man making the deal, most of the time the woman was the one who influenced the decision. That is what I have done differently from day one.

So how do you reach this huge, overlooked market?

We basically capitalize on that in our sales pitches and especially in our advertising. Our advertising is relationship-oriented. Every message emphasizes "feeling" rather than "doing."

THE MOVE

Let's go back to when you started making the move from management to owning your own dealership.

Once I started getting my promotions and making a reputation for myself, I called a meeting with a Chrysler executive and we visited. I asked him what I needed to do to get my own dealership, and he said, "Sweetie-pie, we'd be talking about your needing a minimum, minimum, of $800,000— at the very minimum."

That must have been so discouraging, but obviously you didn't give up.

I went back to my drawing board. One evening, I was working with a customer, a financial planner, and I asked him how business owners became business owners. I gave him the overview of my dream, and he told me to seek the confidence of a venture capitalist.

THE FUNDING

Venture capitalists always want a business plan with financials, forecasts, and things like that. What did you put together?

I couldn't find much information about venture capitalists. So I decided to put together folders of information on myself. It was a way to organize my qualifications and present my ideas so I could raise funding.

I inserted letters from customers expressing gratitude and loyalty. I also had printed rankings from General Motors Circle, copies of all my sales awards certificates, and newspaper clippings from contests I had won. This was so they could see my determination and the consistency of my performance.

What did you do with these folders once you made them?

I wrote a cover letter that read, "As an executive in a Chrysler Corp. dealership, I am interested in this venture. I've got the résumé, if you've got the financial backing." Then I shipped them out to about fifteen CPAs I had chosen from the *Yellow Pages*. Soon after, I heard from one of these CPAs. He said he had a client who might be interested. He wanted to meet with me before he introduced me to his client.

Tell us about that meeting and how you prepared for it.

I met with the CPA, and then he set up a meeting between me and his client, who was a cardiologist. I realized I really had to show them how well I knew my business.

THE PARTNERSHIP

What was the CPA's main concern?

One of his biggest concerns was that I did not have any service experience, which is often referred to as "back-end" experience. My experience was strictly limited to finance and sales. But, I showed him some of my selling systems for registering details and plotting the patterns of my customers. This showed that I could easily take care of service after the sale.

How was the actual deal structured?

My original deal with my partner called for us to raise $800,000. He came up with $315,000. I borrowed $85,000 on my own. The new corporation secured a capital loan from Chrysler Credit Corp. for the balance. The $400,000 was repaid within five years. I should stress that we did not purchase an existing dealership. We purchased the rights to a franchise.

THE BUSINESS

What happened once you knew you had secured the money?

The first thing I needed was a location. I went to an abandoned motorcycle facility I had heard about. I signed a very short-term lease on it and got to work.

We cleaned the entire place ourselves. Then we went to computer companies and got a couple of bids on a very basic system, and I contacted other dealers and the Chrysler Financial Corp. about acquiring some cars to sell. Soon, I had accumulated a very small inventory.

I hired my son, who took a janitorial-type position. Then, I hired my office manager, and then three salespeople. I also hired a finance manager to work with the banks to acquire the loans for these cars. Lastly, I hired a service manager.

How did sales go?

We have broken our own sales records each year since we've been in business. And within two years, my partner was paid off completely.

THE MARKETING

Tell us more about relationship-oriented advertising and sales tactics.

The need for relationship building in transaction making is why women make good "salesmen." We make sure everything we do communicates that we make that effort to relate to our customers, and that's how we attract a high percentage of women as buyers.

THE EXPANSION

How did you know that it was time to get that second dealership?

On the exact fifth birthday of my first dealership, I knew of a dealer who wanted to retire. I asked him if I could take a close look at the facility first. So I went there and looked at this dilapidated facility. But I knew that it was in a growing community, and I liked the proximity to my dealership. So we took it.

Did you structure the financing on the second dealership in the same way as the first one?

I needed $1 million to secure the second dealership, Love Chrysler Dodge Jeep, LLC. This money was borrowed from Chrysler Credit Corp., leveraging both dealerships. It was a five-year capital loan and was paid off one year early.

We turned things around so fast in the same market because we approached it much more aggressively, increased its advertising, and added to its sales force.

THE ADVICE

What is the key to sales, in your opinion?

The key is relationships. Salesmanship is also a subject that I think should be part of the curriculum in every business school, because it's all about selling.

THE PLAN TO FOLLOW

STEP 1

Gain some type of experience in the field you want to enter.

STEP 2

Create a solid business plan that possible investors will believe in.

NOTE: Brem compiled information that would show her determination and dedication.

STEP 3

Get your startup funding intact.

NOTE: With the help of a CPA, Brem was able to find an angel investor.

STEP 4

Find a location and build up your inventory.

NOTE: Brem contacted the Chrysler Financial Corp. to obtain her cars.

STEP 5

Hire a dependable staff, and start selling!

THE HIGHLIGHTS

- Experience is important, but you can make up for it in other areas.
- Having a solid business plan is crucial.
- Lock in your startup funding. If you believe in yourself, others will too.
- Get your location, staff, and inventory together, and put your skills to the test.
- Recognize the need for relationship-building in transaction making, and make that effort to relate to your customers.

THE RESOURCES

U.S. Small Business Administration (SBA)
www.sba.gov
According to the SBA, "America's 9.1 million women-owned businesses employ 27.5 million people and contribute $3.6 trillion to the economy." Its website offers valuable information, specifically focused on the challenges faced by women entrepreneurs. It includes a women's business center and a women's network for entrepreneurial training.

All Business
www.allbusiness.com
This site contains information on forms and agreements, business blogs, expert advice, and business directories.

Business Know How
www.businessknowhow.com
Particularly rich in small and home business necessities, this easy-to-follow site is packed with solutions and suggestions. Articles include "The Seven Deadly Sins of Selling on eBay" and "12 Reasons to Market with Postcards."

Woman Owned
www.womanowned.com
This international site serves over 1.5 million women business owners. It offers networking assistance, information on setting up, running, and growing a business, and an online search engine of women-owned businesses.

StartUp Journal
www.startupjournal.com
The Wall Street Journal's center for entrepreneurs. It includes tips on franchising, financing, and e-commerce, as well as information from columnists and experts.

More Business
www.morebusiness.com
This site "by entrepreneurs, for entrepreneurs" lists over 4,000 sources for business venture capital. Whether you're already in business, starting a business, or buying a business, this site will help you find the money.

Tool Kit
www.toolkit.cch.com
This site helps you build your business financial profile and offers suggestions on how to find and obtain "smart money."

Met Life
www.metlife.com
The "Starting a Business" page includes "A Capital Idea" and a primer on finding investment

capital for businesses. A great overview of how small business is generated.

SmallBusinessLoans.com
www.smallbusinessloans.com
This site boasts "$57 billion in financing requests handled since 1997." It is a one-stop application process that does the searching for you. Most applications receive a reply within twenty-four hours.

Millionaire Blueprints neither endorses nor recommends any of the companies listed in the resource section. Resources are intended as a starting point for your research.

Andi
BROWN

This entrepreneur made millions in profit by focusing on the well-being of animals.

BUSINESS NAME:
Halo, Purely for Pets®

TYPE OF BUSINESS:
Pet Products

LOCATION:
Palm Harbor, FL

ADAPTED FROM:
Millionaire Blueprints magazine article,
"The Lucky Halo,"
August 2005

U p until 1991, Andi Brown was mothering a cat that suffered from kidney, urinary tract, and digestive problems. Advised to "put the cat down," Brown hooked up with a nutritionist who told her that the animal's diet was to blame. The nutritionist then prepared a stew made of chicken and vegetables. Within four days of eating it, the cat went through a complete metamorphosis.

With that, a light bulb went on above Brown's head. If she could improve her own pet's health, why couldn't she do the same for everyone else's pet?

Now, after about fifteen years of trials and tribulations, Brown's company has culminated into thirty different products being sold in 4,000 stores nationwide. Halo, Purely for Pets® has come a long way since its founder began tinkering around with healthy pet products in her home kitchen.

THE BEGINNING

What previous experience did you have in order to launch a pet product business?

Really it was just the personal contact that I had with so many pet owners who had a multitude of problems with their pets. I worked with them individually—cooking for them and gaining knowledge and experience along the way. Based on their demand and interest, I knew I'd found the perfect business to start.

How much capital did you start with, and what did you use it for?

I started with a $3,000 investment from my savings account and used it to seek out manufacturers who were willing to produce small amounts. Four months later, when Halo was making a profit, I began pumping my profit back into the company.

THE RESEARCH

What kind of research did you do before launching, and how did you document it?

We teamed up with holistic veterinarians who were on the cutting edge of the whole natural pet product wave. We worked to come up with our first product, Dream Coat. Two other products followed—an ear product and a natural flea repellent. I chose my first three products based on gaps I saw in the market at the time. I then coordinated with the nutritionists to come up with the basic formulas. We did a lot of documentation, but it mainly consisted of writing down what we found out. There was no formal process or format.

How did you find a pet nutritionist to work with?

I knew a nutritionist who was very knowledgeable about diet, nutrition, and natural health for humans. I'd say it's harder to find these types of people now since so many are "self-proclaimed" nutritionists. The best way to find a good nutritionist is to ask for referrals from sources you trust.

THE PRODUCT

How did you decide on these products, and who helped you with the formulas?

We worked with nutritionists and herbalists who study, collect, and pre-pare plants that are useful for health and healing. They helped us determine what would be the safest, gentlest, most effective ingredients, and how to combine them correctly so they would work.

How did you get your first batch of product made?

Manufacturers typically want to produce in 5,000- or 10,000-bottle increments, and no one wants to make 150 bottles of product. I promised vendors that if they would make these first few small quantities that we would come back and give them the business when the company grew.

How did you find the raw goods to make your products?

We must have gone out to about fifty different companies to source the ingredients. These companies all have different levels of quality. For example, you can buy watered-down ingredients, pure ingredients, or anything in between. We wanted Grade-A, pure ingredients in the smallest amounts that we could buy.

Who designed the packaging?

We tried using designers. I wanted the look to be a silhouette of a dog and a cat playing with a ball. Some of them designed Disney-like characters for me. Nobody had the right thing. I solved the problem by picking up a pencil and drawing it myself.

THE LEGAL

What regulatory hoops did you have to jump through to get your products on the shelves?

I registered the products with each state's Department of Agriculture, worked through the process of "proving" the facts stated on each label, and obtained the necessary licenses to begin selling those products. All fifty states have different requirements. It can cost thousands of dollars to register any one product in any one state on a yearly basis.

All pet foods have to be fully tested for nutrient content to meet minimal levels to be sold as "complete and balanced." Final documentation also needs to be submitted to the Department of Agriculture before a product is allowed on the market.

Did you also do a product analysis?

Yes, and it was conducted by a laboratory and proved that what's in the package is listed on the label. There are many independent laboratories around the country that will test your formulations or products. Each analysis costs about $2,500 for a complete breakdown.

THE MARKETING

Did you rely on any sort of business model, planning, or program?

I depended largely on "learn as you go." I didn't use any software programs, nor did I use any type of formal planning process.

What was your marketing plan?

At the time, it was sink or swim, so I got out and started marketing by word of mouth and referral. I capitalized on the fact that I was doing this for the good of the pets. I attracted a customer base, and the word spread quickly about our products.

How did you find your first customers?

We called major distributors across the country and told them that we were making natural pet care products for dogs and cats. They all laughed at us. That initial rejection actually created a unique business model of selling directly to retailers of natural foods and pet products.

We used an educational approach to finding those first customers. I talked to pet stores, veterinarians, pet groomers, and health-food stores about the products, and found the latter to be especially receptive to selling natural pet products.

How do you educate the users of your products, and how much capital do you devote to education?

We work continually to help pet owners realize the value of nutritional, natural foods made with no fillers or preservatives. Our educational tools include free product samples and a holistic pet care booklet. We don't devote any certain amount of money or time to education. It's just part of our daily routine.

THE PROFIT

How did you set your pricing?

Our fifteen-ounce can of cat food runs about three dollars. Our foods and treats are more expensive than others because they are made with free-range meats and fresh vegetables in our USDA-approved kitchens. We factor in those costs, as well as the cost of the container, labeling the product itself, shipping, our overhead, and how much the store needs to make a profit, and that's your retail price.

How do you go about adding new products to your lineup?

We went into grocery stores and health-food stores and talked to customers about their wants and needs in terms of pet care.

THE GOAL

How do you set realistic sales goals and meet them?

Right now, we're looking at an aggressive sales goal of $45 million by 2008. We plan to reach it by expanding our advertising and marketing efforts, and adding to our sales force. We looked at how much product the typical salesperson can sell in a twelve-month period, then multiplied that number by the total size of our sales force. That's what we call organic growth.

To reach our current goal, we're also going to start using a direct response television (DRTV) campaign, which will allow us to demonstrate and educate in a 2-minute or 28.5-minute format via television advertising.

THE PLAN TO FOLLOW

STEP 1

Locate experts such as nutritionists and herbalists when formulating a new product.

NOTE: Brown suggests that one way to find these experts is through referral or online resources such as (**www.findanutritionist.com**) or (**http://herbalists.meetup.com**).

STEP 2

Document your research.

NOTE: Government organizations such as the Department of Agriculture will need to test your product. Documentation of research is required before your product can enter the market and be sold.

STEP 3

Locate suppliers for your ingredients and a manufacturing company to produce your product.

NOTE: Brown says that you should look for top-quality ingredients when contacting suppliers. Suppliers' products can range from poor- to excellent-quality materials, so do your research carefully.

STEP 4

Register your product with your state's Department of Agriculture.

NOTE: Brown reminds us that each state has different requirements and fees. Keep this in mind when taking your product on a national level. Also, be sure to have your documentation on hand since your product must be thoroughly tested before being released on the market.

STEP 5

Develop a marketing plan.

NOTE: Identify your target audience and discover the means to show your product's appeal to that market. Brown was able to give samples of her product, and she used education to boost her customer base.

STEP 6

Set competitive pricing and create goals.

NOTE: Brown suggests considering each part involved in the development of your product when you set your price—everything from the price of ingredients, to shipping and labeling. She also suggests creating realistic goals and putting ideas into action to meet those goals.

THE HIGHLIGHTS

- People will do almost anything to improve their pets' lives. It is a ripe industry for new ideas.
- Startup money is not as important as finding companies and people who will believe in your product.
- Document your research. It will benefit your product in the long run.
- Educate customers about your product to boost awareness and future sales.
- Set realistic and aggressive goals for your product and company.

THE RESOURCES

MORE INFORMATION ABOUT ANDI BROWN

Halo, Purely for Pets
www.halopets.com
Andi Brown's company of all-natural pet products for dogs, cats, and birds. Her website also offers a forum.

Brown, Andi. *The Whole Pet Diet: Eight Weeks to Great Health for Dogs and Cats.*
San Francisco: Celestial Arts, 2006.
http://shop.halopets.com/product1.cfm?SID=1&Product_ID=224&Category_ID=48
Andi Brown's new book on feeding your pet foods for health.

ASSOCIATIONS AND INSTITUTES

American Pet Products Manufacturer's Association
www.appma.org
This is the leading trade association serving pet product manufacturers and importers.

American Veterinary Medical Association (AVMA)
www.avma.org
Founded in 1863, the AVMA is one of the oldest and largest veterinary medical organizations in the world.

Pet Food Institute
http://petfoodinstitute.org
As the voice of the pet food industry, this website compiles information on industry meetings, export training workshops, and numerous other services for its members.

National Dog Groomers Institute
www.nationaldoggroomers.com
For over thirty-four years, this association has worked with groomers throughout the world, promoting and encouraging professionalism and education in order to upgrade the image of the pet grooming profession.

GOVERNMENT ENTITIES

American Feed Industry Association
www.afia.org

Association of American Feed Control Officials
www.aafco.org

U.S. Food and Drug Administration
www.fda.gov

Food Safety and Inspection Service
www.fsis.usda.gov

U.S. Department of Agriculture
www.usda.gov

USFDA Center for Veterinary Medicine
www.fda.gov/cvm/default.html

ONLINE RESOURCES

Dr. Goodpet
www.goodpet.com/library/links.html
A natural pet pharmacy for dogs and cats.

Pet Product News International
www.petproductnews.com
E-newsletter for professionals and animal lovers.

Petfood Industry
www.petfoodindustry.com

NetWork Petsforum Group
petsforum.com/PetNews.html

Find A Nutritionist
www.findanutritionist.com
Website offers a practitioner index for nutritionists, a health calculator, health charts, and nutritionist headlines.

Meetup
http://herbalists.meetup.com
Find herbalists and herbalists "meetups" near you. Meet others who are interested in working with herbs for health.

LEARN MORE ABOUT PET FOOD PRODUCT ANALYSIS

The Association of American Feed Control Officials provides test requirements or protocols for manufacturers so they can meet state requirements of proof of safety and nutritional quality before a pet food is marketed.

There are also policies or procedures regarding other aspects of labeling, such as health claims, use of the term "natural," and more. For further information or clarification of these issues, or FDA pet food regulations, contact:

Center for Veterinary Medicine
Division of Animal Feeds (HFV-220)
Office of Surveillance and Compliance
7500 Standish Place
Rockville, MD 20855

BUSINESS RESOURCES

Market Research Reports
www.packagedfacts.com/pub/1006027.html
This report can be purchased from Packaged Facts.

Starting a Pet Product Business
http://starting-up-a business.com/businessproducts/
Starting_A_Pet_Product_Business.html
Offers a pet product business plan for $49.95.

ANIMAL NUTRITIONISTS

Darleen Rudnick
www.purelypets.com

Richard H. Pitcairn, DVM
www.drpitcairn.com

Celeste Yarnall, PhD
www.celestialpets.com

REPRESENTATIVES TO SELL YOUR PRODUCTS

RepSource
www.vmwinc.com/repsourcesalespetsupplyind.
htm
This online resource pairs up sales representatives, manufacturers' representatives, and general sales agents with manufacturers who need to get their products to market.

PET PRODUCT MANUFACTURERS

Abady
http://therobertabadydogfoodcoltd.com

Carnivore Connection
414-248-9256

Flint River Ranch
www.flintriver.com

Natural Life
www.naturallife.net

Nature's Recipe
www.naturesrecipe.com

PHD Products, Inc.
http://phdproducts.net

Precise
www.precisepet.com

Sensible Choice
www.sensiblechoice.com

Sojourner Farms
www.sojos.com

Wysong
www.wysong.net

Millionaire Blueprints *neither endorses nor recommends any of the companies listed in the resource section. Resources are intended as a starting point for your research.*

Doug
CANNING

How an entrepreneur's penchant for creating logo T-shirts for bands and 'boarders turned into a multi-million-dollar clothing empire.

BUSINESS NAME:
Dirtbag™ Clothing, Inc.

TYPE OF BUSINESS:
Clothing

LOCATION:
San Quentin, CA

ADAPTED FROM:
Millionaire Blueprints magazine article,
"Dirtbag Dreams,"
January/February 2006

Most people start a business because they are compelled to earn a profit or to make progress. Doug Canning simply thought that selling T-shirts to surfers and skateboarders would be a cool thing to do. In 1995, Canning saw his brother wearing a shirt with a simple logo containing the word "Dirtbag" on it that a friend had made. He knew it appealed to him and that it had potential beyond the run of fifty shirts the friend had made. But he didn't know he'd stumbled across a multimillion-dollar idea.

Canning and college friend and partner, John Alves, began Dirtbag™ Clothing from a modest apartment in San Francisco. They began production in 1996 with $5,000, a couple of T-shirts, and one simple logo. By selling to society's outsiders over the web, Canning has taken a clothing brand from the fringes to the forefront.

THE PRODUCT

How did you acquire the Dirtbag logo?

I called my brother's friend who had designed the shirt. He didn't have plans to develop it further, so I asked if it was cool with him if I did. Then I bought the rights from him by saying, "If we make money down the road, we'll give you a check," but there's nothing specific or contractual. Then I trademarked the word "Dirtbag."

Over the years, we've had many different logos, and now we're narrowing it down. As we grew, we added variations of our shirts, but it's expensive to carry so much inventory. Plus, the bigger brands stick with one logo for brand recognition.

Do you pay the designer on commission?

He gets a percentage of sales. So if a buyer orders ten pieces of a T-shirt he designed, he doesn't earn much. But if a buyer orders 1,000, he does pretty well. As soon as we get paid for an order, we send him a check.

THE PRODUCTION

How did you begin to produce the product?

Before Dirtbag, I was working for a mountain bike manufacturer, and part of my job was selling T-shirts for the company. I had developed a pretty good relationship with Accent Art (**www.accent-art.com**), the screen printer they used. Accent Art already had relationships with suppliers and the setup we needed. So they agreed to do everything for us. They ordered the T-shirts from the distributor, printed them, folded them, bagged them— everything.

THE SALES

Who did you sell to in the beginning?

We sold most of our product locally in skate and surf shops. We got a list of buyers when we had a booth at the ASR Trade Expo (**www.asrbiz.com**). The organizers gave each booth an Excel spreadsheet after the show with the names and contact information of all the buyers who attended. From the sheet, we took our local shops, and that's who we went to first.

How did you approach them?

We'd walk in with twenty shirts. The buyers are very loyal to the brands they already carry. At that point, all we had were two T-shirts and two hats, which wasn't enough for a buyer to make a financial commitment. But they liked the concept, so they'd let us leave some to sell on consignment.

Did they start placing orders after that?

Over time, they would order more and pay up front. We kept turning that money into new products and expanding into new stores. In the beginning, we paid about $800 for 144 T-shirts. We sold them wholesale for around $10 each and retail on our website for around $20 each.

Was inventory a problem for you?

As a small company, the toughest problem is maintaining inventory. If you sell $100,000 worth of product, you need to have $50,000 to get it into production. With MGR Entertainment, they already work with the same vendors we do, and they have sixty-day terms. A couple of months after we signed that deal, we had someone start approaching licensing companies on our behalf. We got a few offers, and soon after we picked the one we thought had the best deal for cost and payouts.

How do you process orders?

From an Oracle-based application called NetSuite (**www.netsuite.com**). It ties our inventory into UPS (**www.ups.com**). When someone places an order, they get an automatic e-mail confirmation and a UPS tracking number, so they can track their order online. We're also moving to a new fulfillment solution that will take us out of the shipping business completely so the fulfillment house will handle all of our orders.

THE EXPANSION

How did you expand into more products?

We started working with designers, mainly freelancers. Currently, we use about four independent designers.

How did you start expanding beyond local shops?

For a couple of years, we wrestled with figuring out what kind of brand we were. We finally realized we needed to figure out a way to reach the same market as the multimillion-dollar companies without spending any money on advertising.

THE MUSIC

What did you come up with?

I realized the one thing our target audience had in common was the kind of music they listened to. So I decided to market to them through the music. I found a website for bands (**www.byofl.org**). This website contains language that may be offensive to some readers. I went through and extracted every band's e-mail address on the entire website. Then, I sent out an e-mail to the entire list saying Dirtbag was sponsoring up-and-coming bands. We offered a 40-percent discount by giving them a discount code to enter into our online shopping cart when they placed an order. We also gave them a link and a picture on our website.

THE MARKETING

The bands just started signing up and buying things?

Exactly. That was basically all the marketing we needed to do to get started. It was a completely viral marketing scenario. After a year, we had numerous bands contact us wanting to be sponsored. The goal, of course, is to be seen by their audiences, who want to wear what the band is wearing.

How do you decide who to sponsor?

They have to send us a demo tape, a biography, or an electronic press kit, and we review that. If we like the music, we e-mail them and tell them they are onboard.

Are you doing any other marketing now?

I have a database of 100,000 e-mails. We send out monthly updates, promotions, gift certificates, and sometimes discount codes for our existing members. We also market to shop buyers online using Google AdWords (**www.adwords.google.com**). If you go to Google and type in "wholesale clothing" or "punk clothing," on the right-hand side of the screen, our ad will pop up. We pay roughly ten to twelve cents every time someone clicks on that link. When they do, they're directed to our site, where they find a dealer registration form. They fill that out and once they hit "submit," they automatically get an e-mail that has a link to our wholesale page.

How much does it cost to send out so many e-mails?

I can send out 50,000 e-mails a month, and it only costs me $49. We use a web-based service called Direct Aim (**www.directaimsoftware.com**). You just copy and paste the e-mail addresses from your files. I have different categories like wholesale customers, retail customers, contestant entries, editors from magazines, and more. I upload the set I want to send the e-mail to, create the e-mail, upload a picture, and put in links to my site. I hit "send," and it's done. It's one of the least expensive ways to send out mass e-mails that I've found.

What other low-cost marketing methods have you tried?

I approached a website called eBaum's World (**www.ebaumsworld.com**). It's a site full of games and humorous stuff. It attracts 20 million unique visitors a month. I sent them a shirt, a press release, and suggested we do a contest together every month. People just fill out a form online to enter, and all of those names go into our e-mail database. Our cost was only about $500 worth of product.

THE INFORMATION

How does the licensing deal work?

I use Signatures Network (**www.signaturesnetwork.com**). They are now our master licensing agent and have the exclusive rights to go out and find licensees for Dirtbag worldwide. They expect to get about forty licenses for any kind of product you find in a music or retail store.

How much control do you retain over what they attach your name to?

We have final approval on any deal they find, and we get a percentage of royalties.

THE ADVICE

Canning says that finding good mentors is key to creating your own success story. "Having people you can talk to and to mentor you is huge," he says.

THE PLAN TO FOLLOW

STEP 1

Develop a product. Play around with logos and designs until you figure out what you like best.

NOTE: Keep in mind who your target audience will be.

STEP 2

Have your logos, words, and designs trademarked.

STEP 3

Find a screen printer to produce your products.

NOTE: Canning used Accent Art (**www.accent-art.com**).

STEP 4

Take your product to trade shows specific to your product to gain exposure and contacts.

NOTE: Canning started at the ASR Trade Expo (**www.asrbiz.com**).

STEP 5

Develop your website, begin contacting potential customers and industry peers, and start taking orders.

THE HIGHLIGHTS

- Developing your product for a specific market is crucial to your success.
- Be prepared to spend a good amount of time perfecting your product.
- You can accomplish great marketing without a lot of money. Just be creative.
- Implement a mature and dependable business plan to secure funding. Use strong marketing strategies.
- If you don't ask, you'll never know your potential for success. Canning asked for a name and a design.

THE RESOURCES

MORE INFORMATION ABOUT DOUG CANNING

Dirtbag Clothing
www.dirtbagclothing.com
Check out Canning's website that is full of apparel for men and women. Sign up for the chance to win free items.

Dirtbag Music
www.dirtbagmusic.com
Canning's music community site.

WHERE TO GO

ASR Trade Shows
www.asrbiz.com
ASR gathers over 500 action sports brands and 7,000 retail buyers for surf, skate, snow, swim, moto, and youth culture.

Imprinted Sportswear Show
www.issshows.com
Dedicated to the decorated apparel industry, including sportswear, embroidery, screen printing, and promotional products.

Decorated Apparel Expo
www.daxshow.com
Embroidery and screen printing industry regional shows. Seminars, exhibiting suppliers, and great networking opportunities.

BAND MERCHANDISING AND LICENSING COMPANIES

IMC Licensing
www.imclicensing.com
Licensing agency specializing in consumer product brands. Seeks licensees for your brand.

MGR Entertainment
www.mgrentertainment.com
The place for rock-and-roll T-shirts.

Bandmerch
www.bandmerch.com
Features B2B marketing.

Cinder Block
www.cinderblock.com
A full-service merchandising and licensing company.

Signatures Network
www.signaturesnetwork.com
Well-known master licensing agency.

SERVICES

NetSuite
www.netsuite.com
E-commerce products and services for managing orders, purchasing, customer contracts, and financials.

Direct Aim
www.directaimsoftware.com
Web-based e-mail marketing tools.

Google AdWords
www.adwords.google.com
Pay-per-click advertising.

eBaum's World
www.ebaumsworld.com
Full of games and humor, this website attracts 20 million visitors a month and can be utilized as a creative marketing tool.

FULFILLMENT CENTERS

Specialty Fulfillment Center
www.pickandship.com
Specializes in helping small- and medium-sized companies develop and execute web-based order fulfillment strategies.

Webgistix
www.ifulfill.com
Warehousing, packaging, and shipping of products, literature, and related items to your customers, distributors, retailers, or salespeople.

Innotrac
www.innotrac.com
Order processing and fulfillment, warehousing, and inventory control from multiple distribution facilities nationwide.

PRINTERS

Accent Art
www.accent-art.com
Screen printing and embroidery for sportswear and accessories. Dirtbag started out with this screen printer.

Douglass Screen Printers
www.dsp-cando.com
Full-service screen printer for decals, posters, banners, signs, tags, wraps, and facia.

Printing Industry Exchange LLC
www.printindustry.com
Get quotes from multiple printers.

SUPPLIES

Beneficial T's by Patagonia
www.beneficialts.com
Organically grown cotton blank T-shirts, tote bags, and caps made by Patagonia.

Blank Shirts
www.blankshirts.com
Wholesale apparel ready for imprinting, including T-shirts, polos, sweats, headwear, outerwear, and woven shirts.

T-Shirt Links
www.T-shirtlinks.com
Links to sites selling blank wholesale T-shirts, apparel, and screen printing supplies.

Blick Art Materials
www.dickblick.com
Discount art supplies, screen printing tools, chemicals, inks, and machines for individuals or small shops.

Ryan Screen Supply
www.ryanrss.com
Full range of screen printing equipment and supplies.

Millionaire Blueprints *neither endorses nor recommends any of the companies listed in the resource section. Resources are intended as a starting point for your research.*

Amanda
KENNEDY

How a former model, actress, and therapist tapped all three careers to find success in the competitive and lucrative lingerie market.

BUSINESS NAME:
Sassybax Bras

TYPE OF BUSINESS:
Women's Lingerie Products

LOCATION:
Los Angeles, CA

ADAPTED FROM:
Millionaire Blueprints magazine article,
"Self-Esteem Marketing Brings Surprising Rewards,"
October 2005

A manda Kennedy was getting dressed for a dinner date with her husband when she caught a glimpse of her back in the mirror. She didn't like what she saw. "Usually from the front, I looked fine. But from the back, I looked ten years older. This sweater was especially frustrating because it was cashmere and was very unforgiving, especially with a bra that was creating a bulge on my back. I tried every bra I had, and they all caused the same problem."

Her inventive, spur-of-the-moment solution was the idea for a product that women are now raving over. It's the smooth silhouette that Kennedy's Sassybax bras create under today's close-fitting fashions and fabrics. After navigating the challenges of entering this tough market, Kennedy is reaping the rewards of her innovative thinking with $2.4 million in wholesale sales and growing.

THE BEGINNING

When did you devise the fashion solution that later evolved into Sassybax?

The lightbulb flashed on Valentine's Day 2003. I was trying to put myself together for dinner, and I wanted to wear a blue cashmere sweater. I hated the bra strap bulge on my back. In a moment of frustration, I turned a pair of control-top pantyhose upside down, cut off the legs, cut out the gusset, and slipped it on instead of my bra! When I put the sweater back on, my back was completely smooth. I began to laugh, but it started me thinking.

So what did you do first?

I started researching how I could make something that was an alternative to a bra. I got on the Internet and did a search of hosiery manufacturers. I found The Hosiery Association with dozens of phone numbers. I called every one of them, described my idea, and asked if they had any interest or information that would help me develop it as a product. One woman knew of a machine that would knit around the torso without a single seam. This was the Santoni machine from Italy.

Once you found the right technology, what did you do next?

I investigated factories that had these machines in this country and found a very small number. I wanted to do my manufacturing domestically, because it's so much simpler to get to the factory quickly. The less complicated I could make it, the better.

THE PROTOTPYE

What was the first step in making your idea a reality?

Armed with just my drawings, ambition, and enthusiasm, I went to several interested domestic factories and talked to them after they agreed to sign a nondisclosure document.

What was their response?

They were skeptical and asked for some kind of assurance that they would not invest money in developing my idea and lose money if I couldn't sell it. There was one lone guy who was impressed with my idea.

So what did you do to capitalize on this interest?

I produced a prototype for the product. Then we spent nine months perfecting it. We had an understanding that they would get the order once I had a finished product.

Did you get any other opinions on these prototypes?

I gave them to friends to wear and critique, and I put together an informal focus group for about twenty strangers. These women came and tried on the samples, and they ended up sitting around in them all evening—not taking them off. They didn't know I was the designer. I heard comments like, "It's so comfortable. When can I buy this bra?" That was all I needed to hear. I knew I had a winner.

What did you do with the feedback?

I didn't go through the whole corporate thing with a hundred people and a research firm. I didn't have that kind of money to spend. Everything had to be done on a shoestring budget. Besides, this group told me what I wanted to know.

THE MONEY

What do you mean a shoestring budget?

I did everything I could by myself, or through friends, to keep my costs down. For example, I spoke to several logo companies and they wanted around $20,000. That, to me, was insane.

A friend of mine said she knew someone straight out of art school. This extremely talented art student was happy to have the work—and the experience for her portfolio. So I got a great logo for $1,500, and I still love it.

And how did you come up with your name?

Just like there are logo companies, there are naming companies. But they are expensive too. I decided to do it myself. The independent woman in me liked the image I think of when I hear the word "sassy." And, because of what this bra actually does, its name needed to have something to do with the back. So Sassybax seemed like a catchy solution.

THE MARKETING

What were some of the other pieces of your marketing strategy?

I searched for a web designer by asking people I knew who had websites. I spent $1,500, but I found a designer who was willing to work hourly. I did the graphic design myself.

With your special understanding of marketing to women, what was your strategy?

I was marketing Sassybax as a comfortable and functional garment that accommodates you. You don't have to accommodate it. That slogan plays back into the woman's psyche. Women are tired of squeezing themselves into garments like corsets and bad bras.

I marketed from a gut level, and from the truth about what my product does. I have learned that women are much more alike than we are different. Body issues are so deeply ingrained in all of us.

How did you create packaging that would complement this marketing?
Since this is a bra, it had to be seen, touched, and tried on. So I put it on a hanger with a great hang-tag that shows what the product does for you.

THE LEGAL

Did you get a patent?
No. I didn't apply for one because, in my business, proving anything in patent law can take up to fifteen years and thousands of dollars.

But doesn't it protect your product from being copied?
No. Fashion is a knockoff business, and everyone in our industry knows that. Enforcing a patent is an endless stream of legal bills and an exhaustive ordeal.

THE PRODUCT

So you've got your product, your website is up, and your marketing strategy is in place. Then what?
Next, I needed to find someone to represent and sell Sassybax. I went to the LA Mart (**www.californiamarketcenter.com**) and shopped my product around to different lingerie representatives. I walked in the showrooms and asked for a minute of their time. Then I showed them my

samples. Everyone I talked to said, "I don't want to take on anything new right now."

Then what did you do?

Someone told me about a book called *Purple Cow*. This is a book about marketing a product that is unlike anything else on the market. It provided just the encouragement I really needed.

What did you do next with your purple cow?

I decided to go to the Las Vegas Magic Show. This is one of the biggest clothing shows in the ready-to-wear industry. After a few rejections, I finally found one woman who invited me to the upcoming October market to rent a space in her showroom.

How did that go?

More than twelve hundred people saw my product. By the end of market, I had ten customers and $3,000 worth of sales. Best of all, I had a list of stores that were now familiar with Sassybax.

What opportunities grew from that market exposure?

I approached a representative who sold lingerie exclusively. She loved the product, and I knew she could sell it to her stores. In February, she and I went to the Neiman Marcus buyer. They bought it, and we walked out with a test order for ten stores. If it sold well, they would start adding stores in a couple of months. They tested it, and it sold so well that they put it in all of their stores within a month.

THE ADVICE

What is your best advice to someone out there who has a great idea for a new solution?

The main thing is you just can't get discouraged. You have to believe in yourself, believe in your product, and, for me, believe in the power of prayer. I didn't do this business just for fun—I really needed it to work.

THE PLAN TO FOLLOW

STEP 1

Develop a prototype for your invention.

NOTE: Kennedy researched companies that manufactured products like her invention, and she approached them to provide support in creating a prototype.

STEP 2

Decide on your target market and construct a plan to reach that market with your product.

NOTE: Kennedy was able to connect her product with her target market by providing a solution to a real need.

STEP 3

Conduct focus groups to test your product and to give feedback.

NOTE: Your focus group should consist of people within your target audience who examine and give their opinion of your product.

STEP 4

Display your product at trade shows in order to boost awareness.

NOTE: Kennedy suggests finding a company to represent your product in their showroom at trade shows. If you are on a shoestring budget, partnering up with another company can save you time and money.

THE HIGHLIGHTS

- Some of the best inventions are the ones that solve a need.
- Find companies and people to work with who believe in your product.
- Develop a marketing plan that will reach the heart of your target audience.
- When on a tight budget, use friends and family networks to get the job done.
- Failure should not be an option. Try, and try again.

THE RESOURCES

Sassybax Bras
http://sassybax.com
Amanda Kennedy's business is selling self-esteem to women in the form of lingerie.

TRADE SHOWS

In addition to the Las Vegas Magic Show (**www.magiconline.com**), and the LA Mart (**www.californiamarketcenter.com**), *Millionaire Blueprints* researchers found additional fashion trade shows around the world at **www.biztrade**

shows.com/apparel-fashion. For more information about any of these shows, go to this site and click on the link to each individual show.

Hong Kong Fashion Week
Hong Kong Convention & Exhibition Centre

Munich Fashion Fair Men
Dahmit Park Forum

India International Garment Fair
Pragati Maidan

Body Look
New Exhibition Centre

Global Fashion Dusseldorf
Dusseldorf Fairgrounds

CPD Dusseldorf
Dusseldorf Fairgrounds

Dallas Fabric Show
Dallas Market Center
SA Fashion Week
Sandton Convention Centre

ASSOCIATIONS

The Hosiery Association (THA)
www.hosieryassociation.com
This is the most detailed and complete directory on U.S. hosiery manufacturers. THA supplier members and international knitter members are also included.

American Apparel and Footwear Association (AAFA)
www.apparelandfootwear.org
AAFA is the national trade association representing apparel, footwear, and other sewn products' companies and their suppliers. AAFA's mission is to promote and enhance its members' competitiveness, productivity, and profitability in the global market.

INDUSTRY RESEARCH

First Research
www.firstresearch.com
Providing more than 150 industry profiles, First Research delivers clear, consistent, and timely knowledge to its customers, allowing them to demonstrate their insight and understanding. Industry profiles can be purchased online or on a subscription basis.
Industry profiles are updated quarterly and include:

- An industry overview
- Financial benchmark data
- Industry opportunities
- Business trends
- Credit and risk issues
- An industry forecast

Easy-to-use, quarterly industry profiles provide you with the industry analysis you need to better understand any particular business. Industry analysis gives you invaluable information about your target market and highlights critical industry statistics and issues, changes that have taken place since the last quarterly update, and key concerns that can have negative or positive impacts on investments. Utilizing the financial and forecasting data, while simultaneously learning from educational business overviews, can help you and your customers plan more effectively and invest wisely.

INDUSTRY FORECASTS

Economy.com, Inc.
www.economy.com/research/default.asp
Economy.com, Inc., is a leading independent provider of economic, financial, country, and industry research designed to meet the diverse planning and information needs of businesses, governments, and professional investors worldwide. The research has many dimensions: country analysis, financial markets, industrial markets, and regional markets.

Reports by topic:
- Business costs
- Country analysis
- European city analysis
- Industry analysis
- Living costs
- North American Industry Classification System (NAICS) employment
- Real estate
- U.S. metro areas
- U.S. states

Each concise, four-page report costs $225. Sample reports are available, and they can be purchased online. Each single report includes:
- Extensive written analysis on current and anticipated trends
- Up-side and down-side risk factors
- Four charts with commentary
- Five-year forecast details for approximately forty to fifty financial variables
- U.S. Macro forecast summary and outlook
- Forecast assumptions
- General industry outlook
- Industry indicators for comparisons across industries
- A user's guide

PROTOTYPES

Lectra
www.lectra.com

Lectra is the world's number-one designer, manufacturer, and supplier of software and equipment to large-scale industrial users of textiles, leather, and other soft materials.
Its products and services span a broad array of major global markets such as fashion, apparel and retailing; footwear; luggage and leather goods; furniture and furnishings; the automotive, aerospace, and marine industries; and industries that handle industrial fabrics and composite materials. Lectra's unrivaled, full-line technology comprises software, CAD/CAM equipment, and a secure Internet communications platform, providing solutions to its customers' major strategic challenges and responding to the specific needs of each of its markets.

SPECIAL-PURPOSE TEXTILE MACHINERY

The Santoni Machine
www.santoni.com
A profile of Santoni products and services, including customer support, news, information on expositions, and textile industry e-commerce.

Pinnacle Converting Equipment
www.pinnacleconverting.com
Pinnacle is a manufacturer of converting equipment for a wide variety of industries. It is a designer and builder of custom equipment solutions for general manufacturing productivity, as well as a consulting service provider and implementer of manufacturing equipment and process solutions for a wide range of challenges. It is also a custom converting service provider, offering a standard line of slitters, rewinders, sheeters, and core cutters.

La Meccanica S.P.A.
www.la-meccanica.it
Textile machinery, products, news, and promotions.

USED TEXTILE MACHINES

Used Textile Equipment
www.usedtextileequipment.com
A worldwide supplier of all types of textile equipment.

Inteletex
www.inteletex.com
Online textile equipment market. More than 3,500 items listed.

BOOK

Godin, Seth. *Purple Cow: Transform Your Business by Being Remarkable.* New York: Penguin USA [2003]
This book, which is about marketing a product unlike anything else on the market, provided just the encouragement that Amanda Kennedy needed to launch her own business. Maybe it will for you as well.

Millionaire Blueprints neither endorses nor recommends any of the companies listed in the resource section. Resources are intended as a starting point for your research.

Kathy
PHILLIPS

One wooden candleholder equals $1.4 million for this entrepreneur.

BUSINESS NAME:
Primitives By Kathy, Inc.

TYPE OF BUSINESS:
Gift Industry and Home Accessories

LOCATION:
United States, Canada, Australia, and United Kingdom

ADAPTED FROM:
Millionaire Blueprints magazine article,
"One Wooden Candleholder Equals $1.4 Million,"
March/April 2006

Kathy Phillips was bored with her career. She'd put in ten years work-ing in her mother's gift shop in Lancaster, Pennsylvania, learning the business, chatting with customers, observing buying habits, and con-sidering pricing strategies. In late 1996, Phillips decided to start her own busi-ness. With a single product—a wooden candleholder—she took her shoestring concept to market.

"I was sold out after the first day," she says. And she had more orders than she thought she could produce. "I went back the second day of the four-day show and put up 'sold out' signs on my tiny half of the booth. My exhibitor neighbors came running, telling me to take those signs down," she laughs. They said, "Take orders, and worry about how you're going to fill them later."

So that's what she did. In four days, with a single product, Phillips had credit card imprints for $85,000. That first full year, Primitives By Kathy, Inc., grossed $1.4 million with the wooden candleholder. Today, Phillips, who is only thirty-six years old, projects $13 million in earnings with a catalog of 2,800 products.

"Our Primitives are in all the big catalogs where you find home accessories and gifts, especially rustic, homey, handmade-looking items," Phillips says. "It's a fast-paced business in that your products only have a unique appeal for about six months. After that, you'd better have something new because at the next trade show, you'll see knockoffs of everything you made in other people's booths."

Phillips sat down with Millionaire Blueprints to explain how her homespun business evolved to the point where it's getting attention from major players in the gift industry. To hear Phillips tell it, the success of Primitives By Kathy, Inc., in the fickle gift and home accessories market was simply a matter of good sense and good luck.

THE BEGINNING

What gave you subtle encouragement to eventually try your hand at starting a business?

I will say, with modesty, that I believe I have some innate talents—for observation, seeing what sells, and being intuitive about why it might be selling. Plus, I learned so much about gifts and home accessories in my mom's gift shop—pricing, quality, and trends. Once I started Primitives By Kathy, I walked through trade shows looking at every single piece of merchandise and taking notes on color trends or finishing trends. I go to flea markets and estate sales and buy antiques that are special, and that are easy to reproduce for our line. I read magazines, looking for trends in home furnishings. When building my staff, I selected only people who felt the same way about ingenuity and quality that I did.

THE TRADE SHOW

Tell us about that first trade show with the single product.

Well, the candleholder was small, with four wooden sides, and an open top where the candle fit in. We made one in a dark country blue, one in barn red, one in a golden mustard yellow, and one in hunter green. Each had a different cutout design—a star or a heart. I had already taken them to local craft shows—some at the high school—and they did very well. I knew from all my research that I wanted to begin at the professional Market Square Show in Valley Forge. I rented half a booth that measured about five-foot by nine-foot and set up my candleholders. The investment was $750 for the booth space, and the products were already made. My catalog for that show was a plain piece of paper with spray adhesive holding four photos. Those were all gone the first day, so I had to run out and make some more copies. That's when I felt overwhelmed and had the bright idea to put up a "sold out" sign. Everyone around me ran up to say, "You can't do that. Just take orders and figure it out later." That was scary. So was the $85,000 worth of orders secured with credit cards over a four-day show. When I got home, I was really happy. But panic soon set in.

THE PRODUCTION

You had to figure out how to produce the products for the orders, right? What did you do?

First, I had to go talk to the bank about a start-up loan. I took them my credit card orders and borrowed against the $85,000 in orders for materials, labor, shipping costs, and more. Then I went to the local Goodwill to try to assemble an "instant workforce" to produce candleholders and fulfill the orders. The developmentally disabled people who reported to the Goodwill workshop every day were able to accomplish the assembly of each piece of my products. My candleholders were perfect for them too—simple to explain and containing straightforward, progressive steps to produce. Goodwill offered me a fixed price on each piece. All those first orders were made in the Goodwill Industries (**www.goodwill.org**) workshop. Eventually, I leased a no-frills warehouse space for a year that ran about $750 a month. Goodwill sent fifty workers, some trainers, and supervisors. The trainers and I provided incentives, like certificates or small gifts, for people to learn all parts of the assembly. We were able to fill those first orders on time and on budget—and we were able to say our candleholders were "All American Made."

THE CRAFT

Now that your catalogs to wholesalers include 2,800 products, it would be hard to list them all. Still, can you give us an idea of what's hot now?

Our hottest products now are tin signs, gently antiqued or not, with large words on them such as "Dream" and "Imagine." We sell quite a few birdhouses that one artist designed with crackled paint that makes them appear to be made from old barn boards. Oh, and another very hot item is any sort of stitchery, such as the old-fashioned alphabet samplers. We have these made by hand in China now. Our "All American-Made" days didn't last as long as I'd hoped.

Tell us about that.

When we were American made, it was hard to find things to make that were affordable. All the designs and prototypes by our artists were wonderful, but they would push the unit cost way over the retailers' preferred price point. I was acutely aware that we needed newer, more innovative things, and that quality was as important as ever.

THE INTERNATIONAL MARKET

Did you know the ins and outs of buying in international markets?

No, not really. There, in fact, was my biggest learning curve in building my business. I got burned at first, using a factory that required prepayment and then shipped poor quality goods. To get started in Asia, most people attend a very large trade show in Beijing called the Canton Fair.

So you're not simply buying overseas, you're manufacturing there? What is that process like, and how long does it take?

We'll get prototypes from our artists around the country in all different media. We give the artists a deadline based on the time it will take in China. Then we photograph the prototypes for our reference, or the catalog, and airfreight them to China. In three or four weeks, we receive several samples back that we carefully check. We get on the phone and get a price, or start to negotiate a price or a discount. We plan on sixty days of production time, and then thirty days travel time for delivery. That's ninety days total after we make the deal.

THE MARKETING

How many of your products are seasonal? How far ahead do your customers place orders?

That's the secret—keeping way ahead with new things—since so much of what we sell gets knocked off regularly. I'd say we change about 30 percent of our products every time we produce a catalog. Our main catalog contains everything so our customers can see seasonal merchandise and evergreen items at the same time. Our large department store customers order way ahead of schedule. In fact, we often have the China factory ship directly to the distribution centers for Nordstrom, TJ Maxx, and other big clients. That saves time and money. Our smaller, mom-and-pop stores work closer on seasonal merchandise. We usually see most of our customers at the trade shows and begin the ordering process there.

What are some of your marketing tactics?

We market only to wholesalers, at trade shows, and through mailing our catalogs. We have in-house advertising and marketing.

THE PLAN TO FOLLOW

STEP 1

Attend local, regional, and national trade shows, crafts fairs, and flea markets.

NOTE: When designing your prototypes, try to stay at least six months ahead of home accent and gift industry trends to reduce knockoffs from your competition.

STEP 2

To get started in Asia, attend the Canton Fair. When choosing a manufacturer, try to find one that will act as a broker. If they can't make something themselves, they'll scout other factories and make arrangements to have your designs made. Try to develop a mutually beneficial relationship so their personnel will function as customer representatives for you. Once you become one of their big clients, urge them to make sure the sample products look as good as the prototype, to evaluate potential materials, to find other factories and high-quality resources (if necessary), and, in general, to coordinate everything from start to shipping.

NOTE: After choosing a manufacturing company, Phillips stresses the importance of planning ahead. Understanding that the lead time for manufacturing to take place in China is paramount to your success.

STEP 3

Do research, attend events, and develop long-term marketing tactics based on repetitive customers. Build your own mailing list from people who have asked to be put on it, and send out a catalog. Develop a marketing campaign for customers you haven't heard from for a while—usually six months. Find out how you can help these customers by e-mailing, sending postcard mailers, and phoning them.

NOTE: In order to produce original ideas and stay ahead of trends, Phillips walks the trade show floors. She and her staff attend events annually, and they pass along what they've seen to her artists.

THE HIGHLIGHTS

- Embrace your innate creative talents, and sell your products at flea markets, trade shows, and local craft exhibits.
- Utilize your local Goodwill for an "instant workforce," and help others gain skills.
- Stay six months ahead of a trend on new products and designs.
- Build on what you know, and learn what you don't know. Recognize that you'll have a learning curve.
- Find a trustworthy company to manufacture your products, and develop a long-term professional relationship.
- If using a factory in China for manufacturing, make sure they have their own quality-control procedures.
- Develop long-term marketing strategies for repetitive customers and wholesalers.

THE RESOURCES

MORE INFORMATION ABOUT KATHY PHILLIPS

Primitives By Kathy, Inc.
www.primitivesbykathy.com
Kathy Phillips turned her gift shop experience into a multimillion-dollar grossing retail business in just a few years.

WHERE TO GO

Market Square Traditional Wholesale Shows, Inc.
www.marketsquareshows.com
These shows are run by Market Square, Inc. These arts, crafts, jewelry, and specialty foods exhibits are held across the country throughout the year.

The Canton Fair
www.chinacantonfair.com
Now in its 99th year, this commodities export show is a great place to connect with manufacturers who can cheaply produce goods for the American market. A recent fair resulted in contracts worth $27.2 billion.

Openair-Market Net
www.openair.org
Two college professors started this World Wide Guide to Farmers' Markets, Flea Markets, Street Markets, and Street Vendors, which includes links to numerous markets and organizations.

Festival Network Online
www.festivalnet.com
An online state-by-state listing of craft shows and art festivals.

About.com
http://artsandcrafts.about.com/od/promotershow listings/
The informational website provides an extensive online directory of craft shows held in the United States.

WHO TO KNOW

The National Craft Association
www.craftassoc.com
This information and resource center for the professional arts and crafts industry offers a newsletter, show listings, and wholesale and marketing sources.

The National Flea Market Association
www.fleamarkets.org
Made up of flea market owners and managers, the association promotes initiatives such as anti-counterfeiting protection with the help of its national lobbyist, and holds an annual convention. The website includes state-by-state links to markets.

Goodwill Industries International, Inc.
www.goodwill.org
800-741-0186
Goodwill, an established nonprofit, believes in work. It aids disabled or disadvantaged people with education and career services. It provides businesses with contract employees for packaging, mailing, assembly, and other work.

The American Chamber of Commerce—China
www.amcham-china.org.cn
8610-8519-1920
"AmCham China" represents companies and individuals doing business in China, and it can be a great resource for every aspect of working with this Asian superpower.

Home Furnishings International Association (HFIA)
www.hfia.com
800-942-4663
An industry group for furnishing professionals, HFIA offers links to suppliers, a store/designer locator, and articles about trends.

THINGS TO GET

A-AAccess OnLine Payment Systems
www.aaaccess.com
This merchant services firm provides credit card and Internet payment processing, and it sells processing equipment. The website has a glossary of credit card processing terms.

Leaders
www.rockbottommerchantaccounts.com
This registered Independent Sales Organization of JPMorgan Chase Bank is another merchant services company offering payment processing and equipment.

VeriSign
www.verisign.com
This Internet and telecommunications company also provides online and point-of-sale payment processing services for credit and debit cards.

Nolo
www.nolo.com
This Berkeley, California, company provides do-it-yourself legal solutions for consumers and small businesses. The website has a bounty of useful legal information including explanations of artwork licensing contracts.

PrintUSA
www.printusa.com
An online directory that provides quotes from a large number of professional printers for business catalogs or other printing jobs.

Red Clay Media
www.redclaymedia.com
Looking to build a marketing mailing list or conduct a direct mail advertising campaign? This marketing data provider might be able to help.

Vertexera
www.vertexera.com
This company sells e-mail and postal mailing lists targeting specific consumers or professionals by industry, geographical area, job functions, or other categories.

HyperPublish
www.hyperpublish.com
This software enables users to create a print catalog or CD to promote their businesses.

Find Legal Forms
www.findlegalforms.com
Offers hundreds of contracts available to download for a small fee, including copyright and sale of goods contracts that could be used by crafts artists and distributors.

The Estate Sales Company
www.estatesalesco.com
This company conducts liquidation estate sales, where aspiring crafts and antique salespeople might pick up some interesting items.

eBay
www.ebay.com
The popular online marketplace that directly connects 100 million global buyers and sellers is an endless flea market on your computer.

U.S. Commercial Service China
www.buyusa.gov/china/en
This government organization promotes American and Chinese trade with tips on marketing and industry data for the Chinese market.

OTHER HELPFUL SOURCES

China Commodity Net
http://ccn.mofcom.gov.cn
Funded by the Chinese government, this is the online arm of the *China Business Guide* in its efforts to promote trade. It is a good source of information and contacts. (Click on "English.")

Millionaire Blueprints neither endorses nor recommends any of the companies listed in the resource section. Resources are intended as a starting point for your research.

Keith Daniels
SCHWARTZ

A set of ugly polyester ties launches a million-dollar business.

BUSINESS NAMES:
Keith Daniels Designs, Divinity Boutique, and
On Target Promotions

TYPE OF BUSINESS:
Men's Accessories and Promotional Products

LOCATION:
Warrensville Heights, OH

ADAPTED FROM:
Millionaire Blueprints magazine article,
"All Tied Up,"
May/June 2007

Many people would never dream of finding high-quality apparel for just dollars in their local grocery stores. But it is this very paradigm that helped Keith Daniels Schwartz build a multimillion-dollar business.

At only forty-two, he's running a company with international offices and products in supermarkets and drugstores across the country. He currently sells belts, ties, wallets, and socks. Every year, he adds new products. Purchase one of his belts, and you'll find a tag that reads, "Department store quality, without department store prices."

Schwartz has also expanded that quality to Divinity Boutique. His brand of Christian-themed ties, belts, and socks have become number one in Christian retail stores in their respective categories.

Moving from a daring purchase of ugly polyester neckties in 1990, to more than 4 million customers today, Schwartz has definitely made a name for himself as a savvy entrepreneur. Through his On Target Promotions, he sells his Keith Daniels Designs and Divinity Boutique lines of accessories. The Keith Daniels product line can be found in more than 6,000 stores in the United States. Divinity can be found in more than 1,000 stores worldwide, with locations in the United Kingdom, Australia, New Zealand, Africa, Canada, the Netherlands, and many other countries around the world. And the company is constantly expanding.

But Schwartz said his business idea is nothing new. It's simply a new take on tried-and-true products.

"I haven't really recreated the mousetrap. I've just taken things, marketed them at the right prices, and created niches," he says.

THE BEGINNING

Around 1988, you were a top salesman. Why did you consider something different?

I was bored. I wanted something else to do, and I needed to make more money. It became clear to me that I was not going to move any farther up the ladder in my current situation.

What was your first step in looking for something new?

I asked the buyer at a small Drug Emporium division in Cincinnati, Ohio, what I could get for her. Drug Emporium, which is no longer in existence, had at that time small franchises all over the country. This particular franchise had thirteen stores. She said, "I need a men's gift item for Christmas." So I found out that she wanted men's ties. She wanted them to retail for five dollars.

Was this the first time you sold an item on your own?

This was how the company actually got started. I started by buying sales rep samples and reselling them to small food and drug stores. I founded the company with $700 and sales rep samples that I purchased and resold at a profit.

THE SEARCH

How did you find the men's ties?

I found a flea market magazine with an ad that read: "Ties for Sale." It was sort of like a classified ad. I think they still have them at a lot of flea markets. So I picked up the phone and called them. Then I flew to Florida to meet with them and see what I was getting. They were the ugliest polyester ties you've ever seen and, truth be told, they sold like hotcakes. But it wasn't about what they looked like. It was about having a five-dollar tie. And a five-dollar tie was unheard of. It still is today.

THE NEXT STEP

After you sold the ties for Christmas, what did you do next? Did you go back to the same Drug Emporium buyer?

After Christmas, when the ties were all gone, I tried to convince the buyer to carry them year-round, instead of just as a promotion for Christmas, and she agreed. Then we needed to build an inventory. We also started to expand into other retailers and other franchises within the Drug Emporium channel.

How long did you stay with ties before you added additional products?

I stayed with ties for four or five years. We were growing very, very, very slowly. I kept my full-time job for more than a year while expanding into some small stores here and there. And I did everything. I packed the boxes. I shipped them. I did the accounting. You've got to remember that, in the beginning, it didn't really start as a business. I started it to make extra money and provide some additional challenge. It grew into a business.

THE CHALLENGE

Did you think of throwing in the towel after losing your top customers and 60 percent of your sales in the same week?

There have been points in time when I've thought that maybe I should just give up. Then somebody would sit me down and say, "You know what? Business goes in cycles. Sometimes those cycles are up; sometimes those cycles are down. You have to wait it out, work through the bad times, and live to enjoy the good times." So when this happened, my thinking was, "It's time to get back out and sell."

And I was able to replace those two customers within twelve months. My sales did not decrease the next year, even though I had to replace those two customers. We actually saw a sales increase in the next year of 20 percent. Because we grew sales slowly, and based on existing cash flow, we had lots of customers to approach and a great success story to tell buyers. They like to buy programs that are proven winners in other retailers.

How long did you continue purchasing ties from the company in Florida?

We continued for about a year, and then we started to spread our wings. We looked for tie manufacturers that could sell us cheaper and better, and we started to buy department store closeouts. In other words, at the end of the season, when they had to develop a new product line, we would buy the season-end closeouts.

I'm sure there are a lot of people who want to buy closeout items. Do you bid on them?

No. It's a first-come, highest price paid. Let's say the wholesale cost was twenty dollars. Coming to the end of the season, they'll sell at ten dollars. Six months later, if they still have some left, they'll sell them at five dollars. A year later, they'll sell them at three dollars. Eighteen months later, they'll come into a price point that I can look at.

Have you always been able to obtain enough ties through closeouts?

No. At one point, around 1993, I no longer had the ability to get enough season-end products. There wasn't enough supply to support the demand I had. So I went overseas to mainland China to meet someone I had met over the Internet who said he could help me find a tie manufacturer. He was a young guy who was willing to do some sourcing and product representation for me.

What was the result of being in China?

We increased our quality and lowered our cost of goods. We developed department-store quality, handmade silk ties that could be retailed for five dollars in food and drug stores nationwide. Most Americans feel like the most important part of buying in China is the price. The truth is that price is only one element of the negotiation. We need factories that can deliver high quality, deliver on time, and that are easy to deal with when errors happen, or when we need something urgently.

THE FORMULA

What is the secret formula that made your company successful?

Value. It is the formula that works for my company. We develop products that offer value to the consumer. Who else sells a handmade silk tie for five dollars? We've most recently developed and introduced coffee mugs in decorative gift boxes that retail for five dollars. This style of mugs in boxes normally retails for ten dollars in Christian bookstores and general market gift stores. By putting the same quality product on the shelf for five dollars, the product is selling very well.

THE ADVICE

What is one of the lessons that you learned while your company was growing?

I learned that people are the most important part of any company. Without good people who have the same commitment level to make the company succeed, you cannot succeed. People who interview with my company immediately feel that the company is warm, caring, and loving. All of my employees embody that character and spirit.

THE PLAN TO FOLLOW

STEP 1

Look for a potential niche market. Then look for a buyer in that niche to develop a business relationship with. Ask that buyer what you can do to help solve a retail need that he or she has.

STEP 2

Once you know what the buyer needs, start researching to find that product—one that offers value to the consumer and is priced competitively. Then look for other buyers in the same niche who have the same need, and repeat your success with them.

STEP 3

Start your business small, and grow and expand your product line slowly. Use wisdom, keep your full-time job while you're getting established, and take educated, calculated risks one step at a time.

STEP 4

Look for manufacturers that do more than just offer you a product you need at a good price. Remember, the price is only one element of the negotiation. You need factories that can deliver high quality, deliver on time, and that are easy to deal with when errors happen, or when you need something urgently.

STEP 5

Hire good people. They are the number one reason why the company will succeed.

THE HIGHLIGHTS

- Price an item to sell by always asking for more than you paid and by compromising the price down.
- After turning a profit, always put a percentage back into your business.
- Buy anything—valuables are to be found at the most common garage sale and thrift store.
- Do your research, and learn from other sellers on eBay. Review completed auctions for market values and bidding trends.
- Be forward and decisive in your actions when bidding and importing.
- Look for a niche market, find a buyer in that market with a retail need, and fill it successfully.
- Once you meet the first buyer's need, build on that success with other buyers with the same need.
- Use wisdom, and take educated, calculated risks one step at a time, and build your business slowly.
- Look for factories that will deliver a good price, high-quality products on time, and that will work with you when errors occur.
- Remember that without good people who have the same commitment level to make your company succeed, you cannot succeed.

THE RESOURCES

MORE INFORMATION ABOUT
KEITH DANIELS DESIGNS

NOTE: At publication time, these websites were under construction. Watch for the completed websites. They're coming soon.

Keith Daniels Designs
www.keithdanieldesigns.com

Divinity Boutique
www.divinityboutique.com

STARTING A BUSINESS IN
THE APPAREL INDUSTRY

Men's Dress Furnishings Association, Inc.
www.shirtsandties.org
This was formerly known as the Neckwear Association of America.

LOCATING CLOTHING MANUFACTURERS
IN THE UNITED STATES AND OVERSEAS

Keith Schwartz helps companies find manufacturers in China that will produce items they want to sell in the United States. If you can buy a substantial quantity, pay cash up front and provide design and material specifications, Schwartz can help. He also provides consulting services. Contact Schwartz at 216-581-9933, or e-mail him at **otpcustomerservice@yahoo.com**.

Hong Kong Trade Development Council
www.tdc.org.hk
www.tdctrade.com
By joining the council, you can be placed on a sourcing list for products you wish to manufacture.

Chinese Embassy in the United States
http://us2.mofcom.gov.cn/index.shtml
The commercial section of the embassy website includes valuable information such as a "Supply and Demand" section. The website may also have embassy contacts who can direct you to potential manufacturers.

LOCATING DEPARTMENT STORE CLOSEOUT
ITEMS AND WHOLESALE PRODUCTS

Aid & Trade
http://usatrade.url40.net/
This website is for suppliers in the United States and Canada.

LOCATING RETAILERS TO PURCHASE
YOUR PRODUCT

Finding a Retailer
www.star.com/cfm/?go=retailerLocator.retailer Search&
This is a search engine specifically for retailers.

Marketing Guidebook
www.progressivegrocer.com/progressivegrocer/ business_resources/print_directories/marketguide book.jsp
This website includes a list of chains, distributors, and buyers for supermarkets.

LOCATING BUYERS
WHO WORK WITH RETAILERS

Marketing Guidebook
www.progressivegrocer.com/progressivegrocer/ business_resources/print_directories/marketguide book.jsp
This site includes a list of chains, distributors, and buyers for supermarkets.

Trade Shows
www.tradeshowbiz.com
www.tradeshowweek.com
Trade shows are a good way to meet buyers. You can find additional websites by conducting an Internet search on "trade show directories."

CLOTHING DESIGN

Guru.com
www.guru.com
This is a great website where you can search for freelance workers, including fashion designers.

DOING BUSINESS IN CHINA

ManageChina.com
www.managechina.com
The website provides a wealth of information on doing business in China, including resources, good corporate structures, establishing a virtual presence in China, and more.

HIRING EMPLOYEES

U.S. Department of Labor—Minimum Wage
www.dol.gov/dol/topic/wages/minimumwage. htm

Minimum Wage Laws in States
www.dol.gov/esa/minwage/america.htm

Employment Law
www.law.cornell.edu/wex/index.php/Employment
This website provides a comprehensive overview.

Millionaire Blueprints *neither endorses nor recommends any of the companies listed in the resource section. Resources are intended as a starting point for your research.*

5

True Stories of SERVICE INDUSTRY Millionaires

Dr. Daniel T.
DRUBIN

How a chiropractor turned his thriving single practice into a multimillion-dollar national consulting firm.

BUSINESS NAME:
4th Dimension

TYPE OF BUSINESS:
Consulting Business

LOCATION:
Tucson, AZ

ADAPTED FROM:
Millionaire Blueprints magazine article,
"Find the Need and Fill It,"
June 2005

A s a boy from New York, Dr. Daniel T. Drubin remembers his South Bronx upbringing well. He says he recalls growing up not only with hand-me-down clothes, but also with "hand-me-down food." But the main thing Drubin says he distinctly remembers from a very early age was his desire for more out of life. It was then that a larger vision for his life began to formulate.

He chose chiropractic school as the path to this bigger and better life. Drubin became very successful in that field. For the next seventeen years, he developed systems and methods for optimizing efficiency and practice profitability that drew the interest of his colleagues. Soon, his practice grew to include multiple doctors, all following the same systems with the same profitable results. Drubin knew then that the systems he had created could be adapted to other practices with the same results. So, with a good friend and colleague, Drubin started a six-month program to teach other area chiropractors what he had discovered about building and running a successful practice—the business end of health care so often overlooked in formal training. The response? They wanted more and more.

Sixteen years later, the resulting practice management organization that Drubin and his colleague built encompassed five bases of operation, a thousand doctors as members, thousands of assistants, and huge seminars every month. Then, in 1996, Drubin sold it all and took his family west to Park City, Utah, and did it all over again. After building the second practice management consultation business—aptly dubbed Chiropractic Elite Organization (CEO)–to its own spectacular pinnacle, Drubin sold it all again and moved to Tucson, Arizona. There, he began his third consulting business called 4th Dimension, which was geared more toward private sector businesses.

Although Drubin's efforts have largely been centered on building successful health care practices, he says he believes his approach applies to any business in any field. If you have discovered a better way to do what you do, and you would like to teach it to others and become a consultant in your field, here's the best advice Drubin has to offer to make that change become your reality.

THE BEGINNING

You were a successful chiropractor. What made you want to become a consultant?

It occurred to me that, as a solo practitioner, or even as a doctor in a large practice with many associates, I am only able to help a limited number of patients. But in teaching other doctors how to better care for their patients and build better practices, I could ultimately help hundreds of thousands of patients.

What made you think you could be a consultant?

I realized I had discovered some processes and systems that seemed to work in other practices. It was so successful that I then bought two more, and the system still worked.

THE BUSINESS

What is a consultant, anyway?

No matter what industry you are in, if you know how to get more clients or customers than everyone else in your field, you can be a consultant in that industry and you can charge people to tell them how you do it.

Once you knew you had the basis of a good consulting business, what did you do then?

Step one for me was to get to the doctors and show them that I had discovered a better way to build a practice and attract patients. This involved writing down all my systems, scripting how it could be taught, and writing down practice protocols and procedures. Then, I started guest speaking everywhere I could to explain what I had to offer my potential market.

THE MARKETING

What did you do differently when you first started your practice that made it so successful—and created the base for your consulting business?

I marketed like a banshee. Besides asking for referrals and giving extra cards to every patient who happened to stop in—and that, of course, started my referral chain—I started patronizing local merchants including delis, gas stations, and dry cleaners. I gave cards out to as many people as possible—every day. I knew, even then, that marketing anything is a numbers game. Soon I realized that for every 500 cards I handed out in a thirty-day period—16.6 cards every day—I generated fifteen to twenty new patients.

What else did you do?

I also started giving educational talks to my patients. These talks were constructed in such a way that required them to bring in a partner. So for every ten new patients who would come to my talk—I'd have ten additional people to market to. I averaged three new patients a night when eight to ten patients brought a guest. It was then that I also started gaining confidence as a speaker and knew I could get up in front of groups and teach.

So what did you do to capitalize on this experience?

I started soliciting local organizations. I called up and offered to speak for free. I spoke on health topics and introduced chiropractic as an alternative to traditional medicine. These talks converted a lot of people to patients.

THE NEED

How do you figure out what each client needs?

Find the need, and fill it. That's what I do. That's what all good consultants do. Within the confines of each business, finding what could be more, new, better, or different is my model of success. My job is often just to remind them that the amount of attention paid to details is what makes the difference between success and failure. Everything depends on the quality of service they provide.

THE PROFIT

Once they signed up, what did they have to do, what did you do for them, and what did they pay for this service?

In the early days, it was telephone consulting. We were on call with unlimited help with anything management-related. Our fee for this was $250 a month. By the time I left, it was $600 a month. We helped them with everything from office design, color schemes, forms, procedures, billing, filing, and even scripting what to say to their patients. Our clients were never left alone. If you give people enough value and substance, there is no limit to what they will pay. Just call up some people in your business and ask them, "If I was willing to spend time with you and teach you what I know to help you grow your business, what would it be worth to you?" Ask this over and over, and at some point you will start to see a trend.

THE SOLUTION

So how do I get new clients?

I figured out how many people I could to talk to every day—and how many new patients that meant per month. Then I realized that getting in front of groups dramatically increased the number of people I could reach in one sitting. Once I saw an average return on that, I knew how many groups I needed to talk to in order to reach the quota I had set for myself. Sales is a numbers game no matter what industry you are in. If you approach ten people, you may sell one. If you approach a hundred people, you may sell ten. If you approach a thousand people, you may sell a hundred. The problem is there are very few people who have what it takes to approach a thousand people—knowing they will probably be turned down by nine hundred of them. But those few people are the ones making the money, while all the others are trying to figure out an easier way to succeed.

THE ADVICE

What's next?

For me, knowing that I'm making a difference to other people is very motivating. But my real mental stamina comes from loving what I do so much that it doesn't seem like work. When you take the jump in your career from what is expected and comfortable to the path that leads you in the clear direction of your goals, who has the time to get burned out?

THE PLAN TO FOLLOW

STEP 1

Instead of a business plan, start with a formula that is simple and thorough. Just write out what you want, when you want it, why you want it, and how you're going to do it—with specific action steps.

STEP 2

Find out what could be more, new, better, or different within the confines of your clients' businesses. Your job is to remind them that the amount of attention paid to detail is the difference between success and failure.

STEP 3

Market with relentless passion. Spread your message to doctors and businessmen, and show them that you have discovered a better way to build a practice or business and attract patients or clients.

NOTE: This involves writing down all your systems, scripting how it could be taught, and writing down practice/business protocols and procedures.

STEP 4

Then, start guest speaking everywhere you can for free to explain what you have to offer to your potential market.

STEP 5

Deliver what you promise. If you give people enough value and substance, there is no limit to what they will pay.

THE HIGHLIGHTS

- Decide what you want, when you want it, why you want it, and how you're going to do it.
- Find the need and fill it.
- Show potential clients that you have discovered a better way to build their businesses.
- Market your concept with relentless passion, speaking for free everywhere you can.
- Deliver the value that you promise.

THE RESOURCES

INFORMATION ABOUT
THE CONSULTING PROFESSION

Kennedy Information's Consulting Central
www.consultingcentral.com
One of the leading research firms on the consulting profession. To request a sample issue of *Consultants News,* call 800-531-0007 or 603-924-0900, ext. 773, or e-mail **CNsample@kennedyinfo.com**.

Institute of Management Consultants USA
www.imcusa.org
Contains informative articles and book resource suggestions.

Association of Management Consulting Firms
www.amcf.org
Association members share experiences, build relationships, develop alliances and partnerships, and create knowledge with those who share their commitment to professionalism.

BECOME A BETTER PUBLIC SPEAKER,
OR FIND A SPEAKER

www.speakersnetwork.com
www.brooksinternational.com

PLANNING BUSINESS CONVENTIONS

www.2chambers.com
A nationwide directory of chambers of commerce, convention centers, visitor's bureaus, tourist boards, maps, and hotels that can help in planning conventions for your business.

ASSISTANCE WITH DIGITAL PRESENTATIONS

Opus Presentations
www.digitalworkshop.com

GLOBAL OPPORTUNITIES IN CONSULTING

www.top-consultant.com
Search by firms, sectors, locations, industries, areas, or salaries.

Millionaire Blueprints neither endorses nor recommends any of the companies listed in the resource section. Resources are intended as a starting point for your research.

Chris
HAAS

His blue-collar background gave this entrepreneur the stamina to succeed.

BUSINESS NAME:
All Pro Freight Systems, Inc.

TYPE OF BUSINESS:
Freight Hauling

LOCATION:
Cleveland, OH

ADAPTED FROM:
Millionaire Blueprints magazine article,
"$40 a Week to $40 Million a Year:
All Pro Freight Hauls in a Fortune,"
March/April 2006

T*he idea of door-to-door cold calling strikes fear in the minds of most salespeople, but not Chris Haas. Compared with working in a cowhide factory, cold calling is a breeze. "Here I was, a kid who did blue-collar work growing up, and all of a sudden I put on a suit and tie, and all I had to do was talk to people. To me it was a joy," Haas says. That attitude may well be the secret to his success.*

After cutting his teeth as a salesman in the freight business in Ohio, Haas began All Pro Freight Systems from his home, doing paperwork in the morning and sales calls in the afternoon. Today, All Pro is a $40 million company, running 165 trucks out of four warehouses, with 250 trailers and over 100 employees. These days he leaves most of the client calls to his eight salespeople, but he never goes a day without meeting a customer for lunch.

THE BEGINNING

What was your first job in the trucking industry?

I started as an assistant to the director of operations at a trucking company. Six months later, he left to run his own company and I was offered his job.

How did you get into the freight business?

One of my clients told me he thought I was in the wrong business. When I asked him what he meant, he said, "We move about seven people every year, but we move fifteen to twenty-five loads of freight every day." It turned out he had a friend who owned a freight company in Cleveland. I interviewed with him, and he hired me on the spot for $100 more a week, plus a company car.

THE BUSINESS

What did you move on to from there?

I met a guy who owned a company called Rush Transport. We had a lot in common, and I decided to come on as a partner with him.

How did you grow the business?

The biggest part of our business was the brokerage. We matched up truckers and loads. It wasn't cash intensive. We needed a phone, a computer, and a desk. When I hired my first employee, I had to decide if I wanted to do the operations or the sales. I chose to go out and sell. We leased a truck terminal and began to grow rather quickly.

How does a freight brokerage work exactly?

We find carriers for the loads of freight our customers give us. The carrier invoices us, and we invoice our customer. That's a broker deal. When the trucker delivers the load, our job is done.

How do you match up truckers with loads?

There are websites that list loads all over the country. There are organizations you can subscribe to online and pay a monthly fee or a per-posting fee. The DAT system (**www.datconnect.com**) is one of the largest.

How long was it before you became All Pro?

After about two years, the partnership with Rush Transport wasn't working out, so we decided to split up and go our separate ways. I got to keep the trucking operation in Cleveland, but I had to come up with $250,000. I was going to continue operating under Rush Transport, but my attorney told me I needed a different name. So I incorporated under the name All Pro Freight Systems.

THE MONEY

So where did you get the money?

From the man who owned the truck terminal I was leasing. I think he believed in me because I had followed through on everything I said I would do. I was talking to him about my dilemma, and he said he'd loan it to me—but at 15-percent interest. Then two months later, I ran into an acquaintance playing golf. He was a banker, and he refinanced the loan at a lower interest rate.

THE GROWTH

Were most of your customers large or small companies?

I grew my business based on a lot of small companies, which meant we didn't have all of our eggs in one basket. After about seven years, a local business newspaper did a story on us. One thing led to another. All of a sudden, I was getting shipments from the Fortune 500 companies. That really fueled our growth.

How did you go from being a brokerage to owning lots of trucks?

My customers started telling me they couldn't rely on us since we were just a broker. So I started buying equipment and getting owner-operators. They don't have authority or insurance, so they sign on with different companies around the country. We put our logo on their cabs, and they haul for us.

How did you find drivers?

We put ads in the classifieds section of local newspapers saying we were recruiting drivers with their own rigs. We also placed ads in truck stop publications.

How did you start your warehousing operation?

Customers kept asking us to store their freight for a while, and pretty soon we could barely move. I realized I could run a trucking operation out of a warehouse, but I couldn't run a warehouse operation out of a truck terminal. I went looking, and found a 100,000-square-foot building. To every customer I could, I said, "Anybody who needs warehouse space, I've got it. I'll make the price right." By the time ninety days were up, we had the place filled.

What's the typical charge for warehouse space?

It's usually by the space, by the freight, and by the month. Typically, a truckload of freight generates a couple hundred dollars a month for storage. The in-and-out charges might be seventy-five dollars to get it in or out.

What was the next major step?

After two years, we were so full that I bought another 60,000-square-foot building. We put a 40,000-square-foot addition on it, and now we have just over 200,000 square feet of warehouse space within a half mile. Our trucking company operates out of one of them.

How did you start your on-site storage operation?

Many companies wanted on-site storage, so we rented old trailers to them. We charged $100 a month per trailer, and they just used it as a storage facility.

Where could someone buy used trailers for this purpose?

There are several trade publications with used trucking equipment, and there are lots of dealers selling used equipment. (See resource section.)

THE MARKETING

How did you get your first customers?

I had a cold calling system. I stopped by about thirty companies each day. When I walked in, I'd ask, "Who handles your freight?" Or I'd say, "Who's your traffic manager? I'd like to see him." The receptionist would usually say, "That's Joe Smith, but he's by appointment only." Or she'd say, "He's busy." So I'd say, "Can you write down his name and phone number?" At the end of the day, I'd have a whole list of contact information. I knew out of thirty calls, only one or two would see me without an appointment, but the goal was to compile information.

What did you do with that information?

The next time I was planning to be in that area, I'd get my list out and start calling until I had three or four appointments. I'd say, "Hey, I stopped in to see you. I know you were busy, but I'm going to be out there next Tuesday. Would you have fifteen minutes to let me introduce myself and my company?" So I'd make sure I had three or four appointments spaced evenly throughout the day, and then I would just cold call around them. Little by little, I established relationships.

How did you improve those relationships?

They used to call me the bagel king because I'd get ten dozen bagels, go to the industrial parkway, and pass them out. By paying three dollars for a dozen bagels, you can take care of a whole office. It comes back tenfold when the manager you're dealing with leaves and the new manager already knows you because you did things like that. I've probably bought 10,000 T-shirts over the years. I had my logo silk screened on them and passed them out to everybody. I also gave out ball tickets.

THE ADVICE

What advice do you have for people out there?

There's no substitute for hard work, and make sure you make money. Some of the best decisions I made were deals I turned away. For example, if someone gives you an opportunity for a ten-truck deal, it may sound great, but always run the numbers. Sometimes you'll realize you wouldn't be making any money. There are "paper" rates in our industry when it comes to brokers. That means a broker might quote a company a low rate, say $500 for a shipment, but then has trouble finding a truck. Then that company calls us because they know we have a truck and they say, "I can get this load for $500. You can have it if you can match that." We run the numbers and say, "No, $500 isn't enough; we'll do it for $700." They turn you down, but come back when the broker can't deliver. Always keep an eye on the bottom line.

THE PLAN TO FOLLOW

STEP 1

Find customers who need to have freight hauled.

NOTE: Haas suggests visiting companies and asking who handles their freight or who their traffic manager is. Then ask to see them, or get their contact information.

STEP 2

Subscribe to an online freight matching service to find carriers to haul your freight. You can post loads to carry and find trucks that are available.

NOTE: Haas says the DAT system (**www.datconnect.com**) is one of the largest.

STEP 3

Always be aware of your customers' needs and adapt your business accordingly.

NOTE: Haas hired owner-operators to haul freight when customers suggested they couldn't rely on just a brokerage. Then he added a warehousing operation and on-site storage trailers to accommodate customers with their freight storage needs.

THE HIGHLIGHTS

- You can launch this business with very little startup capital.
- You can start from your home with a computer and a phone.
- Be kind to your clients and your employees. They will remember you for doing so.
- Adapt your business to your customers' needs, and heed their suggestions for improvement.
- Be personable to gain customers and keep clients. Give away items to keep your business name in the forefront.

THE RESOURCES

MORE INFORMATION ABOUT CHRIS HAAS

All Pro Freight Systems, Inc.
www.allprofreight.com
Chris Haas' highly successful freight hauling company.

INDUSTRY ASSOCIATIONS

American Trucking Associations
www.truckline.com
Dedicated to serving every facet of the trucking industry.

National Association of Independent Truckers (NAIT)
www.naitusa.com
Supporting the needs of independent contractors and small business owners in the trucking industry.

America's Independent Truckers' Association (AITA)
www.aitaonline.com
Offers discounts on products and services regularly used by today's truckers. Also gathers information useful to American truckers and provides it free of charge.

INDUSTRY PUBLICATIONS

Transport Topics
www.ttnews.com
Weekly publication covering the news of the freight industry, including fuel prices, major manufacturer news, and economic indicators affecting the industry.

Truck News
www.trucknews.com
Canada's leading trucking industry newspaper. News stories, trucking resources, directories, jobs, and equipment.

Over the Road and *Pro Trucker*
www.otrprotrucker.com
Two industry magazines featuring stories about truckers. Site also includes lots of links and resources for the industry.

Trucker's Connection
www.truckersconnection.com
Industry magazine for professional truckers. Includes all kinds of industry links for jobs, weather, traffic, and events.

FINDING AND LINKING LOADS

DAT Connect
www.datconnect.com
One of the industry standards to help you find and move loads. All the connections you need to reduce empty miles, avoid costly driver layovers, and quickly find equipment.

TransCore Link Logistics
http://loadlink.ca
A wealth of products for the trucking industry. Owner of DriverLink, LoadLink, and ProMiles, as well as various other tools and products to keep your trucking company moving along and keeping up with the latest technology.

Freight Getter
www.freightgetter.com
Built by and for truckers, this site allows free truck and load posting. Easily post and find loads nationwide.

Truckers Edge
www.truckersedge.net
A wealth of services designed for the small trucking company and owner-operators. Find and connect with loads, keep records, and track fuel purchases. Available through various access points, including kiosks located at 350 truck stops in the United States.

NEW AND USED EQUIPMENT

Kenworth
www.kenworth.com

Freightliner
www.freightliner.com

Peterbilt
www.peterbilt.com

Mack
www.macktrucks.com

American Trucker
www.americantrucker.com
Search for dealers nationwide by state or name. Includes company name, location, and phone number. Also has extensive listings on used trucks, trailers, and parts.

GS Net
www.gsnet.com
One of the largest sources of used machines listed online, including machinery. Search listings, or post equipment for sale.

Trailers.com
www.trailers.com
Nationwide source for renting, leasing, or purchasing used semi-truck trailers, with or without maintenance agreements. All kinds: flatbed, refrigerated, road, or storage trailers.

OTHER HELPFUL LINKS

Truck Miles
www.truckmiles.com
Truck routing and mileage website. Use it to calculate best routes for a load and to evaluate the profitability of a load based on several factors. Also contains daily fuel rates and road conditions nationwide.

ProMiles
www.promiles.com
Truck mileage and routing software.

Driver Link
www.driverlink.com
Source for finding truck driving jobs across the United States and Canada. Serves both owner-operators and company drivers. Also includes resources for driving schools, and weather and road conditions.

Truck Down
www.truckdown.com
Free service for location towing companies, mobile repair services, truck repair shops, trailer repair shops, truck-friendly motels, emergency services, and other providers.

Millionaire Blueprints *neither endorses nor recommends any of the companies listed in the resource section. Resources are intended as a starting point for your research.*

Barbara
MARCUS

Barbara Marcus turned a babysitting venture into a million-dollar business.

BUSINESS NAME:
Parents in a Pinch

TYPE OF BUSINESS:
Temporary In-home Childcare and Corporate Childcare

LOCATION:
Brookline, MA

ADAPTED FROM:
Millionaire Blueprints magazine article,
"Parents in a Pinch,"
January/February 2007

B arbara Marcus never expected to be an entrepreneur. Her father was an interior designer, and her mother was a stay-at-home mom who, at age fifty, got a master's degree and worked with the elderly. Marcus attended the University of Michigan and went to graduate school at Tufts University. She majored in urban and environmental planning. Her first job was with the Office for Children, a part of the Commonwealth of Massachusetts. There, she developed programs for children who had been abused or neglected. After two years, she worked for the Department of Social Services and finally for a private children's counseling center. In all that time, she never seriously considered starting her own business—until 1986.

Two of her friends had started a business called "Parents in a Pinch" that provided backup in-home babysitting. When one became pregnant with her second child, she decided to sell her half of the business.

"I never thought I would go into business. This came out of left field. I realized this kind of opportunity doesn't come along often, and I'm always up for a new adventure!" Marcus says.

The rest is history. Today, Parents in a Pinch is a million-dollar business operating out of most major U.S. cities, Canada, and the United Kingdom. Parents in a Pinch offers in-home childcare services to individuals and is offered as part of company benefit plans.

THE IDEA

How did the idea for Parents in a Pinch come about?

Two friends of mine started the company in 1984. While working in social service agencies, they identified a need for trustworthy short-term childcare providers.

THE BUSINESS

And when did you get involved?

By the beginning of 1986, one of the women had her second baby, and I had an opportunity to buy her half of the business.

What changes did you make when you started with Parents in a Pinch?

After I arrived, we concentrated more on efficient systems to keep track of childcare providers and parents. We also standardized our training program for new caregivers and our interviewing techniques, and we developed a better bookkeeping system.

THE CHILDCARE PROVIDERS

What types of childcare providers did you use?

Temporary childcare is a perfect job for college and graduate students. We also attracted people who moved to the area after college and were seeking a career. Making money in the meantime by babysitting was a lifesaver for some. We also used professionals who were changing careers and taking evening classes. Finally, we found that new immigrants who might have advanced degrees from their countries but who had to study to pass exams for working in the United States were excellent. We've had Chinese doctors, Russian physics professors, and African school principals doing childcare for us.

How did you find the students?

In the beginning, we took out large display ads in the college newspapers. But then we got more creative and advertised in college coupon books. In the early days, we offered a fifteen-dollar bonus if a student became a babysitter. For years, that was one of our very best recruitment tools. We still use the coupon books, and now offer a fifty-dollar bonus.

Do you screen your childcare providers before hiring them?

We are all too aware that these caregivers are unsupervised, so we have to get the best of the best. Our requirements are very stringent. To attract the best, we always paid our childcare providers more than they would get if they babysat on their own. We still have the reputation of, "They're a little expensive, but they're the best."

Is there much of a turnover with your students?

We must constantly recruit new providers, which is very expensive. But we like the turnover because it keeps our services fresh and our sitters active, fun, and enthusiastic.

THE MARKETING

How did you advertise to parents about your business?

Whenever there was an event geared to families, we would walk up and down the line at the ticket counter and hand out fliers. Posters and fliers were sent to every pediatrician and pediatric dentist's office. We also sent fliers to all daycare centers and kindergartens. They were happy to point out our service to parents who were bringing in coughing and feverish children. Because of the catchy name and the uniqueness of the service, newspapers were happy to do articles about Parents in a Pinch. Very soon, growth came as a result of word of mouth.

What other methods did you use to find parents who needed childcare?

We advertised heavily in parents' papers and publications, and we donated dozens of "four hours of childcare" for school fundraisers or auctions. We also donated our services to community events and set up a play space for children.

THE GROWTH

When did you decide to expand your business and also offer nanny services?

One year after we opened, a more experienced agency warned, "You'd better be prepared for the summertime; things are going to dry up. In the summer, parents can get the kids down the block to babysit!" Because of the seasonality, we added a service for placing part-time and full-time nannies. When our temporary service was slow, the nanny placements picked up and helped with cash flow.

What's the difference between a childcare provider and a nanny?

A childcare provider is a person who provides supervisory care of children on an irregular, full-time, or part-time basis. A nanny is employed by a family on either a live-in or live-out basis to undertake tasks related to the care of the children on a regular, ongoing schedule.

At one point, you shifted the entire paradigm of your business, correct?

We began working with corporations to offer backup childcare as a company benefit in 1989. Now, with more than sixty companies employing more than 125,000 people as our corporate clients, we provide care more often to corporate clients than individual parents.

How did you make the switch to working with corporations?

In the late '80s, we got a call from a publishing company called Little, Brown and Company. They asked, "We know that you do backup childcare. Do you do it as a benefit through companies?" And I thought, "Sure, we can do that." The CEO at the time did not do anything for working mothers (his wife was a stay-at-home mom), until his son married a lawyer. Turns out that grandma was being called upon every time her daughter-in-law was "in a pinch." The CEO then understood the need for a safety net for dual-working families. So we developed a model of providing our service as an employee benefit. We were particularly enthusiastic about this request because we felt the service would be more affordable for a broader range of families who could not afford our private family rates.

How did you find more corporations to work with after the initial phone call?

After we began our contract with Little, Brown and Company, we received a lot of press in the business pages. Law firms, hospitals, universities, and management consulting companies were just at the beginning stages of trying to find programs that would recruit and retain working women. At the same time, several companies in New York City were doing the same kind of program and generating national press.

What are some of your selling points for corporations?

Working parents lose up to eight days each year due to disruptions in their childcare routine, whether it is because they have sick children, the schools are closed, because nannies became ill, and so on. The numbers may be even higher because parents are reluctant to admit that their absence is because of a family disruption. In addition, studies show that new recruits, recently out of college, are as concerned or more concerned with company benefits over wages.

How do you charge corporations for your service?

Each company is charged one fee that gives each employee up to twenty uses per year. We charge companies based on the number of employees and how many offices they have around the country. Typical corporate annual fees now range from $10,000 to $50,000. In addition, we have added backup eldercare to the benefit and allow employees to use childcare or eldercare.

How did the employees contact you?

Employees simply called our central number, no matter where they lived. We had a local number. Outside of Massachusetts, we have an 800 number.

Do most corporations call you, or do you have a marketing team that calls them?

When we decided to become a national company, we stepped up our marketing efforts considerably. We attend trade shows, advertise in human resource journals, send out mailings, and have hired a public relations consultant. We also realized that we have a gold mine in our private client business. Over the years, we have provided backup childcare to many CEOs and others in top management. We use our relationship with these clients to get to the benefits personnel.

How do you approach people in human resources?

We usually are referred to the HR department by employees who have used our service, those who are usually at the top level of the organization. Or we collect business cards at trade shows and follow up. When we get a foot in the door, we have a fifteen-minute PowerPoint presentation. Since this will become part of their benefits package, the decision to use us has to be made early in the budgeting process. Therefore, the sales cycle is a very long one. Between our meeting and their decision, we send articles of interest to the HR people, e-mail notes on a subject involving children, and sometimes send a small gift—like a gourmet brownie with the note, "You'll get brownie points if you provide backup care."

THE ADVICE

Can your community support your business?

A nanny business and a backup childcare business are most successful among white-collar professionals. People of middle and upper income are more likely to let strangers into their homes. Providing backup care is expensive, so your fees will be high. Nanny agencies are more successful in bigger metropolitan cities, rather than in communities where people rarely move in or out. In those communities, families can usually find friends, family, or neighbors to care for their children.

THE PLAN TO FOLLOW

STEP 1

Recruit and train childcare providers and nannies to provide temporary in-home childcare.

NOTE: Marcus says that temporary childcare is a perfect job for college students. She also suggests recruiting professionals who are changing careers and new immigrants who may have advanced degrees from their countries but who have had to study to pass exams to work in the United States.

STEP 2

Visit child-oriented businesses such as daycares, schools, pediatrician's and dentist's offices, and post flyers about your temporary childcare services.

NOTE: Marcus says that most daycares and schools are happy to point out temporary childcare services to parents with sick or injured children.

STEP 3

Contact human resources departments to pitch your corporate childcare services as an employee benefit.

NOTE: Marcus suggests that you mention the fact that working parents lose up to eight days each year due to disruptions in their childcare routine. She says the numbers may be even higher because parents are reluctant to admit that their absence is due to a family disruption.

THE HIGHLIGHTS

- College students are excellent candidates for childcare positions.
- This business has a higher focus on quality than on price.
- Advertise in child-oriented businesses that can refer your services.
- This type of business is more successful in metropolitan areas.
- This business has a high employee turnover rate, so you will constantly recruit childcare providers.

THE RESOURCES

MORE INFORMATION ABOUT PARENTS IN A PINCH

www.parentsinapinch.com

CHILDCARE AND NANNY SERVICES GENERAL INFORMATION

Childcare Resources
www.parentsinapinch.com/Resources.aspx
This website offers detailed resources about running a childcare business.

Child Care Online
www.childcare.net
This website features forms, registry, licensing, hiring worksheets, health and safety information, classifieds, and more.

HOW TO FIND GOOD CHILDCARE PROVIDERS

Newspaper Advertising
www.nationwideadvertising.com
The website offers classified and display advertising in more than 21,000 newspapers.

The Employer's Guide
to College Recruiting and Hiring
www.naceweb.org/info_public/recruiting.htm
This guide offers tips about hiring college students.

Coupon Books
www.entertainment.com/save/advertising
This website offers advertising in the Entertainment Book.

SCREENING YOUR CHILDCARE PROVIDERS

Parents in a Pinch Screening
www.parentsinapinch.com/Nanny-Check.aspx
This site offers nanny screening packages.

Questions to Ask
www.caringnannies.com/nanny_interviews.htm

DataCheck, Inc.
www.datacheckinc.com
This service offers pre-employment background screenings.

Background Network
www.crimcheck.com
This site offers a nationwide screening service.

Verify Social Security
www.socialsecurity.gov/employer/ssnv.htm
This site offers information from the official government website.

TRAINING YOUR CHILDCARE PROVIDERS

Nanny Orientation Tips
www.parentinguniverse.com/Nanny/NOrientation Tips.html

Childcare, Health & Safety
www.ironhorsemothersclub.com/Resources/ healthandsafety.htm#Childcare
The site links to educational Web pages.

Childhood Development from Zero to Three
www.zerotothree.org

FINDING PARENTS WHO NEED CHILDCARE PROVIDERS

About.com
http://childparenting.about.com/library/weekly/ aa100699.htm?terms=canada+computer+ future+shop
This Internet page lists numerous parent resources that might provide avenues for advertising.

Parents' Papers
A Google or Yahoo! search on "parents' paper" and the city of interest will reveal if one is available in your community.

Columbus Parents Paper
www.columbusparent.com

Community Newspapers
If you are interested in advertising in your community newspaper, a Yahoo! or Google search on "community newspaper" and your city's name will reveal which papers you can contact.

EMPLOYMENT LAWS

U.S. Department of Labor—Minimum Wage
www.dol.gov/dol/topic/wages/minimum wage.htm

Minimum Wage Laws in States
www.dol.gov/esa/minwage/america.htm

Employment Law
www.law.cornell.edu/wex/index.php/Employment
This site offers a comprehensive overview.

BUSINESS TAXES

Household Employer's Tax Guide
www.irs.gov/pub/irs-pdf/p926.pdf

Nanny Tax Help
www.parentsinapinch.com/Resources.aspx
A detailed list of links can be found on this page in the "Nanny Tax Help" section.

THE COMPUTER SIDE OF YOUR BUSINESS

Procare Software
www.procaresoftware.com
This management tool is for more than 16,000 childcare providers worldwide.

Childcare Manager
www.childcaremanager.com
This software is for managing a childcare business.

Additional Childcare Software
A Yahoo! or Google search on "childcare software" will reveal a myriad of choices.

Quick Biz Builder
www.quickbizbuilder.com
A great Internet page for creating your business website.

Millionaire Blueprints *neither endorses nor recommends any of the companies listed in the resource section. Resources are intended as a starting point for your research.*

Matt
MCINTYRE

A simple approach to serving seniors reaps big-time rewards.

BUSINESS NAME:
Puritan Financial Group, Inc.

TYPE OF BUSINESS:
Insurance and Financial Planning

LOCATION:
Addison, TX

ADAPTED FROM:
Millionaire Blueprints magazine article,
"Simple Approach to Serving Seniors Reaps
Big-Time Rewards,"
Spring 2005

When it comes to the highs and lows of a career in insurance and financial planning, Matt McIntyre has seen it all. He's been rich—living as he does now in spectacular homes, driving the finest and fastest of cars, and living a life with all the bells and whistles of extreme success. And he's been poor—homeless, bankrupt, struggling to keep the phone and electricity on, the rent paid, and food on the table.

The dominant lesson McIntyre says he learned from his roller coaster of business and financial experiences is that the people in your life are important—not money or the things money buys. He says he remembers how he wanted to be treated when he was first learning his business, and that is how he treats employees. He has also discovered a genuine appreciation and respect for senior citizens. This, he says, is the foundation of how he conducts his business. A return to core values of service and love began to drive his business decisions in a new and better direction. Not surprisingly, McIntyre says, the money just followed.

McIntyre's business concept is simple: He has formed a company whose mission is to help senior citizens create safe, workable plans for designing their retirement. With an approach that addresses health care, investments, and estate planning, McIntyre has tapped into an important and lucrative market. In doing so, he is also providing a valuable service to senior citizens.

THE BEGINNING

McIntyre knows the unique needs and special personality of the senior market. He discovered a great love and respect for what he calls "the greatest treasure we have in this country today." He directs his efforts to serve senior citizens and helps them realize a safer, more secure retirement.

THE BUSINESS

What separates you from your competition?

Our service work is really what separates us from the competition. It is routine for our representatives to go out of their way to do what others don't consider "their job."

So if you are not selling insurance, what are you trying to sell?

The selling is really minimal. The important thing is communicating our sincere interest in helping seniors think through issues and make decisions that will make sure things are set up the way they want them to be regarding estate planning, provisions for their own health care, and investments that will make sure their money outlives them.

THE MONEY

What is a fixed annuity?

An annuity is a type of investment that pays the investor a set amount of money each year for a number of years—often the investor's lifetime. A fixed annuity—not to be confused with a riskier variable annuity—if properly done, is the only financial vehicle in the world in which a person cannot outlive his or her money. During the accumulation stage, a fixed-rate annuity earns a certain stated amount of interest. With what is known as an equity indexed annuity, investors can receive gains when the market goes up, but cannot lose past the amount of their original investment if the market goes down.

So when do the checks start coming to clients, and how does that work?

During the annuity's payout phase, beginning at a certain agreed-upon age when the annuity begins producing income, payments begin being disbursed on the schedule the investor chooses. We recommend monthly payments because that is how most people's bills run, but some choose to receive their checks quarterly, semi-annually, or annually.

THE NEED

How do you present your product information?

Well, let's say I'm talking to a couple. He's a retired engineer, and she's a retired teacher. They have all their money in the stock market. I say, "Suppose next year you gained $200,000 in the stock market. Would it change your lifestyle?" Ninety-nine percent say that after a nice vacation and maybe a new car, everything would pretty much stay the same. Then I say, "Well what if you lost $200,000 in the stock market next year? Would that change your lifestyle?" And almost all of them would say, "Of course, it would change everything. We'd be broke." So then I say, "Then why are you continuing to take that kind of risk?"

Once you establish that the prospect has a need, then what?

We go over the estate, financial, and health care (EFH) presentation, discussing the prospect's issues and concerns. We discuss how our products and services could help. We always encourage any adult children to be present so the entire family is comfortable with the process.

What is in the EFH presentation, and how was it developed?

We keep it simple. We lose all the financial jargon. We break down these complicated, often intimidating, issues into simple and understandable choices based on their own values and priorities. First, we go over the basics of an estate plan. Next, we talk about their financial planning. We ask a series of questions that helps us determine their market losses, taxes, rates of return, IRA planning, and creditor situations. Finally, we talk about their health planning.

Can you give me an example of how this works?

We ask them, "If you became incapacitated, who would you like to take care of you?" They'll name someone—their daughter, for instance. And we say, "Now, does she work? What are her resources to be able to do this? Would you rather be taken care of at home or in a nursing home?" They'll probably say at home. And we say, "Let's just look at the costs for a minute to make sure you're covered. Let's say your daughter works full time, and you have a nurse come in to help you during the day for four hours. If the nurse makes $30 an hour, that would be $120 a day, $600 a week, and $31,200 per year. In just three years, that would be a problem."

THE PROFIT

How does the client pay, and to whom?

The client writes the check directly to the carrier, and the carriers pay us based on whatever terms we have negotiated. We keep it simple and only use two or three companies. Depending on what the client purchases, you may earn from 3 to 10 percent in commission.

How do you gain your clients' trust?

We develop that trust by showing our clients in writing that nobody who has invested with us has ever lost a dime because of how we do business, and how we choose the products best suited to the senior market. A change in thinking can make all the difference in the security of their future.

THE MARKETING

Who is your market?

We generally speak to people age sixty-two to eighty.

How do you approach them?

We generally have to take a two-call approach. During the first visit we need to see if the prospect has a need for our services—and why they responded to our direct mail piece. The need may be in estate, financial, or health-care planning. In addition to determining the need, the purpose of this first meeting is to establish rapport.

THE LEGAL

What kind of education and formal certification does one really need?

Formal education is not as important as specialized training and educating yourself on things like long-term planning and fixed annuities. Research, and learn everything you can about Medicare. I have people working for me who are MBAs and some who just barely finished high school. The most important thing in this business in terms of education is the ability to learn and to have an appreciation of seniors.

THE ADVICE

In addition to serving the needs of your clients, what would you say is the biggest key to success in this business?

A good lead company. One that is honest, available, and that knows the special personality of the senior market. They need to be able to tell you what is pulling in each area, and why.

Tell us how you choose your products and which ones you recommend.

In the health portion of the plan, if long-term care insurance is what we determine a client needs, I usually prefer Penn Treaty American Corp. (**www.penntreaty.com**). For fixed annuities, I'm presently choosing National Western Life Insurance Company in Austin, Texas, (**www.national westernlife.com**) for its attention to seniors.

What is your secret for choosing those fixed annuities for your clients who have never lost a dime?

We only use A-rated or better companies. We research them through A.M. Best Company (**www.ambest.com**) or Standard & Poor's (**www. standardandpoors.com**). In addition to the rating, we look for other criteria such as financial position and financial surplus. We monitor the rating closely and carefully. (A.M. Best Company offers a monitoring service for

$140 a year, and they keep you updated and send out alerts if ratings change.) If a rating drops below A-, we move our clients' money out and put it somewhere else.

What other options are out there for seniors that people may not know about?

In the estate planning area, one option is single-premium life insurance, which means for one large, single payment, a client can provide a tax-free benefit to his or her heirs. (For this option, McIntyre recommends Shenandoah Life Insurance Company at **www.shenlife.com**). Also called estate maximization, this option is only for sums of money the client knows he or she won't ever need.

Although laws governing these things have become more consumer-friendly, if something drastic happens, investors can get some or most of their investment back. It still should be used only for funds that are truly "extra."

THE PLAN TO FOLLOW

STEP 1

First and foremost, you have to have a good background and an interest in dealing with seniors. It takes a real conviction to help them and to do what it takes to see that their needs are met.

NOTE: Educate yourself on long-term planning and fixed annuities. McIntyre recommends reading *All About Annuities* by Gordon Williamson. Also, perform in-depth research on Medicare via **www.medicare.gov**, or get relevant information on Medicare from fourteen search engines at **www.info.com**.

STEP 2

Find a good lead company.

NOTE: McIntyre says the leads he requests are people age sixty-two to eighty, who live in single-family dwellings with an annual income of $30,000 or more. Rather than selecting zip codes, he mails to entire counties.

STEP 3

Contact your market by sending them direct mail product information. First, send a simple direct mail piece with a reply card. When they send in a reply card, call and make an appointment to see them.

NOTE: McIntyre buys leads from a lead company called America's Recommended Mailers, Inc., (ARM) at 972-420-6100. Another good lead company is AdSource Enterprises at 630-406-7861.

STEP 4

When you choose a carrier, look at the services it provides to senior citizens. Is there a live person to talk to if you call with a question?

NOTE: McIntyre prefers small carriers to big ones because he's found bigger carriers don't seem to care as much about seniors. You want to know that the carriers understand this market. Some even have special-service teams dedicated to handling senior business.

STEP 5

After you have delivered the policy, then you need to provide annual free financial and administrative reviews to the clients.

THE HIGHLIGHTS

- Be dedicated to helping senior citizens with insurance and financial planning.
- Become a Certified Senior Advisor (CSA).
- Know the system of benefits from every angle.
- Understand long-term planning and fixed annuities.
- Be personable and honest with your clients.
- Find and develop long-term relationships with good lead companies.
- Choose carriers that are committed to senior citizens.

THE RESOURCES

MORE INFORMATION ABOUT MATT MCINTYRE

If you're interested in joining McIntyre's network or would like more information, please contact Puritan Financial Group, Inc., at 800-513-3243. Or visit them online at **www.puritanfinancialgroup.com**.

How to Obtain CSA Designation
www.society-csa.com

Medicare
www.medicare.gov

Shenandoah Life Insurance Company
www.shenlife.com

Penn Treaty American Corporation
www.penntreaty.com

Puritan Financial Group, Inc.
www.puritanfinancialgroup.com

National Western Life Insurance Company
www.nationalwesternlife.com

A.M. Best Company
www.ambest.com

Standard & Poor's
www.standardandpoors.com

THE LEAD COMPANIES

America's Recommended Mailers, Inc.
www.armleads.com
972-420-6100

Millionaire Blueprints *neither endorses nor recommends any of the companies listed in the resource section. Resources are intended as a starting point for your research.*

Dan
NEWMAN

For Dan Newman, courtesy and persistence led to wealth.

BUSINESS NAME:
Aeromedical Collections Service, Inc.

TYPE OF BUSINESS:
Medical Service Reimbursement Management

LOCATION:
Shreveport, LA

ADAPTED FROM:
Millionaire Blueprints magazine article,
"Courtesy and Persistence Lead
to Collecting Wealth,"
Spring 2005

W*hen you see Dan Newman coming down the stairway of his new multimillion-dollar home in Benton, Louisiana, you would never guess that not too many years ago, he was a guy who couldn't even afford to buy groceries. Before that, there were many other days when he hated to get out of bed, just knowing he had to go to work selling cars. Throughout his career, Newman has always worked hard, pushed hard, and tried his hand at many business ventures that looked promising at first, but for whatever reason didn't quite pan out. But Newman is, and always has been, an entrepreneur at heart, so he didn't let that get him down.*

Newman met a man at his church who was doing very well in the collections business. "I asked him a lot of questions and he was very open with me," Newman says. "So I decided to give it a try."

Today, that "small collections agency" has become the key source of Dan Newman's considerable fortune. By working hard, asking questions, finding answers, and staying true to his principle of "doing it right," he has transformed his collections business into a highly specialized enterprise.

THE IDEA

Tell us how you started your business.

I started the collections agency in the spare bedroom of our home. The economy was really tight at that time. When the economy is bad, the need for collections goes up.

Why try the collection business?

A guy from church actually approached me with the idea of starting a collections agency with him in another area he didn't deal with. Throughout the learning process of finding out what was involved, I realized I could do it by myself. It took a lot of work and a lot of phone calls. But, from what I learned, money could be coming the very next day.

THE BUSINESS

How did you get started?

I had some friends, doctors, and vets that I went to and explained what I was doing. I negotiated rates with them and did everything by the book. I got the clients, did the telephone collections work, and sent letters that must go out to debtors when you take their accounts. After a few months, we moved into a small office and hired a small staff.

When you say you negotiated rates with them, what do you mean?

I collected the money owed to them, and I kept between 25 and 50 percent of what I collected. That is normal, and we negotiated the percentage.

From your experience, tell us how we can start our own collection business.

For the next ten years, the medical industry is going to be the most wide-open field for collections. Every doctor, dentist, hospital, and clinic has trouble collecting money from patients and insurance companies. I believe that over the next decade, so much money will be made in this particular industry that it will blow you away.

So, if we want to start a medical accounts receivable management company, walk us briefly through the proper steps.

The first thing you need to do is contact the secretary of state in your state. (To find the number for the secretary of state, do an Internet search and insert your state's name.) Tell them you want to start a collections agency in that state, and ask them to send you all the rules and guidelines you have to follow to set one up. Then you would need to get the computer software for the collections business.

You can do an online search for "Collections Agency Software." This software will show you everything from filing claims and keeping essential records, to informing patients that their bill has been turned over to you for collection.

THE CLIENTS

How do you get clients? What do you actually say?

Most places have trouble collecting their money. Approach doctors and tell them you are in the collection business and that you are different because your main focus is to get their claims paid. Tell them you want a chance to show that you can increase the money being brought in. Then all you need is a small portion of their billings to show what you can do. Then ask them to pay you the same percentage of monies collected that they pay others who are collecting for them.

You will make a polite, daily call to the collection agencies. Tell doctors things that will gain their confidence, like how you know what it takes to get their money from the insurance companies and the patients. Tell doctors how Centers for Medicare and Medicaid Services (CMS) works. All this information gives you credibility—enough for the doctor to give you a try.

Okay, the doctor gives us a try. Then what?

You follow all the rules and regulations, and then you get on the phone with each entity that owes this doctor money. You don't harass or talk down to anyone. You sympathize with them. Ask them if there is anything they can do to start a payment plan that will take care of the bill. It's shocking how many people will start a payment plan when you treat them with respect.

THE EXPANSION

Explain how you went from a small collections agency making $100,000 a year, to processing the billings for ambulances and helicopters and making millions?

While I was doing my collections from my house, I was approached and hired by a small, municipally owned ambulance service that was having a horrible time collecting the money owed to them. They heard about us from one of our doctor clients, and the owner called me and asked if we had any experience collecting money for ambulance services. My response was, "No, but we can do it." Then we took over their collections.

Who did this company collect from?

They collected from insurance companies, Medicare and Medicaid, and patients who had been transported. Insurance companies are no-pay or slow-pay on purpose, and I have a multimillion-dollar company to get them to pay. What you have to remember is that, at this time, I didn't know the laws and regulations regarding insurance payments, insurance companies, and the government payers, Medicare and Medicaid. When I waded into the problem that this system was having, I found out they were not getting paid because of some inadequacies in their billing practices to insurers.

How did you go about finding all of this information?

Through trial and error. We would get the paperwork on a patient, call him, and he would say he had Blue Cross and that they should have paid that bill. We would then call Blue Cross, and they would tell us that it wasn't paid because the claim was filed incorrectly or that they needed more information. We were making tons of money, but what we found out is that this medical emergency company could have saved themselves all that money they were paying us, if they simply had the staff fill out everything correctly and send it in to the insurance company themselves.

Did they know that?

Yes. Because it was municipally owned, I had to go to a police jury meeting and explain to them what we were doing. I told them that I lived in the parish and I loved getting paid for collecting their bills, but if they handled everything correctly, they wouldn't have to pay me or anyone else to collect their money. They told me they didn't have the staff to do that and wanted me to continue collecting their money for a fee of 50 percent. From that night on, I began to research the industry and realized the tremendous need for this service for a multitude of reasons—at every level in the ambulance industry. Everyone had the same problems.

Let's say a California reader thinks he or she can bring in hospitals and clinics, but doesn't have the time, money, or patience to set up everything you have set up. Can he or she contact you and maybe set up a deal and earn commissions by bringing in clients with you working their accounts?

Sure they can. We have hospitals all over the country, but they are only a small percentage of hospitals needing this service. It's wide open right now, and I'm open to anyone's proposal.

THE CONCLUSION

Sum up for us what your company does.

Every company can either cut their costs or bring in more money, and we do the latter. We maximize their cash flow by getting those people or insurance companies to pay their bills as quickly as possible to these emergency medical services (EMS) companies.

You sound passionate about what you do.

I am, because I know we can make a difference in the cash flow of any hospital or clinic we work with. We basically invented this specific industry. Hospitals hire us to increase their cash flow by collecting money that is owed to them, and that's exactly what we do.

THE PLAN TO FOLLOW

STEP 1

Obtain a list of clientele and negotiate your rates.

NOTE: Newman kept between 25 and 50 percent of what he collected.

STEP 2

Find a location to set up shop, and hire a staff.

NOTE: You will need to invest in collections agency software.

STEP 3

Begin to collect for your clients.

NOTE: Newman stresses the importance of courtesy and respect while dealing with customers.

STEP 4

Continue collecting for your regulars, but be on the lookout for ways to expand your business.

THE HIGHLIGHTS

- There is a huge need for this business that most of the industry is unaware of.
- You can start this business with very little capital.
- When collecting, always speak on a personal level with people. This will help you earn more profits in the end.
- Build relationships with clients to keep them coming back.
- Learn all you can about Centers for Medicare and Medicaid Services (CMS).

THE RESOURCES

MORE INFORMATION ABOUT DAN NEWMAN

Aeromedical Collections Service, Inc. (ACS)
www.acs-ems.com
Newman's medical service reimbursement management company website.

Medical Management Associates LLC (MMA)
www.med-man.org
A wholly owned subsidiary of ACS.

STARTING A COLLECTION AGENCY

Starting a Collection Agency
www.startingacollectionagency.com
Find tips and general information about everything you need to know to get started on this site.

HowToAdvice.com
www.howtoadvice.com/CollectionService
Information about starting your own recession-proof collection service.

Credit & Collections Association LLC
www.credit-and-collections.com
This site helps promote the significance and teaching of a vigorous credit environment in our society.

COLLECTIONS AGENCY SOFTWARE

Collect!
www.collect.org
Automates and streamlines collection, administration, reporting, letter writing, and accounting functions.

Parmar Systems, Inc.
www.parmarsystems.com
This company has been providing recovery software for debt-collection agencies, merchants, lenders, and other service businesses since 1980.

Collection Works
www.collectionworks.com
A project to develop an economical solution for in-house collection departments and collection agencies, utilizing the latest in software and hardware technology.

Athenahealth, Inc.®
www.athenahealth.com
This is a subscription service. This site gives a variety of incorporated business services over the Internet on an accommodating subscription basis.

GOVERNMENT CONTACTS

Centers for Medicare and Medicaid Services (CMS)
www.cms.hhs.gov
The federal agency responsible for administering health-related programs and part of the United States Department of Health and Human Services.

SECRETARY OF STATE

Do an Internet search, and insert your state's name to find this information.

COLLECTION AGENCIES:
INFORMATION YOU NEED TO KNOW

Learn Direct: Career Advice
www.learndirectadvice.co.uk/helpwithyourcareer/ jobprofiles/profiles/profile885/
Information regarding what it takes to be a debt collector.

The Institute of Credit Management (ICM)
www.icm.org.uk
Based in the United Kingdom, this professional body represents the interests of people in credit management. ICM is committed to recognizing the importance that credit professionals place on their studies, their careers, and the industry.

Credit Service Association (CSA)
www.csa-uk.com
CSA is the only national association in the United Kingdom for companies active in relation to unpaid credit accounts, debt recovery agencies, tracing, and allied professional services. CSA is committed to improving communications and relations with all organizations and individuals.

Millionaire Blueprints *neither endorses nor recommends any of the companies listed in the resource section. Resources are intended as a starting point for your research.*

Kevin
SUMMERS

Starting with only a hammer and some nails, Kevin Summers built a multimillion-dollar business that turned "wood" into "gold."

BUSINESS NAME:
Pallet Supply of America

TYPE OF BUSINESS:
Pallet Manufacturing and Recycling

LOCATION:
Dallas, TX

ADAPTED FROM:
Millionaire Blueprints magazine article,
" 'Palletable' Profits,"
May/June 2007

W*hen he first started out, Kevin Summers had no business plan and no particular goals. What he did have was a strong work ethic and the dedication to give top-notch service to his customers. Though he never meant to make a career out of selling pallets, he discovered along the way that there was great opportunity in this business. As things progressed, he refused to take on any debt or investors. His customers became his friends and the profits were unbelievable.*

*Summers' success goes to show that the simplest businesses are sometimes the best. Now, thirty years later, he's come full-circle. During that time frame, his company grew step by step to annual revenues of more than $10 million. It was acquired in an industry roll-up in 1997, and Summers decided to retire two years later. But when the five-year noncompete agreement he had signed came to an end, he jumped headlong back into the pallet business. This time, he partnered with a friend and former competitor, Ed Ostrovitz. Together, they created Pallet Supply of America (**www.pallet-supply.com**).*

THE BEGINNING

What's your background?

I was born and raised—and still live—in Dallas, Texas. My mom and dad were entrepreneurs. They started a direct-mail company called Summers Mailing out of the garage of our old house. I got to see the start-up process firsthand by working for them from the time I can remember. They unknowingly inspired me.

What kind of work did you do for them?

You name it, I did it. When I was old enough, I graduated to driving a truck. That's what got me into the pallet business. It was my job to haul the wooden pallets that the printing materials arrived on out to the landfill. I knew the pallets were coming from the printers. So I thought, "Why can't I just resell these back to the printers at half the price of new ones?"

THE IDEA

How old were you when this idea hit you?

Probably about seventeen years old. I created this closed-loop system where I captured the used pallets at my parents' mailing company, repaired them, and sold them back to the printing companies. I knew there were other direct-mail companies in the area that probably had the same situation, so I called on them. Some paid me to haul these things off; some gave me the pallets for free.

THE BUSINESS

What was your pitch to get customers?

I knew that when printers bought pallets, they usually bought brand-new ones. So my pitch was, "I can sell you a pallet. It's not brand-new, but it's half the price of a new one." A new pallet might have cost eight dollars, and I'd sell used ones for four dollars. And remember, I had no cost into them except my own labor.

Did you have any employees?

When I first started, I was the only employee for a couple of years. I repaired the pallets, drove the forklift, and drove the truck. Then I hired my first employee. One by one, I kept adding on.

What did your employees do?

They mostly repaired the pallets. For the longest time, I answered the phone, typed the invoices, made the deliveries, and saw the customers. It was a good thing that I made the deliveries myself because I was able to see the customers one-on-one and build long-lasting relationships.

THE PROFIT

Were your profit margins pretty good?

No question. My accountants used to laugh about it. They'd tell some of their other clients, "I've got this one client and you're not going to believe the margins he's making." But eventually, people caught on to it, and I decided to start offering a little money for the pallets.

THE GROWTH

What was the next major growth point for you?

In 1991, I landed the Sam's Club distribution center in Dallas. They'd been doing their own pallet repairs and supplying their own needs, and not doing a very good job of it. So they were putting it up for bid. They contacted me, and I went out and met with them—and landed the business. We had a history of good service, and we were able to impress upon them through our reputation what we had already accomplished.

How did you convince them of that?

Just by showing our track record, and I told them about my history in the business. We invited them out to our facility because we were proud of it and wanted them to see it firsthand. There's no magic bullet. I always did everything I said I was going to do, and I was always honest—and I think that's what it takes.

THE MARKETING

Do you think personality has anything to do with success?

I believe in myself, and I suppose I convey that to others. I've definitely got a can-do personality, and I think people want to deal with positive, energetic people. I always want to do a little extra too—something to separate myself from the pack. I buy sporting tickets for everything: baseball, basketball, and more. I take my customers to games. When you spend so much time with people, it's just natural for you to become friends. And I was always there for them when it mattered, like when they called at five minutes before five o'clock on a Friday, or on weekends, and needed pallets.

You'd deliver them?

You bet. Since we're friends, I'm that much more motivated to make sure they get what they need. But the flip side of that is when a competitor comes around, they're not just switching from Summers Pallet, they're switching from their friend, Kevin Summers. If I'm there for them when it counts and I've built that loyalty on both sides, then I'm more likely to keep those customers.

THE NEED

Why did you start making new pallets?

Some of our customers demanded it, and they became a nice complement to the recycling part of it. We built a lot of new, custom pallets. We set up our own little mill on site.

Do custom pallets get recycled too?

Some can be. But as a result of the ones we couldn't resell, we developed a new kind of dismantler saw. The saw can take a used pallet that's an oddball size, dismantle it, capture the wood from it, cut it, and build a new pallet.

THE DEAL

Let's skip ahead to when you sold the company. How did that come about?

In 1997, three major pallet companies decided to merge and create an entity called Palex, and make it the first publicly traded pallet company.

They told me that once they went public, they wanted to acquire me. I think one of the reasons I was selected was because we had the Sam's Club and the Wal-Mart® business by that time, and we had annual revenues in excess of $10 million. After the merger, we were a $110-million company.

What were some of the aspects of the deal you made with them?

I sold it for half cash, half stock—and I agreed to work for them for two years. They also asked me to sign a five-year noncompete agreement.

THE REBIRTH

How did you get started again?

My noncompete agreement ended and I partnered with my friend, Ed, to get back into the business. The barriers to entry were much easier this time because of several factors. One was that Palex had only leased my properties from me. I still owned them. And, as they consolidated, they moved out of some of them. Two, I had stayed in touch with most of my employees and was on a friendly basis with them. And three, I had remained friends with a lot of my key customers, and they had said several times, "If you ever get back into it, let us know."

So you just told people you were back in business again, and it took off?

I did, and it ramped up extremely fast. Now we've got 170 employees, and some days we ship as many as 20,000 pallets. Employees are your other key to success. You've got to have good people, and I've got some good, dedicated people. Our main office is in southwest Dallas, and we also have satellite offices.

After he retired, Summers became involved in real estate investing. He purchased many properties he likes to call "those little green houses" (like the ones from that famous board game about money). And now, he's working on "the red hotels," by investing in some larger developments like shopping centers and *apartment complexes. He is currently considering a merger with a major competitor. Together, they will have combined revenues of about $50 million. That's not bad for a kid who started with a few simple hand tools, a truck, and a great work ethic.*

THE PLAN TO FOLLOW

STEP 1

First start by looking around your local area for companies that throw out pallets, and locate companies that use pallets to ship their products.

NOTE: Summers suggests that you look at grocery stores, direct mail companies, and distribution centers. He also suggests that you drive through industrial parks, and look for places that have pallets stacked up in the back.

STEP 2

Approach the businesses that throw out pallets, and offer to haul off the pallets.

NOTE: Some companies will allow you to haul them for free, some will charge you a fee, and some will pay you a fee.

STEP 3

Find a place to store your pallets.

NOTE: Summers suggests that you find a storage area that is close to your suppliers and customers. This will save on fuel costs and time on the road.

STEP 4

Purchase the equipment necessary to repair and haul the pallets.

STEP 5

Approach businesses that ship their products using pallets, and offer to sell them used pallets for a fraction of the cost of new ones.

THE HIGHLIGHTS

- This business offers huge profit margins and encourages entrepreneurship.
- You can start this business with very little capital. All you need is ingenuity.
- Always pay attention to your customers' needs, and develop a plan to fill them.
- Build your company's reputation through a history of good service, which will keep your clients coming back.
- If you're able to see your customers one-on-one, that's the best way to build long-lasting relationships.

THE RESOURCES

MORE INFORMATION ABOUT KEVIN SUMMERS

Pallet Supply of America
www.pallet-supply.com
Kevin Summers' pallet manufacturing and recycling company.

ASSOCIATIONS AND OTHER INFORMATION

National Wooden Pallet and Container Association
www.nwpca.com
Trade association site packed full of information and resources, including a search feature for finding the equipment and supplies needed in pallet production. Also publishes the trade magazine, *Pallet Central.* For those who live in the North, visit their Canadian counterpart at **www.canadianpallets.com.**

Western Pallet Association
www.westernpallet.org
Representing the wooden pallet and container industry in the Western United States.

The Pallet Board
www.palletforum.com
Online forum for people in the industry to exchange ideas and information.

The Center for Unit Load Design
www.unitload.vt.edu
Helps the pallet and related industries save money and resources.

PalletPages.com
www.palletpages.com
If you're wondering how much competition is in your area, search by zip code to find out. This website also contains links to industry suppliers.

e-Pallet.net
www.epallet.net
Once you're up and running, register here to receive requests for quotes from customers looking to buy pallets.

TRADE PUBLICATIONS AND INFORMATION

Pallet Profile's Recycle Record
www.recyclerecord.com
Monthly magazine offering in-depth information and analysis on the business of pallet recycling.

Pallet Profile Weekly
www.palletprofile.com
Weekly newsletter that mainly focuses on the new pallet market but covers many topics, including pricing, economics, labor, and laws.

Pallet Enterprise
www.palletenterprise.com
Pallet and sawmill magazine. Site has lots of links to other resources.

American Lumber & Pallet
www.amlumber.com
Mailed free to people in the industry. This magazine is a source for new and used equipment, announcements, trade shows, meetings, and information.

EQUIPMENT

Zip Online
www.e-adsolution.com/RFP/rfp_welcome.asp
Serving the wood and pallet industries. This is a quick way to find suppliers and request information.

HAND TOOLS AND POWER TOOLS

The Home Depot
www.homedepot.com

Lowe's
www.lowes.com

NAILS, NAIL GUNS, AND OTHER FASTENERS

Maze Nails
www.mazenails.com
Made from recycled steel, this company boasts

that it has "the world's largest variety of specialty nails."

Stanley Bostitch
www.bostitch.com
Creates and supplies a wide range of fastening products.

Viking, Inc.
www.palletnails.com
Product line includes bulk nails, framing stations, sheathing bridges, custom equipment, and accessories.

FORKLIFTS—NEW AND USED

e-lifttruck.com
www.elifttruck.com
Company claims it is the "largest used forklift classifieds listing online."

ForkliftFind.com
www.forkliftfind.com
Services include matching buyers and suppliers.

Mitsubishi Caterpillar Forklift America, Inc.
www.mcfa.com
Manufactures and sells Mitsubishi forklifts.

Nissan Forklift Corporation North America
www.nissanforklift.com
Manufactures, sells, and services Nissan forklifts.

ForkliftPartsOnline.com
www.forkliftpartsonline.com
Online catalog includes a wide array of manufacturers' forklifts and lift trucks, including parts and accessories.

OTHER EQUIPMENT

MachineryTrader.com
www.machinerytrader.com
Classifieds listing of heavy construction equipment for sale, dealers, and equipment haulers.

ThomasNet®
www.thomasnet.com
Online search for industrial products and services.

TimberEquipment.com
www.timberequipment.com
Online information source for logging, pallet, wood, and sawmill processing equipment.

USED TRUCKS
Ryder® Vehicle Sales
www.usedtrucks.ryder.com
Find used trucks, tractors, and trailers with "complete maintenance histories."

Commercial Truck Trader
www.trucktraderonline.com
Online magazine for commercial light trucks, medium trucks, heavy-duty trucks, and trailers.

Truck Paper
www.truckpaper.com
Classifieds and auction listing for trucks, trailers, and equipment.

WOOD SOURCES

The Lumber Pages
www.palletenterprise.com/maplumberpages
Online listing of lumber suppliers.

Low Grade Lumber
www.lowgradelumber.com
Specializes in buying and selling softwood and hardwood lumber, plywood, oriented strand board (OSB), cut stock, and building material surplus.

TRADE SHOWS

Viking Pallets Assembly Systems Trade Show Schedule
www.vikingeng.com
This website provides information on upcoming trade shows related to the pallet industry.

Millionaire Blueprints *neither endorses nor recommends any of the companies listed in the resource section. Resources are intended as a starting point for your research.*

<u>6</u>

**True Stories of
FOOD INDUSTRY
Millionaires**

Wally
AMOS

Wally Amos models success by persevering through times of trouble.

BUSINESS NAMES:
Famous Amos Cookies, Chip & Cookie™

TYPE OF BUSINESS:
Cookies

LOCATIONS:
Los Angeles, CA, and Kailua, HI, on Oahu

ADAPTED FROM:
Millionaire Blueprints magazine article,
"That's the Way the Cookie Crumbles,"
March/April 2007

W*ally Amos has endured a series of tough experiences throughout his life, both in business and in relationships. Yet he has persevered. In 1975, he opened his own business in Hollywood—a chocolate chip cookie store. His Famous Amos chocolate chip cookie business grew by leaps and bounds and became widely popular. But Amos had tough times ahead. Soon he would face circumstances that would make most people give up. However, Amos isn't like most people. He's an expert at taking life's lemons and making—chocolate chip cookies.*

THE BEGINNING

Where did you grow up?

I was born in Tallahassee, Florida, to Ruby and Wallace Amos. Both of my parents were unable to read or write. I left at age twelve when my parents were divorced, and I moved to New York to live with my Aunt Della. She was the first person to ever make chocolate chip cookies for me. And twenty-seven years later, I would open a store selling chocolate chip cookies!

What types of jobs did you hold over the years?

I worked as the manager of the supply department at Saks Fifth Avenue, and then as a talent agent for the William Morris Agency.

When did you start making cookies?

I started making cookies in 1970. A client came into my office with chocolate chip cookies, and it reminded me of my Aunt Della. All of a sudden, I wanted to make cookies. I asked for the recipe, and I thought she was going to tell me it was some deep, dark secret. She lightheartedly said, "It's just the recipe on the back of the Nestlé Toll House chocolate chip package."

THE RECIPE

What did you do when you found out about the recipe?

After our meeting, I went right to the supermarket and, sure enough, there was the Nestlé Toll House recipe. So I started making cookies and giving them away. It became like therapy for me, and it was a way of having my clients remember me in a favorable way.

Did you change the recipe from the Toll House bag?

I embellished the recipe. And it's more than just the recipe, because your energy, your spirit, and your attitude go into it. I'm convinced that's what makes the difference. I had a love for chocolate chip cookies that no one else possessed, and that made all the difference in the world.

THE BUSINESS

Why did you decide to go into the cookie business?

In October 1974, I had dinner with a friend, B. J. Gilmore. She was Quincy Jones' secretary. He had offices at A&M Records, and so did I. After B. J. and I had dinner, she told me something no one else ever had. "Wally, you and I ought to go into business together selling cookies, and I've got a friend who can put up the money," she said. That sealed it for me. I made the commitment to open one store in Hollywood selling cookies.

What was your first step in starting the cookie store?

I knew the health department would have something to do with it. So I had B. J. call and find out what the requirements were for opening a store selling chocolate chip cookies.

After contacting the health department, what did you do next?

You can't open a store unless you find a place. And I put a business plan together. I attempted to answer in the plan what I was going to do, how I was going to do it, how much it was going to cost, and, hopefully, where I was going to do it.

How did you find a location?

I went to the *Yellow Pages,* and started looking at "For Rent" signs. I found a great location at 7181 Sunset Boulevard. I met with the landlord, and, according to my business plan, I needed $25,000 to open what I decided to call Famous Amos. I had commitments to it. The names of the people who committed money impressed him, so he agreed to lease the place to me.

THE MONEY

How did you get $25,000 in commitments? What did you say when you approached people?

People invest in other people. I approached people I had known for a long time, so they were investing in me. They had also been eating the cookies for a long time!

THE MARKETING

How did you advertise your grand opening?

We hosted a grand opening party on March 9, 1975, for people to taste the cookies. I put a really fun invitation together and sent it out to more than 2,500 people. I only mailed a few, because I didn't have money for 2,500 stamps. I would get employee lists from places like CBS Television, stuff the envelopes, and deliver them with cookies. I knew all the guards and everybody there, so I'd drop boxes off to the mailroom. I blanketed the city with the word that I was opening this cookie company.

How did you set up the store for the grand opening party?

We had a red carpet to the entrance, and there was a big parking lot in the back. I put artificial turf back there and had a strolling band. We had cookies and champagne, and more than 1,500 people came. The only ads I took out were Monday morning in *The Hollywood Reporter* and *Daily Variety.* I used the show business community as my mouthpiece because they have access to the world. After the party, lines began to form, and they kept forming for a very long time. Television stations, newspaper reporters, and magazine writers came. Word of mouth about the cookies spread like wildfire.

THE LOSS

You eventually lost the company in 1989, after being in business for fourteen years. What happened?

I lost control. Being famous isn't important; it's the team of people that helps you succeed. That's important. I didn't know that. I was this cocky guy. Everybody was praising me, and I became famous so rapidly. I was selling cookies in Bloomingdale's and Macy's. I was in the Macy's Thanksgiving Day Parade four years in a row. I was on the cover of *Time* magazine, and I was on every television show.

What exactly happened to cause you to lose the company?

I didn't have any capital. The first day I started, I was broke. I started with a $25,000 investment, and it was gone when I opened the door. I had to generate cash every day to keep the doors open. As we became more popular, the business was never sound enough to support all of the exposure. By 1985, we were taking on investors, and by 1989, I had no equity left in the company. Eventually the Shansby Group had taken over, and we couldn't get along. They didn't want to pay my salary or have me in on it. So I chose to leave the company.

And you're still in a situation where you can't use the Famous Amos name, correct?

Famous Amos sued me in 1992, and the suit was settled in 1994. The long and short of it is that Famous Amos is now owned by Kellogg's. They have the rights to the name Wally Amos for food.

THE REBIRTH

Now you have a new cookie company, Chip & Cookie. Tell us about it.

It's a great concept, easy to replicate, easy to manage, and relatively cost-effective. It has the potential to be a series of stores, whether they're franchised or licensed. But my goal right now is to have this one store on Oahu in Kailua be successful and open a second store in Waikiki. I'm putting a business plan together, meeting with banks, and a minority business development center. I'm going to put more structure into this and get more people involved. I'm working diligently on building a strong foundation because the product is second to none.

Wally Amos has not had an easy life. But he doesn't let life's struggles get him down. "A lot of people get mired down in it. They tell all their friends how bad life is," he said. "But you've got to just keep going. I've got a friend who says, 'When you're going through hell, don't stop to take pictures!'" In fact, the struggles he's gone through have helped him become a better and stronger person—someone who is always friendly, always helpful, and always reaching out to others.

Amos believes everything he's gone through has had a purpose.

"Each experience was vital to get me to where I am today," he says. "Life is like a mathematical equation. If you change anything, even the smallest part, you will change the answer. If I had done Famous Amos differently, I might not be here. But I'm alive, healthy, and have been living in Hawaii for twenty-nine years. I have no regrets at all."

THE PLAN TO FOLLOW

STEP 1

First, check with your local health department to find out the requirements for opening a store selling cookies or baked goods in your area.

STEP 2

Put a business plan together. The plan should cover what you are going to do, how you are going to do it, and how much it will cost.

STEP 3

Then secure the funding or commitments from investors to fund your business.

NOTE: Amos suggests that you first approach individuals who you have known for a long time because people not only invest in business, they invest in the person as well.

STEP 4

Find a location that has enough traffic to support your business. Then research the industry to find out what type of equipment you need.

NOTE: Amos suggests that you purchase bowls, scales, mixers, ovens, refrigerators, and a worktable.

STEP 5

Hold a grand opening party, and invite influential people.

NOTE: Amos suggests that you advertise your event with the local media, and hand deliver invitations with cookie samples.

THE HIGHLIGHTS

- Create a business plan to outline what you want to do and how much it will cost to do it.
- Brand your product to create an identity for it.
- Encourage word-of-mouth marketing by allowing people to sample your product.
- Stay in control of your business and carefully select employees who will help you succeed.
- Never give up. Learn from your mistakes, and keep on going.

THE RESOURCES

MORE INFORMATION ABOUT WALLY AMOS

Chip & Cookie
www.chipandcookie.com
This is the website for Wally Amos' new chocolate chip cookie company. The store is located in Kailua, Hawaii, at 609 Kailua Road. For details, call 808-261-1811.

www.wallyamos.com
This is Wally Amos' personal website.

BOOKS BY WALLY AMOS

The Famous Amos Story: The Face that Launched a Thousand Chips [1983]

The Power in You: Ten Secret Ingredients to Inner Strength [1988]

Man with No Name: Turn Lemons into Lemonade [1994]

Watermelon Magic: Seeds of Wisdom, Slices of Life [1996]

The Cookie Never Crumbles: Inspirational Recipes for Every Day Living [2002]

Be Positive!: Insights into How to Live an Inspiring and Joy-filled Life [2006]

The Power of Self-Esteem: How to Discover and Fulfill Your Life Dreams by Wally Amos and Stu Glauberman [2006]

Live an Inspiring Life: 10 Secret Ingredients for Inner Strength by Wally Amos and Stu Glauberman [2006]

RETAIL SPACE: HOW TO FIND A GREAT LOCATION

Walters, Shari. "Choosing a Retail Store Location."
http://retail.about.com/od/location/a/selecting_site.htm
This short article is about choosing a location and offers links to related topics.

PURCHASING EQUIPMENT FOR A STORE

An Internet search for "food service equipment" will yield a variety of websites where you can order equipment for your store.

Equipment Buying Guides
www.webstaurantstore.com/orderingguides.html
This website offers a series of guides about how to purchase equipment for a restaurant or store.

BUSINESS PLANS

Yahoo! Small Business
http://smallbusiness.yahoo.com/r-article-a-70122-m-1-sc-13-write_a_business_plan_to_succeed-i

HEALTH DEPARTMENT INFORMATION

For information from your state health department, run an Internet search with your state's name.

U.S. Department of Health & Human Services
www.hhs.gov

FINDING MONEY FOR YOUR BUSINESS

America's Home Business Funding Directory
www.businessfinance.com
Search this website for business loan and capital source information.

U.S. Small Business Administration
www.sba.gov
This website offers tips on starting, expanding, and financing your small business.

EMPLOYEES

U.S. Department of Labor—Minimum Wage
www.dol.gov/dol/topic/wages/minimum wage.htm

Minimum Wage Laws in States
www.dol.gov/esa/minwage/america.htm

MARKETING

Quick Biz Builder
www.quickbizbuilder.com
This site is for those who want to build their own websites.

VistaPrint
www.vistaprint.com
This is an inexpensive resource for creating business cards, postcards, flyers, and more.

Proforma
www.proforma.com
This company offers custom promotional products, business forms, commercial print solutions, and more.

FRANCHISING

Williams, Patricia. "Business Tips: Finding a Financial Backer."
www.smallbusinessbible.org/howtostart.html
This in-depth article talks about starting a franchising business, and offers links to additional articles.

Millionaire Blueprints *neither endorses nor recommends any of the companies listed in the resource section. Resources are intended as a starting point for your research.*

Tito
BEVERIDGE

How a geologist-turned-distiller made a $5 million splash in the volatile Texas vodka market, one bottle at a time.

BUSINESS NAME:
Tito's Handmade Vodka

TYPE OF BUSINESS:
Microdistillery

LOCATION:
Luling, TX

ADAPTED FROM:
Millionaire Blueprints magazine article,
"Spirit of Success,"
August 2005

*B*urt Butler Beveridge II entered the beverage business with the introduction of "Tito's Texas Handmade Vodka," which he's now shortened to "Tito's Handmade Vodka." On a whim one day, Beveridge made a case of habañero chile-flavored vodka for his friends. The hot, spicy spirit, served icy from the freezer, was such a hit that he had to explore its commercial possibilities.

Beveridge says his distillery is the first and only legal one in Texas. In his first full year of business, he produced 2,150 cases of vodka and sold it mostly by word of mouth. And in 2004, Tito's made and sold 57,000 cases to the tune of $5 million.

How did Beveridge score such amazing success with his handmade vodka in the face of such formidable odds? Just follow his lead, and build your success one bottle at a time.

THE CHALLENGE

What were some of your initial challenges to getting started in the vodka business?

Nearly everything I've done was "against the odds"—especially selling vodka in Texas. Having a legal distillery in Texas, people said, wasn't possible, nor was getting a distributor, which you have to have for a microdistillery.

I was told "no" more times than I can count. I'd go door-to-door. I'd ride along with a distributor's sales representative. He'd do his thing, then introduce me to the store manager, and I'd tell him about Tito's. If I could get a liquor store interested in trying it, they'd do a free tasting. But in Texas, it's against the law to advertise free tastings. Even that was hit and miss.

THE RECIPE

Tell us about Uncle Phil's method, his recipe, and how you formulated "Tito's Handmade Vodka."

Uncle Phil's idea of making vodka was to buy bottles of the best name brand and put a flavoring agent in it. The habañero chili was the best. He'd just push the pepper in and let the bottle sit around for a while. When I made about twelve bottles for friends that way, they loved it. They said, "You gotta sell this stuff."

How did you go from Uncle Phil's method to handmade vodka?

I knew how to make beer. I'd experimented with home brew—cooking it in the kitchen and cooling it down in the bathtub. Plus, I'm a trained geophysicist, so science is my thing. One of the smartest things I did was talk to people at the local liquor stores. They know what's hot and what's not.

So, I headed to the science library at the University of Texas. This was before the Internet. And since I had made beer, I could take a somewhat educated look at distillation methods and equipment in the reference books.

THE PROCESS

Why did you decide to use pot stills for creating vodka?

I thought it would work well since pot stills have stood the test of time. Also, I wanted to control the quality. After I started putting money into the idea of a handmade vodka business, I did a market study and a business plan.

Could you explain the distillation process and describe your pot still?

Distillation is basically a series of sequences involving heating a liquid, evaporating it, cooling the vapor for condensation, re-evaporating, and re-condensation.

In my still, each re-condensation from the previous vapor state achieves a higher alcohol concentration. That's because alcohol in the vapor is at a higher concentration than it was in the liquid mixture from which it was vaporized. So we cook fermented corn mash with water in the pot, heat it up for evaporation and condensation, and do it all over again. The basic advantage of a pot still is the simplicity—simple equipment with cooking, fermentation, and boiling for distillation all in the same pot.

THE MONEY

Did you buy the setup or make it?

I made it. I found a few suppliers at first, but the cost was really high, maybe $8,000 each. I made hybrids of copper or stainless steel and fit them all together with Teflon tape. You can get everything at the big-box home improvement stores. There are diagrams in all the books about distilling, and you can find some on the Internet.

All of these processes are very hands-on and personal. That goes for making the stills and for making the vodka. It's lonely work and, at first, I was making it, bottling it, packing it, and loading cases by myself. I couldn't afford any help. I never could get any investors.

How did you finance the startup?

I used credit cards. My strategy was to apply for every one I could, get as many as I could, and then juggle the due dates or consolidate. I got started with around $70,000 at a very high interest rate.

Did you try to find investors?

I never knew there was any other way to start a business. I made so many proposals to investors, investment bankers, and "angels." I talked to family and friends—basically anybody I thought would be a possibility. Nearly everyone was nice, but I raised zero. One guy told me I'd never get a distillery permit, because there had never been a legal distillery in Texas. Well, we got one, and we were the first legal distillery in Texas.

THE BUSINESS

Did you try to work out of your house for a while, and is that legal?

No, it's not, and there wouldn't have been enough space. I tried to rent a warehouse, but nobody would rent to me because they thought I would blow up their property. I bought the cheapest piece of dirt in Austin, and I was the realtor on the transaction. No commission. I paid $3,000 for the down payment and closing costs, and I paid $409 a month. We hooked up the water and sewer lines ourselves, and built the first building.

What ingredients do you buy?

We buy corn. We did our own fermenting at first, but now we have producers in the Grain Belt who ferment corn for us and ship it down here. We use about 120,000 bushels a year, or roughly two bushels per case of Tito's.

THE LEGAL

Tell us about permitting and licensing for alcohol in Texas. Does the health department do inspections at the stills?

I got my permits from the Texas Alcohol Beverage Commission (TABC) and the Bureau of Alcohol, Tobacco and Firearms (ATF). The Department of Health argues with me every year about whether vodka is a food. They win, and I pay $500. We're permitted by the ATF, which costs $5,000. Our TABC permit runs $2,000 each year.

They keep a close eye on you when you are starting out, and they can do a site visit whenever they want. They do audits of paperwork, excise taxes, and make sure you're not shipping out the back door. These regulations are different in every state. Also, we are monitored by the Environmental Protection Agency for water and air quality—and there are city, state, and county environmental rules and taxes.

THE DISTRIBUTION

How did you get Tito's Handmade Vodka distributed?

At the time, there were only two major distributors in Texas because a big consolidation had just happened. Then I found a little wine distributing company in Houston called Grand Crew that told me they wanted to expand into spirits. So Tito's began distributing out of Houston, and they got us into some of the major Texas chains—Majestic, Centennial, Big Daddy's, and more.

It's still an uphill battle for microdistilleries—or mom-and-pop wineries and microbreweries—in the big-brand marketplace. Getting one of these multimillion-dollar distributors to pick you up is virtually impossible. It took me almost two years to convince Glazer's Wholesaler Distributors. And after two years, they realized I wasn't going to stop coming back. The only way I would stop was if they gave me a contract.

THE MARKETING

How do you advertise? Do you have a sales staff?

In the liquor industry, advertising absolutely works, but it's expensive. I designed our logo and our label, and the people at the state school, which is a mental health/mental retardation facility, make our labels. A couple of times a year, I run over to some radio stations and record a couple of commercials that I've written. We run a print ad now and then, but I don't really do much advertising. Our website (**www.titos-vodka.com**) has turned out to be a great way to reach people too. We rely on effective distribution and a really excellent reputation.

THE PLAN TO FOLLOW

STEP 1

Experiment to find the alcohol formula that customers will buy.

NOTE: Beveridge used his uncle's method of distilling, as well as habañero chili peppers, to create his vodka. Beveridge also suggests speaking with liquor store owners for their advice on what types of drinks are trendy.

STEP 2

Choose the method for distilling your liquor. For handmade vodka, purchase materials necessary for building pot stills, or buy the stills from a supplier.

NOTE: Beveridge mentions that today's commercial distilleries use column stills, which are petrochemical-type stills. Beveridge says he was surprised that his method isn't used as much. For the handmade experience, he suggests the pot stills.

STEP 3

Acquire the necessary permits and licenses to run a distillery.

NOTE: Beveridge became owner of the first legal distillery in his state. To obtain a permit, contact your state's Alcoholic Beverage Commission as well as the Bureau of Alcohol, Tobacco and Firearms. Regulations and fees differ per state.

STEP 4

Work toward getting your liquor brand distributed.

NOTE: It is an uphill battle for mom-and-pop distilleries in this multi-million-dollar industry. But Beveridge proved that if you have a good product and a lot of determination, it can happen.

THE HIGHLIGHTS

- Unique products are a big thing now. People will pay more for something that is handmade or special.
- Research and apply for the correct permits and licenses.
- Try to get investors to finance your company. Credit cards are risky, even though they worked for Beveridge.
- Save money by doing it yourself—distilling, designing, and advertising.

THE RESOURCES

MORE INFORMATION ABOUT TITO BEVERIDGE
Tito's Handmade Vodka
www.titos-vodka.com
Using his uncle's recipe as a base, Tito makes spicy spirits at Texas' first and oldest distillery.

EQUIPMENT
American Distilling Institute
www.distilling.com
Hosts a collection of progressive beverage, medical, and aromatic distillers, and disseminates professional information on the distilling process.

Brewhaus America
www.brewhaus.com
Has been shipping worldwide to homebrewers and the distilling industry since 1992.

Anon. *Building a World Class Distillation Apparatus: A Step-by-step Guide.*
www.moonshine-still.com
This e-book will guide you in the required hardware for making distilled spirits.

Copper Moonshine Stills
www.coppermoonshinestills.com
Custom, handcrafted copper stills.

SUPPLIES
Homebrew Heaven
www.homebrewheaven.com
Online store for everything you would ever possibly need to make your own brew.

The Home Distiller
www.homedistiller.org
Includes information about all processes in home distillation.

COMMERCIAL BEVERAGE EQUIPMENT LISTINGS
www.ebay.com

www.business.com

www.cocktails.com

www.shopping.com

LIQUOR DISTRIBUTORS AND RETAILERS
The Charmer-Sunbelt Group
www.charmer-sunbelt.com

Glazer's Wholesale Distributors
www.glazers.com

National Wine & Spirits, Inc.
www.nwscorp.com

Planet Liquor
www.planetliquor.com
This is a wine and spirits portal to distributors, retailers, e-businesses, advertising and marketing, software and services, trade consultants, trade fair and exhibitors, and design specialists.

INDUSTRY RESOURCES ONLINE
American Beverage Licensees (ABL)
www.ablusa.org
The monthly *ABL Insider*, an e-newspaper, reports on industry issues for America's beer, wine, and spirits retailers and is delivered to over 18,000 ABL members and industry associates nationwide.

The Distilled Spirits Council
of the United States, Inc. (DISCUS)
www.discus.org
DISCUS is a national trade association representing producers and marketers of distilled spirits sold in the United States. Member products include the full spectrum of distilled spirits, such as bourbon, scotch, and other whiskeys, as well as vodka, gin, tequila, rum, brandy, cordials, and liqueurs.

National Association of Alcoholic Beverage Licensing Attorneys
www.naabla.com
This site is a resource for its members, the national bar, and the industry to assist in locating experienced attorneys in each state.

World Association of the Alcohol Beverage Industries
www.waaabi.org

IMPORTANT AGENCIES
The Bureau of Alcohol, Tobacco, Firearms and Explosives (ATF)
www.atf.gov

Department of Health and Human Services (HHS)
www.hhs.gov

Environmental Protection Agency (EPA)
www.epa.gov

U. S. Department of Agriculture (USDA)
www.usda.gov

Millionaire Blueprints *neither endorses nor recommends any of the companies listed in the resource section. Resources are intended as a starting point for your research.*

Curt
JONES

How a microbiologist turned his professional knowledge into an astronomical future.

BUSINESS NAME:
Dippin' Dots

TYPE OF BUSINESS:
Novelty Concessions, Ice Cream

LOCATION:
Paducah, KY

ADAPTED FROM:
Millionaire Blueprints magazine article,
"Pelletized Profit,"
June 2005

W*ith the creation of Dippin' Dots, the pelletized ice cream, microbiologist Curt Jones managed to create an entrepreneur's dream product. This popular success has equaled financial rewards that have led to an award-winning franchise system with thousands of locations in theme parks, water parks, stadiums, arenas, shopping malls, and movie theatres around the globe.*

Jones earned a bachelor's and a master's degree in microbiology. Then he landed a job with Alltech Biotechnology in Nicholasville, Kentucky. There, he helped start a feed division for growing special bacteria. One step in this process of creating probiotics was to quick freeze the bacteria cultures into a powder. The object was to form the smallest ice crystals possible in order to more completely preserve the bacteria in its freshest state. That's when a completely new idea came to him.

He decided to take a leap, and he landed among the leaders of the global marketplace for ice cream products.

THE BEGINNING

How did it all begin?

I put homemade ice cream through the same freezing process that I had devised for the bacteria. We started making this new concoction in the garage and letting people try it.

THE PRODUCTION

Where did you get the equipment?

I made it. Our equipment was basic with few moving parts. When we grew, we had to have more moving parts for automation. For those, we had to have pieces made to fit the design.

How did your production operation and shipping change along the way?

We made ice cream in a 24-foot-by-24-foot garage with a sealed concrete floor for a year or two. We put a liquid nitrogen tank outside and a cooler to hold the mix. We also did all of our own trucking and distribution.

Where did you get the money it took to get your first store open?

We came up with $80,000 or so of our own money that it took to get started.

With credit cards, we paid ourselves our living expenses by cash advances.

Then finally, we worked with a realtor, found a 2,000-square-foot abandoned building, and then we moved production.

How did you handle distribution and keep the product frozen?

We built an insulated box that held 200 gallons. We bought some old freezers from the neighbors and used dry ice or liquid nitrogen to haul the ice cream in a truck.

Who did you try to distribute through at first?

We distributed through Opryland USA in Nashville, Tennessee. After two years, we spent about $5,000 to overhaul a building they had in order to get better placement. They received 25 to 32 percent of our sales over the years.

So describe your production operation now.

In 1995, we built a 26,000-square-foot plant. It has since quadrupled in size. Our volume right now is about two million gallons a year in Paducah, and a plant in South Korea now makes 250,000 gallons a year.

THE BUSINESS

How did all this change as Dippin' Dots got more popular?

We bought a pallet reefer, which is like a big box with a door on it. It's insulated, and you can load product in it with a fork lift or pallet jack. On top, there's a place to fill it with CO_2. That allows you to keep the product for about four days for shipping purposes. You can buy CO_2 and liquid nitrogen from gas companies.

Is that when you started the dealership network?
The dealership network was a license to buy the equipment to keep and sell our product. The dealership license was a contract that we use to license them with the right to use our logo.

Next, you entered the international market. How did that come about?
In 1995, we were approached at a trade show by a Japanese company called Itochu Trading Company. We wondered whether it could make the trip if we used enough dry ice. We tested this theory in our back lot. When we made it the fifteen days it would take to ship and distribute, we made our first international shipment to Tokyo.

What do you have to do to ship something like that internationally?
We have a container that electrically cools to about fifty degrees below zero, and it costs around $9,000 with 7,000 gallons in it. The shipping cost per gallon actually came down.

THE NEED

What is the key to making it work?
The key to making it work was to get people to try it. If people tried it, they wanted it more and more.

THE EXPANSION

How did you do at the Dade County Fair?

It was 1990, and we made $14,000 at the fair. Now we do about $100,000 at that fair. We took a dipping cabinet and a kiosk, so they gave us a second location.

When did you know that Dippin' Dots was really taking off?

In 1992, we got into the Kennedy Space Center. At the 1991 International Association of Amusement Parks and Attractions (IAAPA) show, we met the food service people at NASA. We took samples, and they liked it. We provided them with a kiosk in their colors, and we had to call our product Space Dots.

THE PROFIT

After you saw success, what did you do from there?

From the IAAPA show we got into the Whitewater Water Park in Marietta, Georgia. It is now a Six Flags Park. A fair is shorter, usually ten days or two weeks. A water park is all summer long, so you can leave your equipment in place for several months.

What do you need to have in order to be a concessions vendor at a park like this?

You need a unique product and a way, or place, to sell it. You need signage and health department approvals once you set up, and sometimes you need labor.

How much does it cost to be in an amusement park?

Typically, somewhere around 40 or 50 percent goes to the park. To set up at one location, it costs around $10,000.

THE FRANCHISE

How did franchising come about?

Most franchise sales were from someone contacting us. They would see it somewhere and want to sell it.

How did your franchises do?

Entrepreneur's January 2005 issue ranked Dippin' Dots number 93 among the top 500 franchise companies in the United States. Dippin' Dots also moved up to number two in *Entrepreneur's* listing of the "Top Fifty New Franchise Companies." We debuted on the list at number one in 2002, and we remain the highest-ranking food franchise.

THE MARKETING

Tell us about your marketing budget and strategies.

At first, everything we did was internally generated. Most of our advertising and marketing was location and demonstration.

Initially, what publicity did you get?

We got press because we were so different. A couple of TV stations did stories.

What else did you do to market your product?

We went to the trade show for the International Association of Amusement Parks and Attractions (IAAPA) in 1989. First we contacted them and leased a ten-foot-by-ten-foot booth for about $1,000. Then, we got a kiosk from Staging Techniques in Atlanta.

Have things changed?

We're now placing ads in teen magazines and other places, and we're also now doing promotions at places like Universal Studios.

THE LEGAL

What did you have to do legally?
First, there were tax permits, and then a permit from the health department. I also met with the Milk Board. All production equipment was inspected at the state level.

Was there USDA involvement?
We had to apply for USDA approval.

THE ADVICE

What is your advice for others who have a unique idea for the concessions industry?
Once you are sure you have a good product, start exposing it to friends and family—and ask for honest feedback. Figure out what field tests you need to do. Talk to other people to get impressions of the market you are going to try to reach, but make the decisions yourself. Above all, follow your gut instinct. This will always be your best guide.

THE PLAN TO FOLLOW

STEP 1

Test market your product. Getting it out in front of people. Asking for their honest opinion will help you gauge potential interest. They must have an opportunity to sample your product.

STEP 2

Contact your local health department to find out what local and state requirements exist for food services.

STEP 3

Protect yourself legally by adhering to guidelines in setup and in future business contracts and agreements. Hiring an attorney should be a priority once you have determined that you are going forward with your venture.

STEP 4

Go where the people are. Look for trade shows, fairs, and amusement parks—any venue where you can get your product in front of people. If possible, you should have a kiosk with your identifying art. This will benefit you exponentially and will be useful time and time again.

STEP 5

Don't settle. Curt Jones could have settled for Lexington and the original store he had there. Instead, he took Dippin' Dots to new heights when he soared with NASA, and he continues to expand his territory, crossing international borders to bring his ground-breaking dessert treat to people everywhere.

THE HIGHLIGHTS

- You can start a business with a good idea if your test market is successful.
- Good placement with high traffic is necessary for your success.
- Look for venues to provide sampling opportunities. Getting people to try the product is the way to sell it.
- Be persistent to get your product out there, even if you have pitfalls. You have to know that it is something people will want.
- Go to your local health department for requirements and permits, and hire an attorney to attend to all legal matters.

THE RESOURCES

International Association of Amusement Parks and Attractions
www.iaapa.org

Staging Techniques
www.stagingtechniques.com

USDA
www.USDA.gov

INFORMATION ABOUT FESTIVALS, FAIRS, AND THEME PARKS

The Festival Network
www.festivalnet.com
The website publishes information about more than fifteen thousand music festivals, craft shows, art festivals, and fairs throughout the United States and Canada. Festival Network memberships start at forty-nine dollars a year.

Miami-Dade County Fair
To speak to someone regarding the rental of facilities at the Miami-Dade County Fair, call 786-315-5266.

Theme Parks Online
www.themeparksonline.org
This online resource for gathering information about nearly every entertainment park in America lists parks by state in alphabetical order. Beneath each state you will find the parks.

FINDING THE RIGHT BUSINESS LOCATION

www.125aday.com

www.amazon.com

www.shoppingcenters.com
Shopping mall carts and kiosks are a far less expensive alternative than the huge startup cost of leasing or buying permanent retail space. Look to these websites for information specifically for the United States and Canada.

SPORTS STADIUM AND FOOD VENDOR INFORMATION

http://beta.collectingchannel.com/?page= welcome/stadiums
This website has a listing of sports stadiums nationwide and their food vendor contact information.

DIRECTORY OF VENTURE CAPITAL FIRMS

My Capital
www.mycapital.com
This website offers a free directory of venture capital firms, searchable by state. The database of private equity investors covers more than three thousand private equity, venture capital and buyout firms throughout the United States, Europe, and Asia.

U.S. Small Business Administration
www.sba.gov

FINDING THE RIGHT EQUIPMENT AND SUPPLIES

Chefs Bazaar
www.chefsbazaar.com
This is a good website for finding just about any equipment you might need for your new food business, ranging from garbage disposal units to cabinets to freezers.

HOW TO INCREASE MARKET SHARE

First Research
www.firstresearch.com
This affordable online resource with food industry profiles offers industry-specific reports and market analysis for individual use.

Millionaire Blueprints *neither endorses nor recommends any of the companies listed in the resource section. Resources are intended as a starting point for your research.*

Paula
LAMBERT

How an American entrepreneur with a passion for fresh mozzarella brought home a slice of Italian culture and now serves up millions in the cheese business.

BUSINESS NAME:
The Mozzarella Company

TYPE OF BUSINESS:
Cheese Factory

LOCATION:
Dallas, TX

ADAPTED FROM:
Millionaire Blueprints magazine article,
"Mozzarella Millions,"
October 2005

P aula Lambert first learned to make mozzarella by hand while she was overseas in Italy. Lambert soon became as enamored of the process as she was of the product. Starting with fresh milk each morning, the mozzarella was ready to sell in the afternoon. Lambert felt this idea would catch on in her native Dallas, Texas, especially if she could capture the charm of Italian life and link it with the cheese's unique, farm-fresh taste.

But when she opened her cheese factory in Dallas, Lambert was the only one eating The Mozzarella Company's fresh mozzarella every day. That is, until the American cuisine scene began to embrace gourmet cooking and artisan-crafted products.

The Mozzarella Company now makes 250,000 pounds of cheese annually. Lambert says her multimillion-dollar business started the way many businesses do—with a dream.

THE BEGINNING

What took you to Italy in the first place?

After college, I convinced my parents to let me learn to speak Italian in Italy. I applied, and I was accepted at a fabulous language university in Perugia.

How did the concept for The Mozzarella Company come about?

That started with a Christmas visit to see our Italian friends, Suzanne and Enrico Bartolucci. The Bartoluccis served a salad containing fresh mozzarella for lunch. That was my lightbulb moment. We could get good Italian wines back home and imported dried pastas, but we couldn't buy fresh mozzarella. I told Suzanne about my idea, and she became one of the two silent partners I have on the spot. The other partner is my friend, Carole Jordan. The three of us invested $50,000 for the startup of The Mozzarella Company.

So what did you do first?

Our friends took us down to the local cheese factory, and I asked the owner, Mauro Brufani, if I could watch them make mozzarella. After a few days of watching, I asked Mauro if he would teach me to make mozzarella. I bought a pair of rubber boots and a little white cotton cheese-maker's hat, and I went to the Caseificio Brufani (Brufani Cheese Factory) at 6:00 AM sharp for three weeks.

Did you tell Brufani what you were up to?

When I told him of my plans, he called a young Italian professor he knew who taught the science and technique of cheese-making. Before I went home, I made arrangements for Professor Giovanni Marchesi to help me design a Brufani-style cheese factory in Dallas.

THE BUSINESS

How did you find a location for your factory?

I went to city hall and found out that a cheese factory requires industrial zoning. Most of the industrial sites were in the suburbs, or in some pretty undesirable parts of south Dallas. Then I noticed an industrial zone called Deep Ellum. As I drove the streets looking for a factory location, I saw a storefront—a classic butcher shop. I went in to talk to them. As luck would have it, they owned a nearby vacant corner drugstore. It was for lease.

How did you go about evaluating this space to see if it would work for the cheese business?

I got the blueprints and called Giovanni. I liked the location because I felt it had the potential for growth and walk-in traffic. In a day or two, Giovanni had received and reviewed the blueprints. So we talked again, and I signed the lease.

What else did you have to do before you could open?

I had a modest business plan, hoping to sell a hundred pounds of mozzarella a week. I compiled a list of local and regional contacts—restaurants, groceries, gourmet shops, and chefs—for my sales calls.

I also reviewed information on licensing, permitting, and inspections from the Food and Drug Administration, as well as from the city and state health departments. And we had to completely remodel the building and install the equipment.

THE INGREDIENTS

What kind of equipment did you have to buy?
Timing and temperature sensitivity are the most critical elements in cheese-making, so we ordered the best heat sources, refrigerators, thermometers, and timers we could find, as well as specialized equipment and utensils.

How did you find suppliers for cheese ingredients?
Our key supply need is milk. For cheese-making, we use fresh-off-the-farm raw milk. Through a list of local dairy farmers and dairy suppliers, I met a dairy equipment salesman in Fort Worth. He helped me not only in finding high-quality used equipment; he also introduced me to people in the dairy business.

THE CHEESE

Did your unique goal of reproducing a "foreign" product for U.S. markets present any unusual challenges?
I'd say the uniqueness of fresh mozzarella proved to be the most daunting challenge. It turned out that the concept was about two years ahead of trends in American cuisine toward fresh, handmade, globally inspired food.

So being a trendsetter isn't all it's cracked up to be?
Well, it wasn't for me—at first anyway. I went personally to specialty grocery stores. Store managers seemed interested, but at first they would

only buy about five pounds, or ten balls, of fresh mozzarella. I would schedule an enthusiastic return visit, and I'd ask, "How many pounds today?"
They'd say, "I have nine out of ten balls still left." This went on for months,
and I was losing money.

So I went back to Italy to see Giovanni. I returned home with the ability
to make excellent new cheeses such as ricotta and caciotta.

Did that help you turn it around?

Yes, and I also began making all the deliveries and talking more with the
old and potential customers. They represented a new breed of chefs, and
each was determined to offer Dallasites access to new and unique tastes. I
didn't realize that a lot of big cities were just beginning to experience the
same thing.

How did you find out that this new trend was beginning all over the United States?

I entered my cheeses in a competition of the American Cheese Society.
I was thrilled to win several awards in the handmade cheese competition.
Later that year, I went to a symposium of the American cuisine in San
Francisco. I took coolers loaded with my new Italian cheeses that I passed
out. It turned out to be pivotal for the success of The Mozzarella Company
because I met a lot of people who were eager to become my new customers—regardless of how far and how fast I would have to ship them
fresh, artisan cheeses.

So the challenge then became keeping up with new orders?

The daunting challenge was threefold. We had to make enough cheese.
We had to negotiate with air carriers for the best price and fastest turn-
around for fresh cheese delivery. And we had to stay on top of the critical
distribution, shipping, and delivery part of our business.

THE MARKETING

How do you market your product and get new customers? What is your advertising strategy now?

My website (**www.mozzco.com**) is really useful for promoting our cheeses. It's quick and direct, so that old and potential customers alike can see what's new. We have an online store, which features some of my best marketing ideas for retail sales.

What are some of those ideas?

We make cheese sampler boxes and cheese gift baskets. The gift baskets often include a Mozzarella Company cap or T-shirt, or some related gourmet foods. We also always make seasonal cheeses with holiday themes.

Do you have a sales effort for your wholesale customers, or do you also rely on the website?

I have had success with some inexpensive postcard direct mail. Each postcard highlights a new cheese or a reminder of a popular cheese. For the wholesale crowd, we do a bit of telemarketing.

Finally, keeping the product interesting, providing high quality, as well as delivering on time, are part of our successful marketing. We're reliable, and we always have something new.

THE PLAN TO FOLLOW

STEP 1

Before venturing into creating your own food product, get some real hands-on experience by learning from an existing company.

NOTE: Lambert volunteered at a local cheese factory while on an extended vacation in Italy. She says that had it not been for the factory owner's willingness to teach her, The Mozzarella Company would not be as authentic as it is.

STEP 2

When looking for a location for your factory, research your area's industrial zoning regulations. Look for an area that will be conducive to the growth of your company.

NOTE: Lambert studied zoning maps for her area and went to city hall to research any requirements for running a cheese factory. She also chose her factory location because of the potential the area held for future growth, as well as for the walk-in traffic to her store.

STEP 3

Purchase the necessary equipment, and connect with suppliers to equip your factory with the right ingredients.

NOTE: Lambert mentions that the equipment for a cheese company defines the layout of the factory. She also suggests doing an Internet search for suppliers in your local area.

STEP 4

Devise a marketing plan.

NOTE: Because Lambert was on the cutting edge of the introduction of gourmet food, she worked to expand her product line in order to boost business. Lambert also found success by adding gift baskets and a monthly club membership for customers.

THE HIGHLIGHTS

- Food products are part of a lucrative industry. There will always be a need for food.
- When recreating an authentic food product, find a mentor to help guide your steps to keep it authentic.
- Public information is freely available from your city hall to find the best location for your factory.
- The Internet is a great way to find suppliers and the equipment you need for your business.
- Market to your customers through their appetites. Good food is a great incentive to come back for more.

THE RESOURCES

MORE INFORMATION ABOUT PAULA LAMBERT

The Mozzarella Company
www.mozzco.com
Dallas-based cheese factory owned by Paula Lambert.

RULES, REGULATIONS, AND REQUIREMENTS

City Departments of Health: Local public health departments may require inspections and permitting for a cheese factory, especially one that offers retail sales. Check local directories or websites for specific information for your area.

U.S. Department of Agriculture
www.usda.gov

U.S. Food and Drug Administration
www.fda.gov

PROFESSIONAL ORGANIZATIONS

American Dairy Association
www.ilovecheese.com
Website managed by Dairy Management, Inc., offers recipes, a "cheese guide," entertaining tips, a cheese-maker locator, and online shopping.

National Dairy Council
www.nationaldairycouncil.org
As a leader in nutrition research and education since 1915, this website showcases nutrition and product information, health professional resources, recipes, health tips, and more.

International Dairy Foods Association
www.idfa.org
Represents: Milk Industry Foundation (MIF), National Cheese Institute (NCI), and International Ice Cream Association (IICA).

American Dairy Goat Association
www.adga.org
Offers a wide range of industry information to members, including posted events.

SUPPLIES AND SERVICES

Following are Paula Lambert's recommendations:

American Cheese Society
www.cheese.com
A searchable database committed to being the number-one resource for cheese! Website lists every cheese imaginable with background information

for each, including country of origin, texture, cheese trivia, vegetarian varieties, and more.

California Cheese and Butter Association
www.cacheeseandbutter.org
This trade organization is useful for any person, company, or organization engaged in the manufacture, sale, promotion, or distribution of cheese or butter in California.

Cheese from Spain
www.cheesefromspain.com
Compilation of cheese producers and recipes with tips on cutting, serving, preserving, and storing a wide variety of cheese.

The Cheese Reporter
www.cheesereporter.com
E-newspaper encompassing all aspects of the cheese industry, including dairy prices, events, a supplier directory, and more.

The Great Cheeses of New England
www.newenglandcheese.com
Embracing the heritage of New England cheese-making, this website offers gourmet recipes, a store locator for purchasing New England cheeses, news and events, nutrition information, and more.

Vermont Cheese Council
www.vtcheese.com
Posts events and offers e-books and newsletters all dedicated to the production and advancement of Vermont cheese.

New England Cheesemaking Supply
www.cheesemaking.org
Paula Lambert's favorite supplier.

BOOKS ABOUT CHEESE AND CHEESE-MAKING

Lambert, Paula. *The Cheese Lover's Cookbook & Guide.* New York: Simon and Schuster [2000]. Lambert's book provides many unique recipes and tips on the culinary delight known as cheese.

Anon. *Wisconsin Cheesecyclopedia.*
www.wisdairy.com/AllAboutCheese/cheese cyclopedia/default.aspx
E-book compiled by the Wisconsin Milk Marketing Board, Inc. It offers everything you ever wanted to know about Wisconsin cheese in an easily searchable format.

Millionaire Blueprints *neither endorses nor recommends any of the companies listed in the resource section. Resources are intended as a starting point for your research.*

Nadja
PIATKA

A struggling single mom found a market for her special cooking talent—and parlayed it into millions in the international food service industry.

BUSINESS NAME:
Nadja Foods

TYPE OF BUSINESS:
Low-Fat Desserts

LOCATION:
Edmonton, Alberta

ADAPTED FROM:
Millionaire Blueprints magazine article,
"Muffins to Millions,"
August 2005

329

The defining moment for Nadja Piatka came as she crouched under her dining room table with her young daughter so the bill collector who was pounding on the door couldn't see they were at home. After her twenty-year marriage ended, Piatka found herself a single mother who was "unemployed and unemployable." But as someone who always had an interest in cooking—and eating—great-tasting food, there was one thing Piatka had learned to do to keep her weight under control. She called it "recipe makeovers." Piatka's makeovers had won the acclaim of her friends and family. And they especially raved about her muffin recipes.

After that moment of supreme humiliation under the dining room table, Piatka made a list of goals on a piece of cardboard. Then, she baked several batches of her low-fat muffins, put them in her car, and drove to all of the local privately owned coffee shops in Edmonton, Alberta, where she lived. She made a deal with the shop owners. "Put my muffins on your shelves, offer people free samples, and if you sell them, pay me ten cents a muffin. Let me know if you want me to bring you more tomorrow," she said. The muffins flew off the shelves, word spread, and little by little, Nadja Piatka climbed out of debt and into the limelight as a successful entrepreneur with more than $20 million in sales for her now-famous low-fat desserts.

THE BEGINNING

Why did you think you were "unemployable?"

I sent out thirty résumés and got one interview. When I didn't pass the interview, I realized that the only person who would hire me was me. I didn't have a blueprint. I didn't know where to start.

Tell us about those goals you wrote on the cardboard from your pantyhose package.

I wrote those goals down that day and then hid the list. In a year, all but one came true. They were: I will own a national company; I will be a best-selling author; I will have my own newspaper column; I will be a public speaker; I will have my own television show; and I will bring value to people's lives.

THE MONEY

Where did you get your money to start this venture?

No money was available to me. I was in the midst of an extreme financial crash. Creditors were literally at the door every day. I just decided to bake and sell my muffins and see what happened. I dreamed big, but I started small.

THE FOOD

Where did you get your recipes?

I started experimenting in my kitchen. My first commercial product was muffins, so I would experiment with different flavors and ingredients for the basic muffin recipe. I'd call the kids to the kitchen to test each product, and when my daughter gave me a thumbs up, I knew I had a winner. Then I took them to local coffee shops.

Once you had a few coffee shops interested, what happened then?

By encouraging shop owners to offer samples, I got lots of people to try them. People were surprised that although my recipes were low fat, they also tasted pretty good and they became very successful.

When were you totally convinced that you had a successful product?

My shop owners would say, "Can you deliver every morning?" Those muffins were selling out the door.

THE BUSINESS

So what was your life like when you were baking and delivering to your local coffee shops every day?

I was waking up at 4:00 AM—baking, loading, and getting the muffins to all the coffee shops. At some point I realized my ability to keep growing was limited by time. I knew I could only bake so many muffins.

So how did you solve this dilemma?

I decided to outsource. I approached a little local bakery to see if I could get them to make the muffins and deliver them for me. And since they were already delivering to my customers, I wouldn't have to get up and do it. I had them sign a confidentiality agreement that I just came up with on my own. I basically said, "This is my recipe, and I'm letting you use it." After I got bigger, I had a lawyer write up an agreement.

How did you know how to set your prices and percentages?

I had them price it for me. Because of their volume, they could price it better, including labor. I took a percentage spread. If it cost thirty cents to make, I would charge forty cents, and so I would make ten cents per muffin. I had been working hard, but not smart, and this way I ended up with much higher margins.

Would your startup strategy work today?

No one today is going to buy something made in someone's kitchen. You'd have to start with a proper facility, and that would be much better for your product. Outsourcing gives you more time to get customers.

THE MARKETING

How did you market your product once you began outsourcing?

The first step was to get my name out there. So I approached the newspaper. I offered to do a column of healthy "recipe makeovers." They said, "Why should we give it to you? Besides, we have no budget."

What did you do?

I offered to write it for free. Getting my face and name out there was worth much more to me than money.

What was the response?

Writing the weekly recipe makeovers was fun for me. After a while, the response was so favorable that the newspaper started paying me. I did that column for a couple of years, and it really did create and reinforce some good branding for me.

THE EXPANSION

How did you make your television show dream come true?

I started with a local television show. I got on by calling the station and setting up a meeting with their program director, and I offered to do some healthy cooking spots for them for free.

Tell us how you got into McDonald's.

We approached McDonald's locally in Edmonton. They were just coming on with a breakfast program and were looking for a great tasting muffin product. They tested our muffins in their markets, and we ended up getting their muffin business and becoming the primary muffin supplier for McDonald's Canada.

Our muffins outsold their higher-fat muffins. I sold the license to use the recipe to Quaker. Under our agreement, they were able to use the recipe. I could still use it as well.

How did you get into Subway?

Subway approached our local development agent in Calgary, Alberta. They tested it in this market, and everyone loved it. At the time, Subway was involved in their low-fat campaign—and our low-fat brownie, at three grams of fat, fit nicely in their "complete meal under ten grams of fat" program.

THE ADVICE

What do people want to know when you approach them with a recipe you'd like them to license from you?

They want to know the facts and figures of how much money it has made. It's very important that you keep up with the monthly and annual sales it generates. That is the key to its value. So, before you try to sell it, you have to generate some sales and show that it is something people want to buy.

If I have a recipe and I want to outsource the preparation of it, what do I need to have in place?

One thing to know is that no outsourcing facility will take your recipe on if you don't already have customers. They have equipment overhead and labor. Most outsourcing facilities also say that they need to know quantities relative to the size of a facility.

THE PLAN TO FOLLOW

STEP 1

Develop a recipe that stands out from the competition and one that customers will want to try.

NOTE: For her low-fat desserts, Piatka says she researched and found nonpreservative and nonadditive products like natural rice bran extract. Piatka also contacted the government to find research entities that were starting up business labs, as well as research facilities for people with food ideas.

STEP 2

Grow your customer base by selling your product through local, privately owned food stores or restaurants.

STEP 3

Get a lawyer.

NOTE: Piatka says you can't patent a recipe, so you should spend your money on protecting your name. If someone else is going to use your recipe, hire a lawyer.

STEP 4

Find a company that will outsource your recipe.

NOTE: Once you have a customer base, Piatka suggests finding a facility that will outsource your product. Have the facility set the price of the food based on labor and equipment needs. Then, Piatka suggests raising the selling price to make a profit.

STEP 5

Do what it takes to get your name out there.

NOTE: Piatka suggests doing almost anything that gets you in front of the public to sell your wares. She was able to garner free publicity for her products by volunteering her time and expertise on television and in the newspaper.

THE HIGHLIGHTS

- Create a product that people are willing to pay for.
- When developing a new recipe, friends and family can serve as your focus group.
- Hire a lawyer to protect your name and your recipe.
- Learn to use free publicity.
- Set some long-term goals, and remember that those dreams can be realized.

THE RESOURCES

Baking Management Magazine
http://bakingmanagement.bakery-net.com
This website offers information on everything from how to automate bite-sized cookie packaging, to how to maximize the lifespan of baking pans.

Baking Business
www.bakingbusiness.com
This is a grain-based foods information website that provides industry links, wholesale products, and buyers guides.

Bakery-Net
www.bakery-net.com
This website is specifically designed for owners, company officers, management, and purchasing professionals in the retail and wholesale baking industries. You will find an online magazine, information about computer systems and service, baking equipment, paper products and packaging supplies, ingredients, showcases, services and management needs, and trade shows.

The American Institute of Baking (AIB)
www.aibonline.org
AIB was founded by the North American wholesale and retail baking industries in 1919 as a technology transfer center for bakers and food processors. It currently serves many segments of the food processing, distribution, food service, and retail industries worldwide. On this site, you'll find sources for education and research, bakery management, equipment, ingredients, cereal science, nutrition, food safety and hygiene, occupational safety, and maintenance engineering.

American Society of Baking Engineers
www.asbe.org

The Retailer's Bakery Association (RBA)
www.rbanet.com
This trade organization creates industry-specific training programs, develops profit tools, and connects retailers with suppliers and experts to help build profitable bakeries.

COMPUTER SOFTWARE

Bakery Machinery & Fabrication, Inc.
www.bakerymachine.com

Stewart Systems, Inc.
www.stewartsystems.com

Food Software
www.foodsoftware.com
This site offers information on menu design software, food software, restaurant pagers and more.

ONLINE PROMOTIONAL OPPORTUNITIES

Big Baking Book
www.bigbakingbook.com
This is the American Society of Baking's new public service directory.

Virtual Showcase
www.asbe.org/exhibitors.html
This site offers quick access to industry websites.

Millionaire Blueprints *neither endorses nor recommends any of the companies listed in the resource section. Resources are intended as a starting point for your research.*

Saul
RUBIO

How a young college student from Mexico made his millionaire dreams come true by bringing Mexican cuisine and a special model of service to Southern Louisiana.

BUSINESS NAME:
La Carreta Restaurant

TYPE OF BUSINESS:
Mexican Restaurants

LOCATION:
Hammond, LA

ADAPTED FROM:
Millionaire Blueprints magazine article,
"Cooking Up Success,"
June 2005

Walking up to the shady, hacienda-style courtyard of La Carreta Restaurant in Hammond, Louisiana, you can't help but feel a little bit special. Servers greet you at the door with genuine smiles, and if you've been there before, they probably remember how you like your iced tea.

Who is the spark of genius behind this unusual model of service? A young man named Saul Rubio, who came to Hammond from the heart of Mexico to open this sleepy little college town's first Mexican restaurant. Today, after weathering the challenges of bringing a new ethnic cuisine into Cajun country, he now serves an average of 700 hungry guests every day. And Rubio didn't stop there. He has replicated his success again and again. Adobe Cantina & Salsa, which is La Carreta's sister eatery, is also in Hammond. In the surrounding area are La Carreta of Baton Rouge and La Carreta of Amite.

If you aspire to restaurant ownership, Saul Rubio is happy to tell you his secrets and show you by his remarkable example what it means to create the kind of service, quality, and atmosphere that keeps people coming back for more.

THE BEGINNING

What made you choose the restaurant business?

My family owns a small restaurant in Queretaro, Mexico, where I grew up. I learned a lot about cooking and running a restaurant and bar from them. Then, in working for several restaurants in different states here in America, I learned what Americans like in Mexican food.

So tell us about the jobs you had with that first restaurant that prepared you to open your own.

Before I was a server, I washed dishes for four months and then started cooking. It was important to me that I learn all the jobs. You have to know about the restaurant business, not just the cooking. I also learned the importance of having a talented staff.

THE MONEY

Tell us how you financed your startup.

I worked for three years at a Mexican restaurant in Milton, Florida, to save the money I needed to open my own restaurant. I made $700 a week—and I saved $500 of it.

How much did it take to start your restaurant?

I started with $35,000 that I had saved up. One of my ex employers loaned me $13,000 to start the business, and he said, "If you need more, let me know." He wanted to be a partner, but the first year of any new business is always hard, so the next year I bought him out. I was able to pay him $26,000.

THE LOCATION

Why did you choose Hammond?

Some friends told me about Hammond, that it was a growing college town, and it didn't yet have a good Mexican restaurant. I contacted the Chamber of Commerce and found out that there were several major employers in the area, so I knew there would be enough people here to support us. From a marketing standpoint, Hammond was the ideal place for a small restaurant. It would have cost a lot more money to go to a big city, and we had to start small.

What deal did you make on your building?

A businessman in the area owned the building I wanted. He leased the building to me for $2,900 per month for the first year with no contract. The second year, he raised the rent 30 percent.

THE MARKETING

Tell us about how you promoted your restaurant in town and how it was received.

The first important thing I did was go to the Chamber of Commerce. The second thing was to be nice to everyone. In many cases, that meant bringing them food so they could try it.

What else did you do?

We hosted a big Cinco de Mayo fiesta. It has now grown to become one of the biggest celebrations in town. Other projects include a CD of "Favorite Music from La Carreta," T-shirts, sauces, and we're now working on our own beer label. We are improving our website and creating a store for our sauces, CDs, and T-shirts.

THE INGREDIENTS

What have you learned after that first year about what goes on your menu and what foods your customers like?

When you get one item working very well, keep it. Chips and fresh salsa are very important. We also use a different kind of tortilla and less oil. We buy the tortillas precut and cook them here, once in the morning and once in the afternoon.

Our hot sauce is the simplest thing in our restaurant. I taste all the sauces personally. If something is wrong, I know exactly what needs to be added. We make fresh hot sauce every day.

What other ingredients have turned out to be important?

I use premium tequila for everything, and we've just started making our margaritas. It's costly, but people drive from other towns just to have one. We make the most money on the simple things.

THE BUSINESS

To serve 700 people a day must require an incredible amount of food. Tell us about your ordering system.

We place a food order daily. For fresh produce, you have to have a close supplier. We have one person who checks prices on every item, every day. Suppliers sometimes give you a good deal initially, and then raise the prices without telling you. So, if one goes up on an item, we can buy it from their competitor. For me to make money, I have to have the best price and quality on the market.

How do you find these vendors, and how do you negotiate with them?

When you first open, they call you. They want to look at your menu and see what kind of things they can sell you, and then they quote you a price. The trick is to find three or four companies to get the best price. For things other than produce, there are a lot of big food service companies to choose from. We use SYSCO and US Foods.

What are some of your best employee relations strategies?

Most of our staff is Spanish-speaking, and people like to come here to practice their Spanish with our Mexican wait staff. And for my Mexican workers who want to learn to speak English, I have a tutor come in twice a week to teach English. I also talk to them continuously about saving money and preparing for their futures.

What other things besides ordering food do you have to keep track of, and how do you do that?

In the first year, we counted by how many trays of silverware we used to estimate how many people we were serving. That was before we had a computer. Now we have a point-of-sale (POS) program that can run reports and track everything for us. With this program, I can even monitor the floor and guest checks from home.

What things, besides food and service, are critical issues in the restaurant business?

Too long a wait to get in, or not keeping your word about how long it will be. It is also important not to give specific times, because you really don't know. If the wait gets long, I send some drinks out to them while they wait. And, if the wait is really long, we may send some appetizers out as well. And we never skip anyone. We want everyone to feel special and appreciated when they choose to come to La Carreta.

THE ADVICE

What do you think is the key to your success?

It's doing what I love and having a talented staff. Customer service is also essential. Balancing time between the restaurant and my family is the hardest part. My wife knows the business well, so she understands how much time I have to spend here. But it is important to spend time with my family, too, so it is a delicate balance and sometimes quite a challenge.

THE PLAN TO FOLLOW

STEP 1

Gain experience in the particular type of restaurant you intend to open.

NOTE: Rubio says experience helps you gain knowledge.

STEP 2

Produce a business plan.

NOTE: This should include the steps you are going to take, how you are going to do them, and how much it will cost you.

STEP 3

Obtain startup funding, whether it is from your own savings, investors, or both. Make sure investors are people you trust to become part of your business.

STEP 4

Find a location that will respond to your restaurant. Look for a void and then fill it.

NOTE: Rubio found a small town that was lacking great Mexican cuisine.

STEP 5

Customer service and employee relations can make or break your business.

THE HIGHLIGHTS

- Create a business plan with your projected actions, and include all costs.
- Establish a menu with a few signature items that will keep customers coming back.
- Promote word-of-mouth marketing by letting people sample your product.
- Carefully select employees who support your vision and who will work hard to make your restaurant successful.
- Learn from your mistakes, and try new ideas.

THE RESOURCES

INDUSTRY TRACKING SURVEY

Restaurant TrendMapper
www.restaurant.org/trendmapper
This website offers a complete analysis of the National Restaurant Industry Tracking Survey, which includes data broken out by industry segment, as well as a host of other economic indicators that impact the restaurant industry.

The Restaurant Industry Forecast
www.restaurant.org
This website provides in-depth analyses of the industry's prospects and reviews trends observed throughout the industry by operators, as well as customers. It provides detailed sales projections for the restaurant and food service industry as a whole, as well as for a variety of industry segments.

RESTAURANT AND FOOD SERVICE TRADE SHOWS

www.foodinstitute.com/tradeshow/searchshow.cfm.
Visit this website for a complete list of restaurant and food service trade shows.

RESTAURANT SUPPLIERS

www.instawares.com

www.restockit.com

www.sysco.com

www.usfoodservice.com

POINT-OF-SALE (POS) PROGRAM

Micros
www.micros.com

RESTAURANT SOFTWARE

www.businesssoftware.com
This website offers a complete restaurant software package for seventy dollars, plus thirty dollars a month for support.

www.pixelpointpos.com
Visit this website for PixelPoint POS, POS, back-office, wireless, web, and enterprise software for restaurants.

www.abcs-international.com
This website offers Billpro: POS, and Wireless Restaurant, and bar software with a free thirty-day trial, and free support.

www.capterra.com
This website offers a restaurant software free directory, where you can compare restaurant management software.

www.posadvisor.com
This website offers Restaurant POS, fast and easy touch screen POS updates, Peachtree, and QuickBooks automatically.

www.valuepos.com
This site offers VPOS Restaurant Software, Restaurant Software POS, and Value POS.

www.posguys.com
This site offers Restaurant POS Software, Nextpos, RP, E, and more.

www.resttech.com
This site offers RestTech—Restaurant POS Touch-screen-driven software systems for all restaurants with good prices.

INFORMATION ABOUT OBTAINING A PRIVATE BEER LABEL

www.beeronthewall.com

www.beerlabels.com

Millionaire Blueprints *neither endorses nor recommends any of the companies listed in the resource section. Resources are intended as a starting point for your research.*

7

True Stories of
ARTS AND ENTERTAINMENT
Millionaires

Billy
CUTHRELL

How music made a difference in one man's life, and inspired him to create a place where that same gift is passed on to others.

BUSINESS NAME:
Progressive Music Center

TYPE OF BUSINESS:
Music School

LOCATION:
Raleigh, NC

ADAPTED FROM:
Millionaire Blueprints magazine article,
"A Business With A Beat,"
July/August 2007

O ur lives can change direction at any moment. For Billy Cuthrell, that moment arrived as he sat in a high school hallway after being kicked out of class for the umpteenth time. He was approached by the school's band director who wanted to know why he was always there. That impromptu conversation earned Cuthrell entry into band class and an introduction to his first drum lesson.

Learning to play percussion transformed this teen into a hardworking, focused young businessman who went on to found a successful band and an entire music school as well. The composition of Progressive Music Center began to take shape after Cuthrell stopped playing full time professionally, and decided to try teaching to earn some extra cash. Beginning with just a few students, he worked his way up to several small locations until he found a permanent home in the Raleigh-Durham area. From there, he used his combination of business and musical skills to expand and create the thriving school he runs today.

THE BEGINNING

Where did you grow up?

In North Carolina. I come from a farming family. My dad was the first in a long line of people who didn't make farming his full-time occupation. He was a Methodist minister for twenty-seven years, and then he retired to go into healthcare administration. My mom is in the healthcare industry as well.

How old were you when you started playing the drums?

I was around fourteen. I played percussion in my high school band.

THE ROCK BAND

Were you also a member of a rock band?

Yes. I started a band called Fountain of Youth in my junior year of high school.

How did you find places to play?

We got a demo tape together. We also developed our image and got some really nice band pictures together. Then we worked with an upstart management company. They began setting up shows for us, calling clubs, and acting in a management role in exchange for a percentage of each show. They also called radio stations and set up interviews for us.

Why did you leave the band?

I was ready to move on. I wanted to be the best musician I could possibly be, and I felt that getting out at that time would help me do that.

THE TEACHING

What did you do next?

I went to work at a local sod farm. The work was fine, but I was only making minimum wage. By the time I paid my rent, I had nothing left. I was still playing music, but not on that same scale. Then a buddy of mine told me he was teaching guitar lessons, so I thought maybe I could find some students of my own.

How did you find your first students?

I made a flyer on a blank piece of typing paper using pictures I clipped out of *Modern Drummer Magazine*. I kind of based it on my dad's old church bulletins. I put the flyers in local stores around town and told my friends to spread the word.

Where were you teaching the lessons?

I was going house to house. Once I got one or two kids in a neighborhood, I'd end up getting three or four more.

THE BUSINESS

How did you decide when to stop making house calls?

When I realized that I had more students than I had time. I went down to a local music store and talked to the manager about getting some space in his store. He said, "The only thing I have is this little room in the back. If you can make a go of it in there, you can have it."

Did you have to pay for the room?

No, but I was sharing it with a guitar teacher. Then, when the music store decided to move down the street, a music academy took over the space I was in. I went to them and said, "I don't want to work for you. I want to work with you." I told them, "I'm not willing to let my company go and turn all my students over to you, so can we make a deal?" I was able to keep the room I had and add one more, so I could bring on another teacher.

THE MARKETING

How did you advertise your business?

I was still doing what I consider guerilla marketing tactics—sticking the flyers wherever I could and getting them into people's hands. Even if somebody wasn't a drummer, it didn't matter to me. I figured they might know someone or would meet someone who was. I'd give them a flyer and a business card. That's still our biggest marketing tool, but now we have a nice brochure and a full color eight-page catalog. We leave stacks of them at grocery stores and places like that.

Do you ever advertise in newspapers?

Our local newspaper does a summer camp circular, so we run an ad in that each year, and we get a lot of calls from it. We do call-to-action ads that read, "Mention this ad, and get 10 percent off." This is so we can track the response. Our best advertising is our monthly e-mail newsletters to our clients.

THE LOCATIONS

What other marketing strategies have you used?

When my wife and I moved to Wilmington, North Carolina, in 1998, I went back to playing in bands. I had added another teacher, so I had time to go on the road again. When a band needed a sub, I would go in and cover the gig for them with little or no rehearsal. And once I realized I had created this niche for myself, I wrote a two-part article called "Effective Subbing" and submitted it to *Modern Drummer Magazine.* They published it and since then, I've written a few other articles for them. At the bottom, I always add my name and contact information.

What happened to your teaching business when you moved?

I opened a studio in Wilmington, too. So I was teaching in Wilmington two days a week, then in Greenville for two days, and spending two days performing on the road. I did that route for about two and a half years until I burned out.

What was the next step in your business?

We moved to Raleigh. I kept teaching in Greenville, but I turned over all my Wilmington students to other teachers, and I went down to a local Raleigh music store and asked to speak to the manager. It turned out that the manager was an old friend of mine from Greenville who I had not seen in five or six years. That reinforced another important lesson to remember. Don't ever burn a bridge. You never know who you're going to run into down the road, or who will be in a position to help you.

How did he help you?

They had several offices in the back that I turned into teaching rooms. I used some of the programs that I had developed in my other locations and started doing clinics and things like that. Within two years, I built a huge practice there at the Music Loft. If I didn't have a lesson going on, I was down on the drum floor talking to potential students.

THE SCHOOL

How did you get your own location?

I teamed up with another well-known teacher. We were both at the point where we couldn't take on any more students, so we joined forces and brought in some more teachers. After about a year and a half, our lease was dropped because they sold the music store. That was in 2001. So we moved across town. We lost some students in the process, but we ended up picking up a lot as well, because there was really no competition in the new area.

How did the company evolve from there?

The growth was tremendous because Raleigh-Durham is such a rapidly growing area. I recognized that and thought we needed to capitalize on it. I also sold the Greenville location to the guy who was running it for me, which alleviated a lot of my time constraints in traveling back and forth. I decided to incorporate, and I made Progressive Percussion Drum Studios our parent company.

Do you think you'll expand nationally?

We work with a studio down in Orlando, and with one in Tennessee, plus I receive a lot of interest from people all over the country to work with them to open schools and stores. My biggest fear is that I don't know if this company would survive a huge, rapid expansion. It will be a gradual road if we decide to move forward with that.

THE FUTURE

What do you think the future holds for you and your career in music?

Cuthrell says he still has plenty of time to explore new directions in music, and that he's always incorporating new and innovative ideas into the classes at the center. That includes videotaping students' lessons so they can download them via e-mail at home to review their performances. He says that this ties in with his goal of making each student's experience fun and challenging while they strive for musical excellence.

"I don't know if I'll be involved in the business aspect of music for the rest of my life," he said, "but I'll always play because I love it."

THE PLAN TO FOLLOW

STEP 1

Create flyers announcing that you are offering music lessons.

NOTE: Cuthrell suggests that you post flyers and hand out business cards everywhere you can. If the people who pick up the cards or flyers aren't into music, they might know someone who is.

STEP 2

Visit local music stores, and ask if you can offer lessons at their store.

NOTE: Some music stores will charge you a percentage of your intake for the space.

STEP 3

As your business grows, you can add teachers and open your own location.

THE HIGHLIGHTS

- Once you establish a business model, you can repeat it in new locations.
- Writing articles about your area of expertise, and submitting them to be published, can be a great marketing tool.
- Call-to-action advertising is an easy way to measure the results of your ad.
- Recognize growth in your area, and capitalize on it.
- Don't burn bridges. You never know who will be able to help you in the future.

THE RESOURCES

MORE INFORMATION ABOUT BILLY CUTHRELL

Billy Cuthrell / Progressive Music Center
www.progressivepercussion.com

ORGANIZATIONS

Many of the following websites contain information for all types of music educators. Look for directories, databases, and links that might help you.

Music Teachers National Association
www.mtna.org
This organization supports music teachers and promotes the study and making of music.

The National Association for Music Education
www.menc.org
This organization for music educators aims to encourage the study and making of music. Their index contains a host of links related to music education.

WHERE TO LOOK FOR YOUR STATE'S MUSIC EDUCATORS ASSOCIATION

www.menc.org.
Click on "About MENC" (at bottom left of the page.) Click on "State Music Educators Associations." Then look for your state alphabetically.
International Association for Jazz Education

www.iaje.org
This organization promotes the growth and development of jazz and jazz education.

Percussive Arts Society
www.pas.org
This organization promotes education, research, and performance of percussionists and drummers. The website also includes educator resources.

Guitar Foundation of America
www.guitarfoundation.org
This organization for guitarists provides information, resources, and teaching aids.

The National Band Association
www.nationalbandassociation.org
This professional association for band directors is dedicated to band music excellence and contains a directory of members, many of whom work at middle schools and high schools.

SHEET MUSIC

Unless you plan to write your own music, you'll need sheet music and music books for your students. Check out these companies that offer a wide variety of products—from the classics to today's top hits. Some are hard copies, and others are available for immediate download. Free sheet music is available on some sites.

The Sheet Music Company
www.sheetmusicco.com

Sheet Music Plus
www.sheetmusicplus.com

Musicnotes, Inc.
www.musicnotes.com

Sheet Music Direct
www.sheetmusicdirect.com

INSTRUMENTS—NEW AND USED

Your local music store is the best place to go for instruments, but we found a few places on the Internet that sell new and used instruments. They also carry equipment you'll need such as amplifiers, strings, stands, and metronomes.

BMC—the Music Source
www.bmcmusicsource.com

Musical Instruments
www.musicalinstruments.com

Guitar Center
www.guitarcenter.com

Guitar Stop
www.guitarstop.com
This website offers new and used guitars and accessories.

Daddy's Junky Music
www.daddys.com
This website offers new and used drums, guitars, keyboards, amps, and accessories.

Musicians Buy Line
www.musiciansbuyline.com
Site for classified ads for new and used instruments and musicians wanted.

HOW TO FIND MUSIC STORES IN YOUR AREA

The best place to look for music stores you might approach about giving lessons at their locations, as Cuthrell did, is in the *Yellow Pages*. A quick way to find local stores in your area is to search a well-known manufacturer's website such as Fender (www.fender.com), and look for dealer locations. Most sites will let you search for stores by city, state, or zip code.

OTHER MUSIC SERVICES

Clarion Associates, Inc.
www.clarionins.com
This website offers insurance for musical instruments.

TigerBill's DrumBeat
www.tigerbill.com
This website offers information and resources about drums and percussion, including free online drum lessons.

Guitar Lesson World
www.guitarlessonworld.com
This website offers free online guitar lessons and exercises.

Millionaire Blueprints *neither endorses nor recommends any of the companies listed in the resource section. Resources are intended as a starting point for your research.*

Jack
FARR

After being "bitten" by the sports car driving bug, Texas entrepreneur Jack Farr decided to fulfill a dream: the nation's first sports car country club—a place where the amateur, weekend sports car driver can let it all hang out.

BUSINESS NAME:
MotorSport Ranch

TYPE OF BUSINESS:
Sports Car Country Club

LOCATION:
Cresson, TX

ADAPTED FROM:
Millionaire Blueprints magazine article,
"Driving Force,"
March 2006

J ack Farr says that his dream was barraged with roadblocks, overwhelming skepticism, negativity, and even ridicule. "Who would want to pay money to join a sports car country club?" Farr heard the question time and time again. But against all naysayers, Farr's "If I build it, they will come" philosophy, coupled with relentless determination, resulted in MotorSport Ranch (MSR), a 300-plus acre complex seventeen miles south of Fort Worth, Texas.

The complex includes two asphalt tracks, a two-story clubhouse, and 200 garages to house the members' Ferraris, Porsches, Cobras, Vipers, Corvettes, and Mustangs—to name a few of the high-speed weekend "hot wheels."

"Some people are stuck in first gear," Farr says. "I, on the other hand, want to be in overdrive. I want to be in the left lane of life. I do not want to lie on my deathbed someday thinking I could have, should have, would have, but didn't."

THE IDEA

What gave you the idea to start a country club racing facility?

I have been riding motorcycles off-road since I was thirteen, and that experience evolved into motocross racing. I wanted to build a place to drive a fast car and a place to be with others who like to drive fast cars.

THE TRACK

Describe the complex for us.

Currently, we have two road courses. One is 1.7 miles long, and the second is 1.3 miles long.

The skid pad is 200 feet by 200 feet and basically is a patch of asphalt to be used to warm up tires, run through a couple of gears, and check the understeer.

The auto storage is currently made up of 200 garages where members store their cars or tools at the track. The covered grid pad is able to hold twenty cars while staging for the next track session. We also have a 5,000-square-foot driver's building.

What did you look for as far as land for the business?

I was looking for at least 300 acres, without too many trees, situated off a good-sized highway, with rolling hills. We like driving over hills and around turns.

So, once you bought the land, what did you do next?

I started building the safety tower and the covered grid area even before the first track was built. I called a local steel building fabricator to build the tower and staging area.

Tell us how you designed and built the first track and about the costs that were involved.

It is difficult to define the track itself, but it includes dirt work, lime stabilization, 400,000 tons of flex base rock underneath the asphalt, the two layers of asphalt itself, the concrete curbing inside the turns, the pit road, the concrete barriers, and the six-foot chain-link fence surrounding the track itself, which is forty feet wide. The cost is about $1 million per mile. The first track cost $1.7 million.

Who designed the track?

I hired a professional track designer. After months of them not being able to follow my design criteria, I finally let the designer go and finished the design myself. Once the track is designed, it's a matter of finding a civil engineer and a paving company.

You have over 200 garages and are building more. Where do you find people to build garages?

You can find local contractors in the *Yellow Pages*.

THE MONEY

How did you finance this venture?

The seed money came from the profits of a digital printing business that I own. And, since most banks do not consider land to be a risk, I got a twenty-year note from a bank for $500,000 on the land. I also put $250,000 on seventeen different credit cards with interest as low as 2.99 percent, and I refinanced my home to keep the Ranch going.

THE MARKETING

How did you promote the club?

I never spent a dime on newspaper, magazine, radio, or television advertising. I did it by word of mouth. It's better that way, because you get people who are genuinely passionate about driving.

With no advertising, how did you get the first members?

I mailed out a questionnaire to Porsche Club (**www.hcrpca.org** and **www.mav.pca.org/mav**) and Corvette Club (**www.clubcorvette.com/clubs.asp**) members to see if they felt the way I did about a road course country club. It came back exactly the way I thought it would. They were very excited about the idea.

Describe those questionnaires for us.

We all know that with direct mail advertising, businesses are tickled pink if they get a 2- to 3-percent response. The recipient ordinarily just fills out a short questionnaire and drops it in the mail with no postage required. For surveys, the response rate is even worse, usually about ½ percent. I sent out 1,000 questionnaires, and there was nothing short about them. I had an introductory letter on the front and even had essay questions. I purposely did not include a return envelope. So, people had to fill out a two-page questionnaire, get their own envelope, address it, and put a stamp on it. The response rate was 47 percent.

Why do you think your direct mailing was so effective, and where did you get the mailing list?

I made sure they were sent to people who would be the most interested in a sports car country club. I contacted the Porsche Clubs, and they would not give me their member list. I sent them the mailing materials, and they sent them out for me. The Corvette Club gave me their list. I hand-addressed all of them. This is how the word got out initially.

What is your market?

For every driving professional, I can find 100 amateurs who want to just dabble and have fun with it. The big hidden market out there is for the person who treats this as a sport.

THE MEMBERS

How many members do you have now? What is the cost of a membership?

We have 560 members, and eleven of those are women. The initiation fee is $3,600, and the monthly dues total $95. To rent a garage costs $175 per month.

How many members did you have after one year in business?

About 100, but I'm sure if I had advertised we would have gotten more. My thinking was if 500 people had shown up on the first day, it would have been chaos. I'd rather grow the business in a manageable way.

THE EVENTS

What events do you hold here?

About a dozen weekends each year, the facilities are rented out to various sports car and motorcycle clubs. The weekends are sold out for the next three years. The cost is $4,000 a day.

Do the clubs come to you, or do you invite them?

They came to me before the track was even built. They remembered the questionnaires I sent out early on. In June 2001, we had 250 Ferraris here. To this day, people are talking about that event. I don't have time to market and promote, and now there's no need because we are booked solid.

Do you hire safety workers for big events? If so, where do you find these workers?

We do hire safety workers for our large weekend events. For about $50 an hour, you can hire a vehicle and two paramedics. Just look in the phone book for businesses listed as standby medical services.

THE INSURANCE

What about insurance costs?

We use K&K Insurance (**www.kandkinsurance.com**), which insures all the major motor speedways.

How much do you pay in premiums each year?

I pay $25,000. Of all the things I had envisioned that we needed, insurance was the only one that came in under budget. But I also have to explain that technically, most of the time, according to the insurance definition, we are not racing.

How does the insurance company define racing?

Racing is defined as passing in the corners. We don't pass in the corners, only in the straightaways. That's the reason we've had six years of members on the track and have never even had two sports cars touch each other.

THE ADVICE

Looking back, what would you do differently?

I've never had a mentor, but I wish I could've had one. There are so many pitfalls, but I would advise anyone to pursue their dream. What's life all about? Is it about not taking any financial risks? I mean, it's not like you're risking your life. What's the worst that could happen if you fail at business? The best thing you can do is pursue your dream, and surround yourself with people who will help you, and, of course, avoid those naysayers!

THE PLAN TO FOLLOW

STEP 1

The first thing you should do is clearly define your market and contact organizations that can reach large groups of people that will be interested in your car club. Then, create a questionnaire about your club and send it to members of these organizations. You can use this feedback to enlist members and gauge interest.

NOTE: Farr sent out 1,000 questionnaires to Porsche Club and Corvette Club members and had a response rate of 47 percent.

STEP 2

You will then need to find a piece of land that suits your car club.

NOTE: Farr needed at least 300 acres, without too many trees, with rolling hills, and that was situated off a good-sized highway.

STEP 3

After you find land, you need to design and build a track, garages, a skid pad, a grid pad, and a tower.

STEP 4

Before you can open for business, you need to have insurance and standby paramedics.

NOTE: Farr says that insurance companies define racing as passing in corners, so rates are lower for passing in the straightaways.

THE HIGHLIGHTS

- Clearly define your market for an optimal response rate in direct mail marketing.
- Avoid naysayers and follow your dreams.
- A questionnaire to your target market is a great research tool.
- The hidden market is the group of people who treat this as a sport.
- The *Yellow Pages* is a great resource for finding local contractors, insurance, and standby paramedic services.

THE RESOURCES

MORE INFORMATION ABOUT JACK FARR

MotorSport Ranch
www.motorsportranch.com
Jack Farr's first-ever sports car country club.

WHO TO KNOW

Specialty Equipment Market Association (SEMA)
www.sema.org
Sponsors numerous trade shows for the performance driving and racing industries. You will find a complete list on the website.

Performance Racing Industry (PRI)
www.performanceracing.com
This website is "the gateway to the worldwide racing marketplace" with links to PRI's magazine, trade show information, and racing.

Bob Bondurant School of High Performance Driving
www.bondurant.com
Information on courses, pricing, gear and apparel, instructor profiles, and various multimedia.

Skip Barber Racing School
www.skipbarber.com
With numerous locations nationwide, this driving and racing school also hosts corporate outings, ride-and-drives, dealer training, and consumer events.

National Auto Sport Association (NASA)
www.nasaproracing.com
In addition to a performance driving and racing school, NASA is a business dedicated to organizing and promoting racing activities for both the aspiring and accomplished racer.

Performance Driver's Association (PDA)
www.pdadrivingschool.com
PDA is an association of automotive enthusiasts and performance car drivers.

Porsche Club of America—Hill Country Region
www.hcrpca.org
Offers members auto events, social events, forums, and more.

Porsche Club of America—Maverick Region
http://mav.pca.org/mav
Offers members a newsletter, classifieds listing, trivia, online shopping, and more.

Club Corvette
www.clubcorvette.com/clubs.asp
This website offers a comprehensive directory of Corvette clubs around the world.

National Auto Sport Association (NASA) of Texas
www.nasatx.com
Racing club, high-performance driving and competition school, time trials, industry media, and a Texas calendar of NASA events.

The Driver's Edge
www.thedriversedge.net
Organizes high-profile, high-performance driving events throughout Texas.

Lone Star Track Days
www.lonestartrackdays.com
This riding school also offers Central Motorcycle Roadracing Association (CMRA) racing licenses.

INSURANCE INFORMATION

K&K Insurance
www.kandkinsurance.com
Brings essential insurance programs and risk solutions into areas such as professional and amateur sports, leisure, entertainment, recreation, motorsports, leisure camps, arenas and facilities, franchised motorcycle dealerships, health and fitness clubs, special events, fairs, festivals, outfitters and guides, and more.

American Specialty
www.amerspec.com
Specializes in insurance and risk services for the sports and entertainment industry.

Sports Insurance
www.sportsinsurance.com
Specializes in racetrack and event insurance.

Deist Safety
www.deist.com
Online shopping for accessories, hardware and materials, stunt equipment, transmission blankets, window nets, crew apparel, driving suits, and more.

Parker Pumper
www.parker-pumper.com
Online shopping for all items related to motor sports.

A-1 Racing Products
www.a1racing.com
The master warehouse for the New York Tri-State area for tools, equipment, import parts, hardware, trailer accessories, and more.

Racesuit.com
www.racesuit.com
Online shopping for race suits, teamwear, gloves, shoes, helmets, and accessories.

MultiVex Mirrors
www.safetymirrorsonline.com
Need safety mirrors? Need an expanded field-of-view? Offering high-performance vehicle mirrors for maximum road safety, this website has what you need to see around blind spots.

SITES TO SEE

Race Industry
www.raceindustry.com
Information on all types of racetracks, vendors, industry updates, and trade show information.

Motorsports Marketing Group
www.raceweektv.com
Marketing and sales consultation, comprehensive sponsorship packages, public relations, and on-site promotions. Also available is professional video editing, copywriting, layout and graphics, vinyl and printing, logo creation, business cards, and letterhead. Marketing and advertising services for race venues, race teams, touring series, and corporate and/or retail events and promotions.

Millionaire Blueprints neither endorses nor recommends any of the companies listed in the resource section. Resources are intended as a starting point for your research.

Benjamin
KNOX

How one former starving artist went from receiving scholarships to giving them.

BUSINESS NAME:
The Benjamin Knox Gallery

TYPE OF BUSINESS:
Art Gallery

LOCATION:
College Station, TX

ADAPTED FROM:
Millionaire Blueprints magazine article,
"Painting a Bright Future,"
August 2005

The Texas oil crash of the 1980s wiped out the money set aside for Benjamin Knox's education. He was enrolled at Texas A&M University to get a degree in architecture, but he barely had enough money to start college, let alone finish. He refused to go into debt, so he turned to scholarships and hard work. Embracing the school's military culture, he fell back on his artistic skill and marketing acumen and found a successful career in the process.

He began drawing and selling pictures depicting his fellow military students. The idea caught on, and soon he was running a studio out of his dorm room. Today, his collective works include hundreds of paintings. Many are of the Texas A&M campus buildings, sports activities, and students. He also owns his own gallery, which he built just two blocks from the university as a reproduction of the town's old train station. Through his connections with other Aggies—a term that affectionately refers to the university's agricultural roots—he's developed a remarkable home base and become friends with such notables as Governor Rick Perry of Texas and former President George H.W. Bush.

THE BEGINNING

Who were your first customers?

My first customers were the guys in my outfit in the Corps of Cadets at Texas A&M. I really was trying to figure out how to pay for my next meal, so I came up with the idea of drawing pictures of the guys in uniform and approached the outfit about buying them.

THE BUSINESS

College students don't have a lot of money. How much did you charge?

Most sold for around twenty dollars. I had a little trick that helped to boost sales—I drew the actual people. Obviously, they wanted to buy one, and so did their parents. It just grew from there. It wasn't long before other groups wanted me to draw them, and then I started drawing the university buildings and scenes from football games. Eventually, I started getting prints made of each drawing. I had a system where I created the original piece of art and then took pre-orders to pay for the prints.

So you used that as a way to finance the printing costs?

It cost around $500 for one hundred prints. I collected pre-orders until I had the $500. Then I'd get the prints made, deliver the ones I had already sold, and keep the rest in inventory until they sold out. At $20 a print, that's $2,000, and after printing I had $1,500 profit to pay for food and living expenses. That's how I was able to generate a cash flow.

THE MARKETING

What other ways did you sell prints while you were attending school?

I set up a booth in the Memorial Student Center during football games. In order to sell items on campus, you had to be affiliated with one of the student groups. So over the years, I had several of them sponsor me in exchange for a percentage of the sales. It started out at around 50 percent of sales and eventually was a 70/30 split. During my senior year, I wore my Corps uniform and my senior boots in the booth, and I had my outfit sponsor me. I also signed and personalized each print as an added bonus.

How much were you selling the prints for at the booth?

They were $20 to $70 per print, depending on what type and size it was. We got bombarded with phone calls afterward, too, because we had brochures people could take. I think it hit me that this was going to be a phenomenal success one day during a signing. I looked up and saw a line going down the hall, through the post office and then back down the other hallway. I asked, "What are all those people doing?" Someone said, "They're all waiting for you." I couldn't believe it.

THE LICENSING

Do you have to pay royalties on the university prints?

Yes. The royalty fees vary, but it's usually around 8 percent. Art Editions is actually set up as my publisher, because they hold the license with the Collegiate Licensing Company (CLC) and Licensing Resource Group (LRG) for all of the universities. They hold the licenses and pay the royalties on my behalf.

THE GALLERY

What happened after you graduated?

I'd become known as the Texas Aggie artist, and by 1993 I had developed a very strong business. I established the Benjamin Knox Gallery, which was the first—and so far the only—artist-owned gallery in College Station, Texas. Texas A&M was my niche, so by then I was doing a lot with the alumni and student groups, and I marketed in the alumni magazines.

Did marketing in the alumni magazines work well?

Yes, that was probably our number-one advertising for about eight years. I bought full-page ads for around $1,000 to $3,000. The ads included the paintings and mentioned any events that were coming up.

How many prints do you usually make of one painting?

I print anywhere from 500 to 3,000. It depends on if it's a limited or open edition. The cost of printing varies, but it can go as low as $5 apiece to print lithographs. I'm basically selling my time. It takes a considerable number of hours to create a painting. I sell most of the prints for $35 to $75 apiece. I like to keep the prices reasonable so the students and alumni can afford them. I also sell the originals, which currently go for $1,000 to $25,000.

Do you sell them framed as well?

Yes, and those generally go for $200 to $500. We recently started doing the framing ourselves. We looked at what it would cost to do it ourselves and discovered it made sense to bring that part of the process in-house.

THE PHILANTHROPY

We heard you donate to a lot of scholarships and charities?

One of the reasons I was able to go to college was because of scholarships. So the first thing I did when my business took off was establish scholarships like the ones I received.

How do you start a scholarship?

You can set up an endowment. You take a sum of money and put it into an investment, like a mutual fund, and the interest earned is awarded as a scholarship each year. Once you start it, it will go on forever. Usually, I start by approaching an alumni or university group and telling them I want to set up a scholarship. Nearly every university has information about endowments on their websites.

Where does the money come from?

I designate a set of prints, and decide what percent of sales will go toward the endowment.

That's a great way to give back. Does the recognition tie in with your marketing efforts?

Yes, alumni groups request one of my prints for an auction. The side benefit for me is that the piece is on display for people who might not otherwise see it. And because only one person gets it in the auction, I might eventually sell fifty more of that same print.

THE GROWTH

You seem to be more focused on marketing than the typical artist.

A lot of artists don't start out with marketing abilities, but that's something you can develop. I've worked hard to develop a marketing sense. I also try to diversify. Texas A&M is my niche, but that's not to say I don't branch out. I've done designs for the Native Texan license plate, the Daughters of the Republic of Texas, the state gift for the governor and the secretary of state, and the Telluride Jazz Festival, along with other universities.

Do you analyze your business?

Of course. I look at the numbers, knowing what I'm about to do. When I'm about to release a new painting, I know how many prints I plan to sell and how much income it should generate. I think every business needs to be viewed from three facets: looking ahead, the day-to-day, and looking behind. My primary job, other than creating the artwork, is looking ahead.

Who takes care of the other aspects?

I have an executive director who takes care of the day-to-day operations, and my financial director takes care of looking behind.

THE ADVICE

What advice do you have for other artists who would like to be as successful as you?

Find a niche wherever you are. Look around to see what large organizations are in your area. Focus on how you could get involved with one of those. Then do direct marketing to build your foundation. Build relationships with your customers. If someone is buying one of your pieces as a gift, find out how you can make it special for them. If you can make the recipient teary-eyed, that will make an impact on everyone involved. Lastly, have a home base, a place where everybody can come together and communicate.

No matter how small it is, keep a presence somewhere, even if you go away for periods of time.

THE PLAN TO FOLLOW

STEP 1

Find a niche in your area. Look for an area or organization that people are attached to, or that they are emotionally connected to. Then paint or draw pictures of it.

NOTE: Knox says his niche is Texas A&M University, and people buy his artwork because they are emotionally connected to the school.

STEP 2

Sell your artwork and/or take orders for prints at functions held by the organization or area you've chosen. You can also sell your artwork through direct mail to people who are involved with the organization.

NOTE: Knox began selling his paintings and prints in the Texas A&M Memorial Student Center during football games. Knox says in order to sell items on campus, you must be affiliated with one of the university's student groups, and you usually pay them a commission from your sales.

STEP 3

After you have enough orders to cover the printing costs, have prints made of your artwork.

NOTE: Knox says that if you are depicting a university in your artwork, you must be licensed by the CLC or work with a publisher who holds a license with the CLC.

STEP 4

After you have established yourself in your community, open a gallery to display and sell your artwork.

NOTE: Knox became known as the Texas Aggie artist.

THE HIGHLIGHTS

- Find a niche and establish a relationship with your niche's community.
- Taking preorders is a great way to cover your cost without accumulating debt.
- Philanthropy is a great way to market your business and build your reputation.
- Every business needs to be viewed from three facets: looking ahead, the day-to-day, and looking behind.
- An emotional response from recipients of your artwork will leave a lasting impression.

THE RESOURCES

MORE INFORMATION ABOUT BENJAMIN KNOX

The Benjamin Knox Gallery
www.benjaminknox.com

LICENSING

Collegiate Licensing Company (CLC)
www.clc.com

Licensing Resource Group (LRG)
www.lrgusa.com
This group holds the licenses and pays the royalties on Knox's behalf.

ART AGENTS AND ORGANIZATIONS

The Arts Business Institute
http://artsbusinessinstitute.org
This nonprofit organization offers educational resources to the arts community. Workshop topics include product development, pricing, and wholesaling.

The Artist Help Network
www.artisthelpnetwork.com
The website lists various resources for aiding artists with their careers.

National Association of Independent Artists
http://naia-artists.org
This organization was established to help enhance the economic well-being of artists.

PRINTMAKING INDUSTRY GROUPS

American Print Alliance
www.printalliance.org

Boston Printmakers
www.bostonprintmakers.org

California Society of Printmakers
www.caprintmakers.org

Chicago Printmakers Collaborative
www.chicagoprintmakers.com

Mid-America Print Council
http://homepages.ius.edu/special/mapc/MAPC.html

The Ink Shop Printmaking Center
www.ink-shop.org

SERVICES

Fine Art Impressions
www.fineartgiclee.com
This company produces museum-quality prints of art and photos using the giclée process.

LIgiclee.com
www.ligiclee.com
This company offers fine art printing, reproduction and other art, photo and Web services on Long Island, New York.

Staples Fine Art, Inc.
www.staplesart.com
Not to be confused with the office retail giant, this Virginia fine art printer offers a trademarked giclée print system, as well as lithography, digital scanning, and archiving services.

SUPPLIES

American Frame Corporation
www.americanframe.com
This company is a source of picture frame kits and supplies.

Cheap Joe's Art Stuff
www.cheapjoes.com
This website offers online sales of fine art supplies and an "Artists' Community" with web discussion forums, links, and event and workshop listings.

Digital Painter
www.digitalpainter.com
This is a manufacturer of fine art printing systems, including hardware and software.

Discount Art Supplies
www.discountart.com
This twenty-two-year-old New Hampshire company has a product line that includes brushes, paper, paints, and easels. The company also offers a free brochure and a monthly newsletter.

FramingSupplies.com
www.framingsupplies.com
This website offers wholesale equipment and supplies, including aluminum and wood frames, mat cutters, and adhesives.

MatShop
www.matshop.com
This is an online wholesaler of mat and framing supplies for bulk custom framing.

Utrecht Art Supplies
www.utrechtart.com
This online retailer has a large product list.

FEDERAL AGENCIES

National Endowment for the Arts
www.arts.endow.gov
This federal agency supports artists with grants and other programs.

United States Patent and Trademark Office
www.uspto.gov
This website includes information on all current trademark legislation.

ONLINE ART GALLERIES AND SALES

Art-Agent.com
www.art-agent.com
This is a commission-free, online broker for marketing fine art.

Arts & Design.net
www.artsanddesign.net
This Internet gallery is where visual artists can display their work free of charge.

PaintingsDirect.com
www.paintingsdirect.com
This is a commission-based website for painters to sell their work.

Millionaire Blueprints *neither endorses nor recommends any of the companies listed in the resource section. Resources are intended as a starting point for your research.*

Lorie
LINE

How a talented musician parlayed popular appeal and flair for promotion into one of the largest independent record companies in the world.

BUSINESS NAME:
Lorie Line Music, Inc.

TYPE OF BUSINESS:
Pianist

LOCATION:
Wayzata, MN

ADAPTED FROM:
Millionaire Blueprints magazine article,
"America's Most Loved Pianist,"
January/February 2006

L orie Line's path to becoming "America's Most Loved Pianist" may have started with a joke, but it proved to be a lesson in supply and demand economics—and the power of giving the customers what they want. Beginning with a handwritten list of 500 people who had requested a CD that she hadn't yet made, Line's list has now grown to a database of over 125,000 ardent fans who line up every year to see what she has created, both visually and musically. She not only owns the company; she runs it. Set designs, musical arrangements, costume designs, distribution deals, recording, manufacturing, ticket sales, tour schedules, music publishing, direct mail marketing—if it touches her music at all, she is in control. And to top it all off, she has retained ownership of all rights to her music. She owns her sheet music, creates her catalog, and distributes her products from a small office building in charming Wayzata, Minnesota.

THE BEGINNING

What made you want to produce that first CD?

I had started playing at Dayton's department store. During this time—over a five-year period—I started taking names from people who asked for my music on CDs. When I had gathered up a list of about 500 names, I thought, well, the risk is pretty low if I make a CD.

THE CD

How did you go about recording the first CD?

I looked on the back of a George Winston CD—because he was really popular—and I found the name of the engineer in California who worked on his album. I called this engineer and asked if he was still in the business. We discussed my ideas, and he agreed to engineer a CD for me. So I flew out to San Francisco and recorded my first CD.

Once you had the CD recorded, what was the next step in getting it to your fans?

The first thing we did was work on artwork for the cover, and then we found the company that duplicated CDs by just calling around.

Is it hard to find someone to duplicate your CDs?

Anybody can duplicate and manufacture CDs. They want your business. It's a per-CD thing. You put your order in, and you pay per CD.

Then once you send them out, do you ever hear from anyone who purchased your CDs?

The original CDs had a "kickback" card in them, and we immediately started hearing from fans. These reply cards simply said, "If you'd like to be on my mailing list, send me your name and address."

How did your second album do?

The second one didn't do as well as the standards and the copy tunes, but I learned a lot from it. My third album was a holiday album, and it took me over the top. At the store where I was playing, I then became both a pianist and a vendor. When they started selling my CDs there, everything became supercharged.

THE BUSINESS

Did they then set up a kiosk for you at the department store?

No. I just set my CDs on the piano. When people requested one, I'd say, "Just take it over there, and they'll ring it up for you." The first day that I put my CDs on the piano I had forty copies, and they were all sold by the end of my shift. So I knew that I was on to something pretty good.

What was the split with the department store per CD?

They paid me $7.50, and they sold them for $15. They made well over $1 million off my CDs when I was playing there. It was a good deal for me, too, because more than 30,000 people would walk by me on busy days.

THE TOUR

How did you decide which cities were best for your tour?

This goes back to those kickback fliers. From the responses that came in, we created a database that showed me where people lived who were buying my CDs. As we started pinpointing these areas, it just started spiraling. Being headquartered in the Twin Cities, we started branching out into the Midwest. That's how I really developed a following.

How did your husband get involved with your music company?

I realized that I was making enough money to pay the mortgage. Since Tim is really good at the marketing and the business side, he took care of that. Then I could concentrate on the music and the creative part of my business.

How do you put the shows together?

We have formed all kinds of teams to pull this production together. We have a lighting designer. We have a choreographer. I have a costume designer, and they all come to my office in Wayzata and meet with me. Since I'm the producer of the show, I give them the direction they need, and off they go.

THE MARKETING

Tell us about your direct-mail campaigns.

My campaigns generally center on a new CD or on a new tour. We don't send out anything that doesn't give me a return on my investment. We are very much enjoying my new e-mail database, as we can send the same information with no printing or postage costs. My e-mail database is growing rapidly. I never do mass mailings to people who do not know me. My database consists purely of Lorie Line fans.

Tell us about your retail sales.

The Music Land CEO walked into his Minnesota store one day and asked, "What's the bestselling item?" The store manager said, "We don't carry her. Her name's Lorie Line. Everybody asks for her, and we don't carry any of her music." The Music Land CEO then called me at home and asked to carry my CD in his stores. By the next week, he had put my music in a thousand stores. We sold our CDs directly to them, cutting out the middleman. They made more money, and I made more money. It continues to be a great relationship. When one major retailer carries you, they all start coming around. That's how I became nationally distributed.

What did you do differently regarding your national retail exposure?

One thing we did correctly was that we never gave up anything to a distribution company. We never gave up control. It was unheard of, but we developed important relationships in the retail world. To this day, Tim still does all that distribution work directly with retailers.

You also sell sheet music. Tell us how your publishing venture evolved.

Music distributors typically own the rights to all the music they distribute. But, although Hal Leonard distributes my music, I am the publisher and I own all the rights to my music—my entire catalog. It's unusual, but they distribute my music; they don't own it.

THE MERCHANDISING

You have described yourself as a mass merchandiser. Tell us what that means and how it works.

I always go out on a concert tour with three hot "gotta-have-them" items. I come up with something spectacular and new every year. When I have a new holiday concert, I also record and have for sale there a brand-new "studio version" CD of the show that they hear that night. My slogan for my holiday shows is, "Be there with bells on." The audience is invited to chime in with the orchestra during the audience participation parts of the show. I created a series of collector bells, and I put a new one out each year. I also publish a book with all the music for the night for all the piano players out there.

Where do you sell the most merchandise?

Well, the most merchandise is sold when I do a campaign. When I come out with a new CD, I use the power of the database. I send out a beautiful direct mail flier announcing the new release. There are always four ways you can order it: via fax, online, by calling, or by mail.

Lorie Line's story is a wake-up call to all the aspiring musicians out there who think making it big in the music business is strictly about talent or the music you make. "Success in today's music business," she says, "means taking charge and keeping control of all the things that can make or break your career."

THE PLAN TO FOLLOW

STEP 1

Start by keeping a list of names, addresses, and phone numbers of anyone who asks to buy your music on CD.

NOTE: By keeping track of fan information, you are beginning to build your mailing list.

STEP 2

Record a CD, have the CDs duplicated, and create artwork for the cover.

NOTE: Line suggests that you include a reply card with your CD asking fans if they want to be added to your mailing list. Line says she collects this information and sends direct-mail marketing pieces to her list announcing a new CD or tour.

STEP 3

Contact the people on your list to buy the CDs. You can also visit local music stores and gift shops, and ask them to sell your CDs.

STEP 4

Track your fans, and schedule performances in areas where you know you have a fan base. You will also want to have merchandise available for your fans to purchase.

NOTE: Line says she always has three "gotta-have-them" items with her while touring, and she comes up with something new every year.

THE HIGHLIGHTS

- The music business is just as much about the business as it is about the music.
- It is possible for the artist to maintain control in the music business.
- Build a strong mailing list of your fans for direct-mail and e-mail marketing.
- If your fans enjoy your music, they will want to buy your products too.
- Always have copies of your CDs available for purchase, whether you're playing a large or small venue.

THE RESOURCES

There are thousands of resources available to musicians of all styles and genres. Many of the websites offer extensive links to an enormous range of subjects. With a general knowledge of all aspects of the music business, you'll be able to do as much as you'd like, yourself. You'll also know if you're getting what you're paying for, if you decide to outsource some of the work.

Music Biz Academy
www.musicbizacademy.com
The music business site for the promotion-minded. It covers everything from music law to CD art, and it offers a free monthly online newsletter, *The Music Biz Digest*. It also has a listing of the Top 20 Articles, which gives a great overview of the business from first-person accounts.

All Music Industry Contacts
www.allmusicindustrycontacts.com
You can purchase or download a file (or CD-ROM) that contains all of America's most successful record label A&R's, managers, producers, and publishers, including their contact information and credits. There is also a glossary of music industry professional titles, what they mean, and how they fit into your music career.

PROFESSIONAL ORGANIZATIONS

The American Society of Composers, Authors, and Publishers (ASCAP)
www.ASCAP.com
ASCAP has a collaborators' corner, which is a free service for music professionals to find collaborators.

Broadcast Music, Inc. (BMI)
www.bmi.com
World-famous BMI is a performing rights organization. It collects license fees on behalf of its songwriters, composers and music publishers, and distributes them as royalties to those members whose works have been performed. As a performing rights organization, BMI issues licenses.

SESAC
www.SESAC.com
As the most innovative and fastest growing performing rights organization in the United States, SESAC can secure your copyright from infringement. This site is especially helpful if you are writing your own music.

The American Federation of Musicians
www.afm.org
This site offers helpful advice about protecting your rights, as well as information about specific brands of musical instruments.

COPYRIGHT

United States Copyright Office
www.copyright.gov
Copyright your creations at the Library of Congress.

TOURING

Concert Coach
www.concertcoach.com
Specializing in leasing entertainment tour buses.

Projection, Lights and Staging News
www.plsn.com
Introduces you to all the latest information concerning your set design. Their slogan speaks the truth: "Without the lights, it's just radio."

GENERAL INFORMATION

All Music Web
www.allmusicianweb.com
Here, you'll find 139 links covering musical equipment to sound libraries.

Songwriter101
www.songwriter101.com
This site has a section titled "Lingo," so you can figure out the terminology and talk like a pro.

Performing Songwriter
www.performingsongwriter.com
This site will keep you informed on all things involving being a traveling musician. Its monthly magazine, *Performing Songwriter*, is a powerhouse of information and includes interviews with up-and-coming artists, as well as industry giants.

Millionaire Blueprints *neither endorses nor recommends any of the companies listed in the resource section. Resources are intended as a starting point for your research.*

Todd
PLISS

Todd Pliss combined his teaching talent with his abilities as an award-winning filmmaker, and discovered the formula for creating record-breaking multimedia sales.

BUSINESS NAME:
New Look Products

TYPE OF BUSINESS:
Direct Response Marketing

LOCATION:
Calabasas, CA

ADAPTED FROM:
Millionaire Blueprints magazine article,
"Show and Sell,"
March 2006

W hen Todd Pliss relocated from Brooklyn to Los Angeles, a lot more changed than just the weather. After becoming a credentialed teacher, Pliss began writing and directing short films. He also had an idea for a book that would help people lose weight. The Catabolic Diet e-book amassed over $2 million in sales via radio and television spots, most of which were paid for by the method known as "per-inquiry."

Then Pliss had an even better idea. "I thought I could tell more stories in twenty minutes than I could in a one- or two-minute slot," he says. Armed with the knowledge from his book and contacts from his filmmaking, Pliss developed a program called the Catabolic Weight Loss System and produced a successful infomercial. He took it one step further and founded a direct-response marketing company called New Look Products. He remains its acting president today.

THE BOOK

Take us from the moment you had the idea to write the diet book to where you are now.

I had an idea for a diet book, *The Catabolic Diet*, that was based on certain foods that cause you to burn calories resulting in a negative calorie factor.

I wrote this book and was trying to set up a merchant account so I could take credit cards. (See resource page.) Once I was set up for that, I started testing paid spots and began doing well. Then I started running on a per-inquiry (PI) basis.

Can you explain what PI does for the seller?

It just means you get a cut for selling things, and the media outlet gets a cut in lieu of the fee that they would normally charge for the spot.

How did you find your information on where and how to run the spots?

We were working with an agency for that. There are only a few agencies that can very easily handle that, and it's well worth the money to use their expertise. (See resource page.)

THE INFOMERCIAL

The Catabolic Diet *system was also a successful infomercial. How did you take it there?*

I could tell more stories in twenty minutes than I could in a one- or two-minute slot. You can also get into more detail and more testimonials, so that is always valuable—especially with something visible, such as weight loss.

What are the risks versus the benefits?

You have to use the infomercial not just to make sales, but to help develop products for the future. It can act as a product survey. We also offered a newsletter, and we were then able to sell a second one to that list of customers.

How do you know where and when to place your infomercial for viewing?

Cable is great for infomercials. If you want a certain market, you've got the golf channels, beauty channels, and all kinds of specific markets. You just pick the channels you want to advertise on.

THE BUSINESS

If I have a product, and I have made my infomercial and would like to approach a cable channel, what are the steps I need to take?

Before anything, you definitely need to have a turnkey operation setup. That means having credit card services. You can set up a system to take a check by phone now for people who don't have credit cards, and the money comes right out of their checking accounts.

So you have to do something extra to do the check by phone?

There are different companies that you can set up with that will take checks. Amerinet (**www.debit-it.com**) is one of them.

THE CALL CENTER

What else would we need?

There must also be a call center. The call centers are West in Nebraska (**www.west.com**) and Protocol in North Carolina (**www.protocolmarket ing.com**). Call centers usually get paid per minute, but there are also performance-based ones that will take a commission. You will also need to look into getting a fulfillment center.

What kinds of questions would we need to ask of a smaller call center?

You want to ask if it is performance-based, or if you can pay per minute. You want to ask how many stations they have, and how many operators are working at any one time. The minimum number of operators you want on the phones is fifteen. If it becomes a successful campaign, you want at least fifty. You might want to research how many operators they typically have when your commercials are going to run, and choose eight different times, being sure to include Saturday and Sunday.

What else would we look for?

You want to make sure that they have tracking software and that it accurately tracks where the orders are coming from, especially by zip code.

Will the call centers help with what the operators will say to a caller?

Yes, they'll help you with the scripts. They will take a look at your products and your offer, and work with you to write the script.

THE FULFILLMENT CENTER

What are the questions we need to ask when we are talking to a fulfillment center?

You want to make sure they have the experience exchanging with call centers, because they are going to be getting all the orders downloaded from the call center. You want to make sure they can do the credit card processing, because they are the ones who are actually going to process the orders.

THE MEDIA BUYER

So you have your credit card merchant account, your check-by-phone setup, and your call center and fulfillment center. Now are you ready to approach the station?

You can try individual calls, but I think it's best to hire a good media buyer. If you are going to do an infomercial, having a good media buyer is definitely important because they negotiate—they buy in bulk—so they get better rates than you can get. Icon Media in Atlanta is an excellent company (**www.iconmediadirect.com**). Not only do they do television, they also do radio, and they do print campaigns. They are going to know what to do and where to best place it based on past experience, and they really can get the best rates for you. Now, if that is a success, then you can test PIs, which is a separate thing—the per-inquiry. So you'll usually want to test the item first.

Who is a good media buyer for PIs? What is the payment structure?

We use different media buyers for PIs. Media Vantage of New Jersey (**www.ad-vantagemedia.com**) is a good company. The agency is usually going to charge about 35 percent. The stations get like 25 percent, and the agents get about 10 percent. But it can be as high as 40 percent. Your cost is about 30 percent and works out to about a 30-percent profit margin.

What does a media buyer cost?

They are usually paid on commission. The standard is about 15 percent.

Should you find a media buyer first and see what fulfillment center they like, or go in the order that we have discussed?

Ask the media buyer who they recommend and who their clients are having success with. I generally do that. It takes a few weeks to get set up. Definitely consult with your buyer. They will have some good feedback.

THE NETWORKING

Where else can you find these experts?
There are people who advertise in most trade magazines that sponsor television and electronic retailing. And again, you can ask around if you are going through a fulfillment house or a media buyer. Also, every September, attend the trade show in Las Vegas (**www.retailing.org**). It's called the Electronic Retailing Association (ERA).

THE UP-SALE

Will you do better with a PI there, or with a paid spot?
Every item is different. If it is not working on a paid spot, then it is probably not going to work on a PI. Up-sales are very important. You should always have another two or three related items to offer the customer. Thirty percent of people will pick up additional products. Whether you are offering the same item or a different item, you always want them to be related.

Pliss ends the lesson like all good teachers. Once he gets you up to speed on one subject, he excites you with the possibilities of a new one. In the process, he makes you aware of what lies below the surface—up-sales and back-sales. You almost hate for the school bell to ring.

THE PLAN TO FOLLOW

STEP 1

The first thing you want to do is set your business up to accept payment.

NOTE: Pliss suggests that you have a means to accept credit payments and that you work with a company like Amerinet (**www.debit-it.com**) to accept check payments by phone.

STEP 2

Find a call center to handle your incoming orders.

NOTE: Pliss says that you should ask if it is performance-based, or if you can pay per minute. He says you should also ask how many stations they have and how many operators are working at any one time.

STEP 3

Find a fulfillment center to ship your product to clients.

NOTE: Pliss suggests that you find a fulfillment center that is experienced in working with call centers.

STEP 4

Hire a media buyer to help you choose television spots and negotiate rates.

NOTE: Pliss says that media buyers buy in bulk—so they get better rates than you can get.

THE HIGHLIGHTS

- You can also use an infomercial as a survey to help develop products in the future.
- Cable is great for infomercials because you can choose spots in specific markets.
- Call centers will help you write your script and provide feedback.
- You should track all incoming calls by zip code to help you select future spots.
- Keep in mind that people who order your product (30 percent) may purchase a related item.

THE RESOURCES

MORE INFORMATION ABOUT TODD PLISS

Pliss, Todd. *The Catabolic Diet.*
www.buymyebook.com/buy/authorinfo.asp?Eb
ookId=1102
Pliss' famous e-book on fat-burning foods.

CREATING AN INFOMERCIAL

Incredible Discoveries
www.incrediblediscoveries.com
A multimedia production company that specializes in half-hour infomercials, including pre-
production, production, and postproduction.
Immediate Capital Group, along with Incredible
Discoveries, will co-fund media ventures involving
half-hour infomercials under the title of Incredible
Discoveries.

Script to Screen, Inc.
www.scripttoscreen.com
Direct thinking, for direct response. Has produced
quality direct response commercial and infomercial campaigns that provide results since 1986.

Stilson & Stilson
www.stilson-stilson.com
Among the leaders in the direct response industry, with twenty-five years of experience. Services
include high-end national quality production,

economical, film, HDTV and video production,
media management—television, radio, and
print—marketing, consulting, and new product
review.

Tara Productions, Inc.
www.taraproductions.com
Tara Productions says it has "the unbelievable
track record of seven hits out of every ten spots
produced." Featured celebrities are Joe Fowler,
Tamilee Webb, Jenilee Harris, Darla Haun, Kathy
Derry, Cameo Bernard, Kathy Kneur, and Randy
White, among others.

Infomercial Solutions, Inc.
www.infomercialsolutions.com
Producers of high-quality, money-making infomercials and direct response commercials. Take their
infomercial quiz to see if an infomercial is the
right choice for you.

Zephyr Media Group
www.zephyr-media.com
Manages all the pieces of an infomercial.

FUNDING THE MEDIA CAMPAIGN

Media Funding Corporation
www.mediafunding.com
This firm provides the capital that direct response

entrepreneurs need to aggressively grow their businesses. Peter Bieler, president of Media Funding Corporation, cofounded Ovation, Inc., to sell products on television in short- or long-form. He found a product called the V-Toner that was a rehabilitative device for injured skiers. He renamed it the ThighMaster, hired Suzanne Somers as spokesperson, and set records for short-form sales. In 1993, he sold his shares and left the company.

Anon. *The Independent Filmmaker's Guide to Film Financing.*
www.fundingfilm.com/page/page/870227.htm
A sixty-page downloadable e-book. Take a look at the rest of this funding site as well.

EVALUATING A PRODUCT FOR AN INFOMERCIAL

Concepts TV Production, Inc.
www.conceptstv.com
Offers criteria (in fifteen steps) for evaluating your product for short-form direct response television (DRTV).

Hawthorne Direct
www.hawthornedirect.com
Try the DRTV product evaluator online to find out if your product is right for DRTV.

Electronic Retailing Association (ERA)
www.retailing.org/new_site/default.asp
The trade association for multichannel marketers using direct response on television, radio, and the Internet.

WORKING WITH AN AGENCY

RainMakers International
www.rainmakersintl.com
Provides the following services: national direct response television and radio, local television and radio direct response, per-inquiry, media campaigns, and remnant media placement.

SPONSORING TELEVISION AND ELECTRONIC RETAILING

Higher Power Marketing
www.hpowermarketing.com
Advertising specialists who create and place per-inquiry advertising for radio, television, newspapers, movies, and the Internet that produce measurable, trackable results.

USING MEDIA BUYERS

Icon Media Direct
www.iconmediadirect.com
Integrated direct-response resource, including direct-response advertising, as well as general rate advertising techniques. Also offers production and vendor consultation, customized client service reporting and support, research, analysis, logistics, and more.

CHECK AND CREDIT CARD PROCESSORS

AmeriNet, Inc.
www.debit-it.com
Offers alternatives to credit card payment solutions. Customers can use their checks just like credit cards.

CyberSource
www.cybersource.com
Offers typical electronic payments including Bill Me Later. Under the resources/downloads section, one can obtain the compilation, *The Insider's Guide to eCommerce Payment—20 Tools.*

NACHA: The Electronic Payments Association
www.nacha.org
A resource for further reading on electronic payments, latest payment news, and various rules.

Merchant Accounts Express
www.merchantexpress.com
Offers credit card processing, free software, and free setup.

CALL CENTERS

West Corporation
www.west.com
West is one of the nation's top providers of outbound, interactive, and inbound services.

Protocol
www.protocolmarketing.com
Offers seamless, integrated direct marketing and customer care solutions.

CALL CENTER SERVICES

BuyerZone
www.buyerzone.com/marketing/call_center/index.html
Helps buyers with purchasing products and services for their businesses. Fill out the eight question survey online, and receive custom responses from national and local call center outsourcing companies.

Five9
www.five9.com
A leading global provider of on-demand telemarketing, customer service, and call center solutions for customer interaction management.

United States Patent and Trademark Office
www.uspto.gov/main/trademarks.htm
Get a trademark registration, enforcements, manuals, laws, and more.

E-BOOKS

Hawthorne, Timothy R. *The Complete Guide to Infomercial Marketing.*
www.hawthorneinfomercialguide.com
E-book authored by chairman and founder of Hawthorne Direct, Inc.

Marcum, Nancy. *Do You Want to Make a Million?*
www.marcummedia.com/book.htm
E-book authored by the CEO of Marcum Media.
Nancy Marcum specializes in helping entrepreneurs and small businesses sell their products
through infomercials. She is a founding member
of the Electronic Retailing Association, the leading
trade organization of the infomercial industry.

Anon. *Everything You Must Know to Make a
Profit from Infomercials.*
www.howtomakeinfomercials.com
Audio training seminar, *e-reference book*, paperwork and legal forms, and mentoring/consulting.

SOFTWARE SOLUTIONS

Cool Conversations LLC
www.coolconversations.com
Cool Conversations LLC, has partnered with
Incredible Discoveries TV to promote and market
Cool C Talking Computer software through direct
response television commercials and other media.
Watch the Cool C sixty-second commercial.

Vendaria Media, Inc.
www.vendaria.com
This visual merchandising company says that by
working with manufacturers to create short
video clips of how a product works, it provides

online consumers with a superior end-user experience. It combines video, audio, animations,
and text into dynamic, rich media presentations.

Take 2 Direct
www.take2direct.com
It's not a matter of if you get a hit, but when
Take 2 Direct fulfills the roles of infomercial production, strategic campaign and marketing
management, expert telemarketing script writing, and DRTV testing and analysis—all under
one roof.

CABLE CHANNEL CONTACT INFORMATION

Warren Communications News
www.warren-news.com/factbook.htm
For telecom and media intelligence, use this
website to find up-to-date information for cable
channels, including addresses, phone numbers,
and contacts.

Millionaire Blueprints *neither endorses nor
recommends any of the companies listed in the
resource section. Resources are intended as a
starting point for your research.*

ABOUT THE AUTHORS

Tom Spinks (1948–2007) was a natural-born visionary who strongly believed that there is an entrepreneur in everyone. During his lifetime, he started up, made successful, and sold four national companies in four different industries. But his dream was to design a publication like no other that would provide individuals with concrete answers about how to create and grow successful businesses. His *Millionaire Blueprints* magazine, featuring step-by-step "blueprints" of how self-made millionaires worldwide achieved their wealth, made its wildly successful national debut in April 2005. After a short battle with cancer, Spinks passed away on August 26, 2007. He realized his own dreams through *Millionaire Blueprints* and *Prepare to Be a Millionaire*. His work has taught entrepreneurs around the world that no dream is impossible.

Kimberly Spinks Burleson is president and editor-in-chief of *Millionaire Blueprints* magazine. She manages the publication's business affairs and oversees its daily editorial operations. Burleson spearheads the magazine's promotional campaigns, including *Millionaire Blueprints Live*—educational seminars featuring guest millionaires—and acts as public relations representative for all magazine-related events. Burleson was also the driving force behind the launch of *Millionaire Blueprints Jr.* magazine and *Millionaire Blueprints Teen* magazine, which present step-by-step articles about child and teen entrepreneurs, respectively. She is the eldest daughter of the magazine's late founder, Tom Spinks, and his wife, Barbara.

Lindsay Spinks Shepherd is executive vice president of
Millionaire Blueprints magazine. Since 2005, she has served as
chief financial officer of the company and acts as financial investment adviser to the editor-in-chief. Shepherd is involved in every
facet of the publication, specifically planning and making decisions on editorial content. She is the youngest daughter of the
magazine's late founder, Tom Spinks, and his wife, Barbara.

Wait One Minute

We've Got Something for You!

MILLIONAIRE BLUEPRINTS

SPECIAL OFFER

Preparation Just Met Opportunity . . . and You're the Winner!
Now that you're prepared to be a millionaire, let our team show you
how to become one! That's right, we've got a FREE gift, valued at $149,
to get you started on your very own Millionaire Blueprint!
Here at headquarters, we are committed to your success.

Just go to **www.MillionaireBlueprints.com/SpecialOffer** to get started.

Develop your very own Millionaire Blueprint with our help!

One last thing . . . be sure to subscribe to *Millionaire Blueprints* magazine,
and be on the lookout for some exciting new offerings and events that
are sure to skyrocket your success!

Code #723X • $16.95

The country's hottest young millionaires
reveal what it takes to rise to the top.